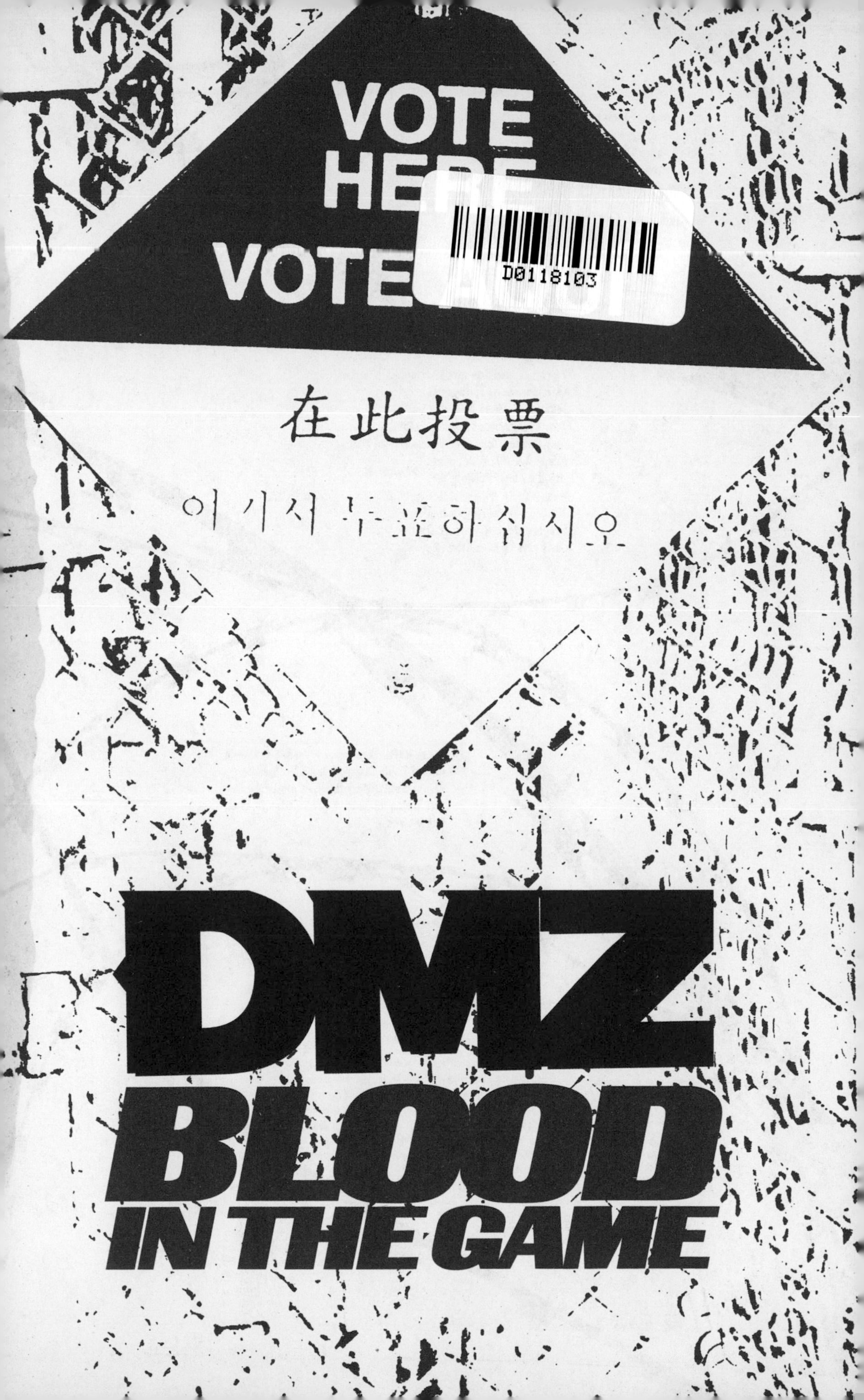
VOTE
HE
VOTE
在此投票
이기서 투표하십시오
DMZ
BLOOD
IN THE GAME

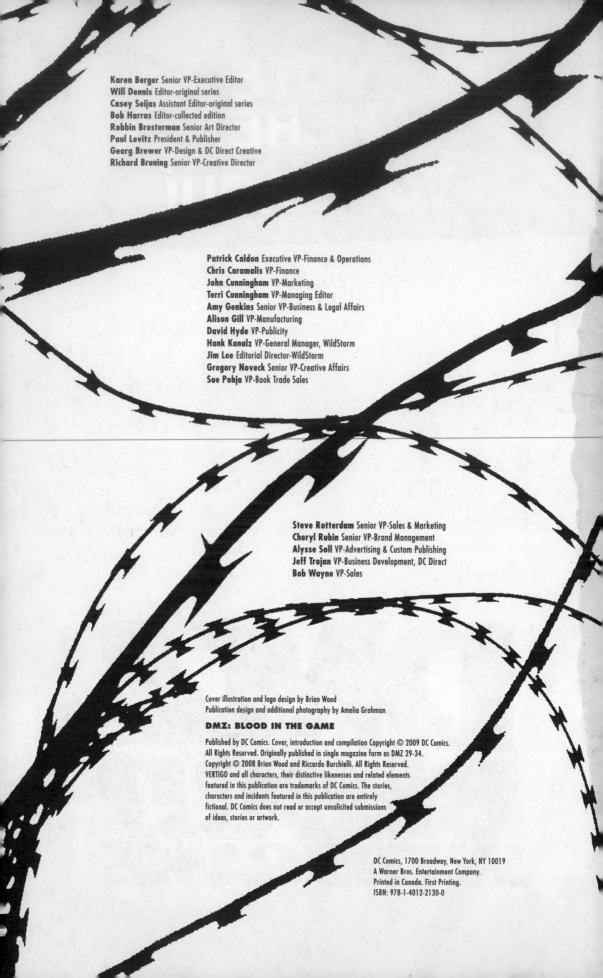

Cover illustration and logo design by Brian Wood
Publication design and additional photography by Amelia Grohman

DMZ: BLOOD IN THE GAME

Published by DC Comics. Cover, introduction and compilation Copyright © 2009 DC Comics.
All Rights Reserved. Originally published in single magazine form as DMZ 29-34.
Copyright © 2008 Brian Wood and Riccardo Burchielli. All Rights Reserved.
VERTIGO and all characters, their distinctive likenesses and related elements
featured in this publication are trademarks of DC Comics. The stories,
characters and incidents featured in this publication are entirely
fictional. DC Comics does not read or accept unsolicited submissions
of ideas, stories or artwork.

DC Comics, 1700 Broadway, New York, NY 10019
A Warner Bros. Entertainment Company.
Printed in Canada. First Printing.
ISBN: 978-1-4012-2130-0

BRIAN WOOD
WRITER

RICCARDO BURCHIELLI
ARTIST

JEROMY COX
COLORIST

JARED K. FLETCHER
LETTERER

ORIGINAL SERIES COVERS BY
BRIAN WOOD

INTRODUCTION BY **GREG PALAST**

DMZ CREATED BY **BRIAN WOOD**
AND **RICCARDO BURCHIELLI**

DMZ
BLOOD
IN THE GAME

"TURN AROUND WHILE YOU CAN! TRUST ME, QUEENS SUCKS TOO!"

THE OCCUPIED TERRITORY OF MANHATTAN IS SUPPOSED TO BE A DEMILITARIZED ZONE — as long as you ignore the blown-apart corpses in front of the bodegas and Trustwell Corp assassins infiltrating the block parties.

This is the revolution and the most revolutionary thing you can do is...vote. Good fucking luck. The useless UN blue-helmets guarding the polling stations in Spanish Harlem can't stop the fix: ultra-right paramilitaries from the "Free States" have locked up with the Corporate Powers to contain the discontented and steal the election.

In the center of the story is a half-assed but earnest journalist, Matty Roth, whose need to voice the story of the voiceless is at war with his reasonable cowardice.

It's New York in the future and looks uncomfortably too much like America today. There's a phony war on terror, a hunt for illusory insurgents and troublemakers which becomes the trigger-point excuse for crushing the heaving, rising underclass.

Except here, in the comic, America's culture war and class war has moved to its inevitable bloody conclusion: a corporate junta pretending to provide safety to war-torn New York while using high-tech military intelligence and scum-bag death squads to hold on to power.

Reporter Roth is sent in to find and cover a charismatic street leader, Parco Delgado, who declares his candidacy with explosives. Is Delgado a greasy, piece-of-shit thug or a savior in a dirty T-shirt? What makes creators Wood and Burchielli such smart storytellers is that they don't make the answer simple, but they don't fail to give the answer.

Reporter Roth is a mess, a fuck-up you have to like. At times he doesn't know his ass from his elbow; he's an emotional fuck-wit, driving his girlfriend crazy, a fly-girl who is sure Delgado's a charlatan. Yet Roth has soul, and gives a shit when he knows a journalist shouldn't. So he fights over stories with editors parked in some distant, safe media tower while Roth gets his ass kicked, literally. Roth puts himself mindlessly in crazy danger while his brain is taking up precious think-time with trying to figure out what the hell his socialite mom is doing in the ghetto playing revolutionary as Parco's PR mouthpiece.

If the story sounds weird it's because any story that's real is weird.

I'm writing this after filing my own story from Eight Mile in Detroit. One foreclosed home after another, weeds to the roof. This guy in the last unemptied house on the street told me his son was just shot dead in his back yard. There's several foreclosure notices on his dinner table. He's working seven straights to keep his kids from having to live in a homeless shelter. But he's fucked and he knows it. He doesn't stand a chance. America is a fixed casino.

In DMZ, the damned and doomed have risen. They don't want to eat this shit anymore — but all they've done is bring out the iron claw from America's democracy glove. The poor are crushed, herded into the Bantustan of Uptown Manhattan and offered the peace of surrender in the class war.

This is a brilliant news report from inside America's skull dreaming into the future. A future closer than you think.

GREG PALAST

Greg Palast is the author of Armed Madhouse *and* The Best Democracy Money Can Buy. *He reports for BBC Television Newsnight.*

CHAPTER ONE

DMZ
VOTO

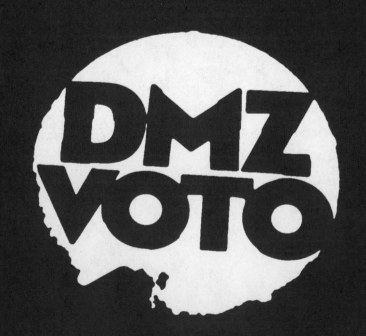

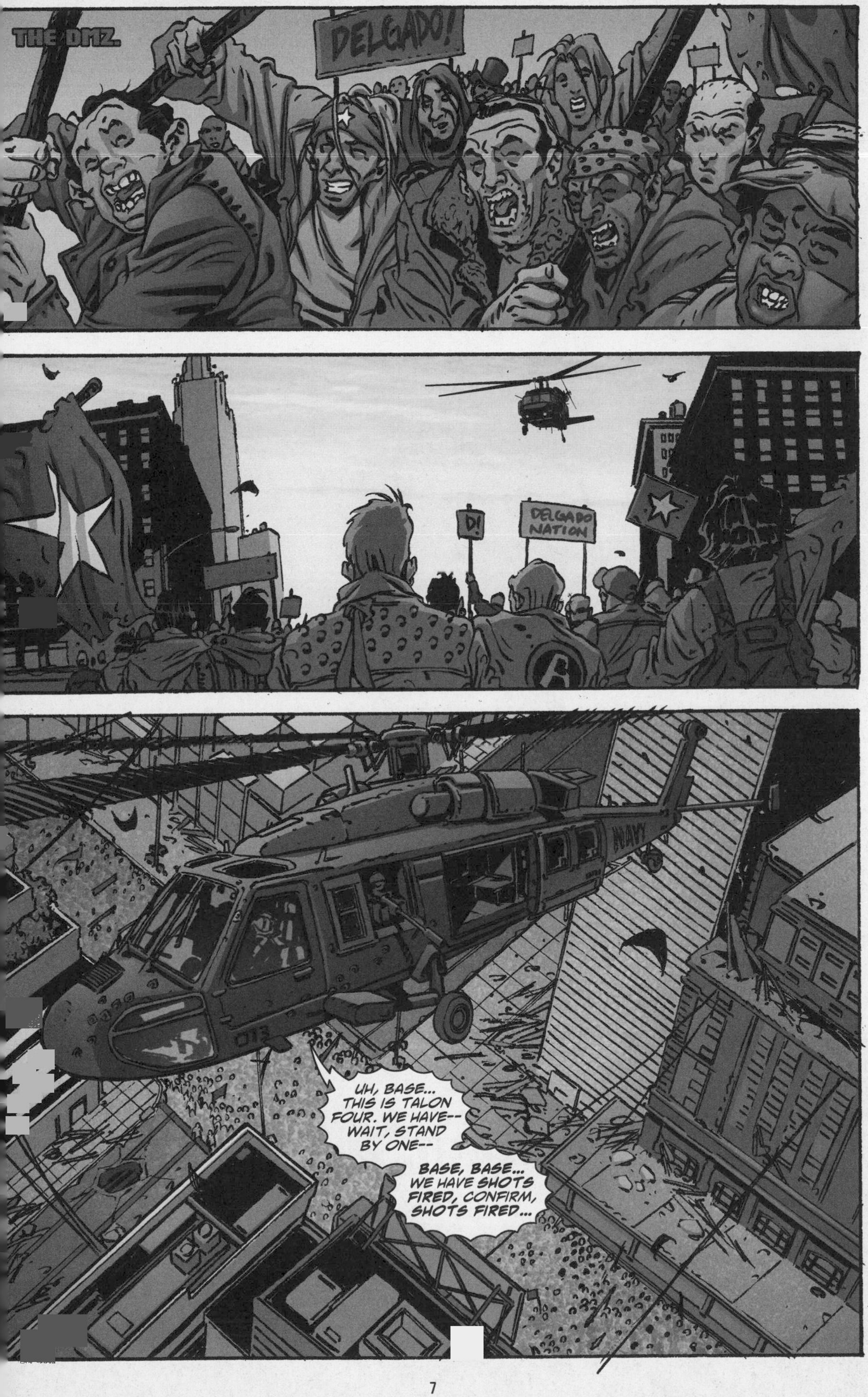
THE DMZ.
DELGADO!
D!
DELGADO NATION
NAVY
013
UH, BASE... THIS IS TALON FOUR. WE HAVE-- WAIT, STAND BY ONE--
BASE, BASE... WE HAVE SHOTS FIRED, CONFIRM, SHOTS FIRED...

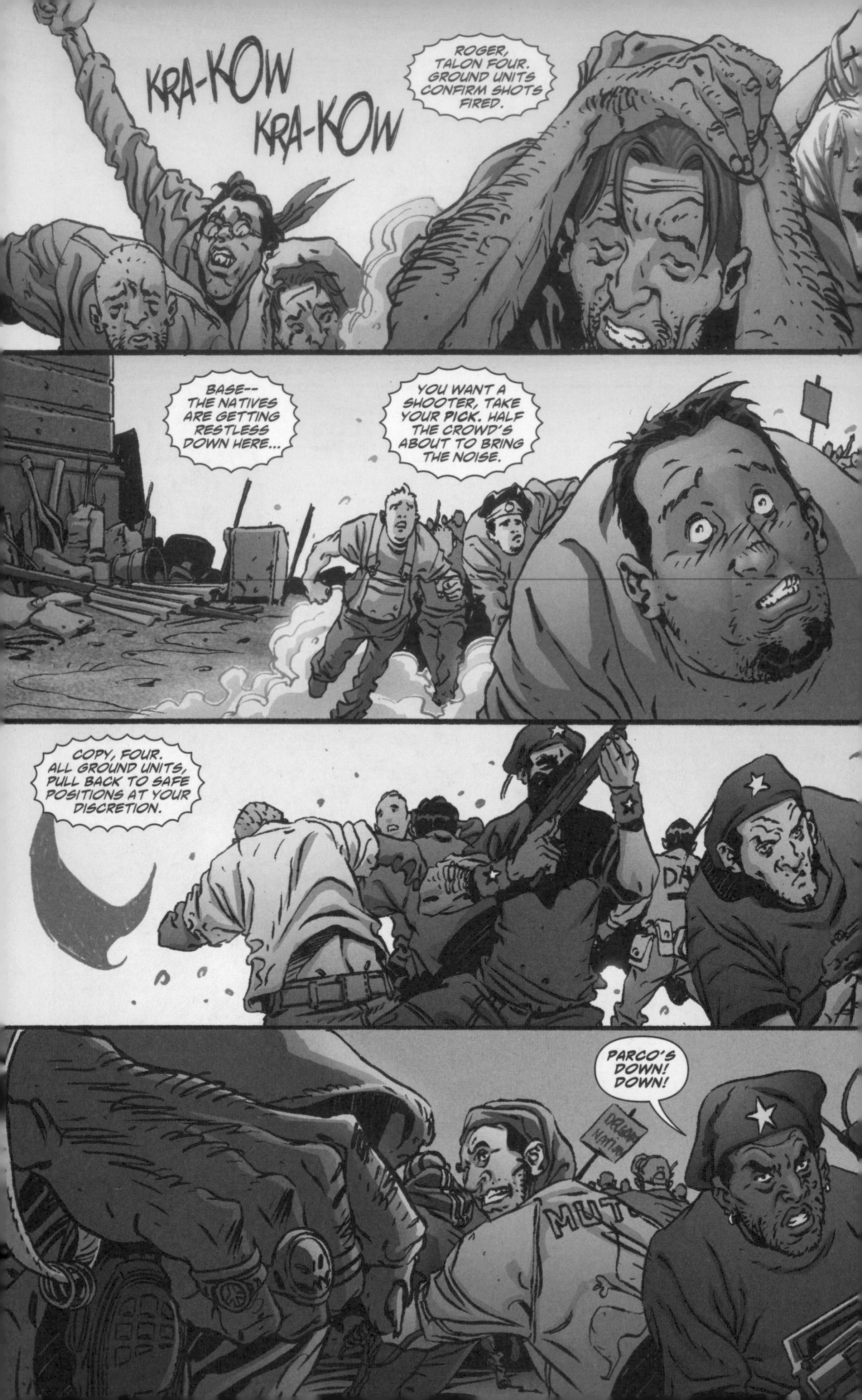
KRA-KOW
KRA-KOW
ROGER, TALON FOUR. GROUND UNITS CONFIRM SHOTS FIRED.
BASE-- THE NATIVES ARE GETTING RESTLESS DOWN HERE...
YOU WANT A SHOOTER, TAKE YOUR PICK. HALF THE CROWD'S ABOUT TO BRING THE NOISE.
COPY, FOUR. ALL GROUND UNITS, PULL BACK TO SAFE POSITIONS AT YOUR DISCRETION.
PARCO'S DOWN! DOWN!

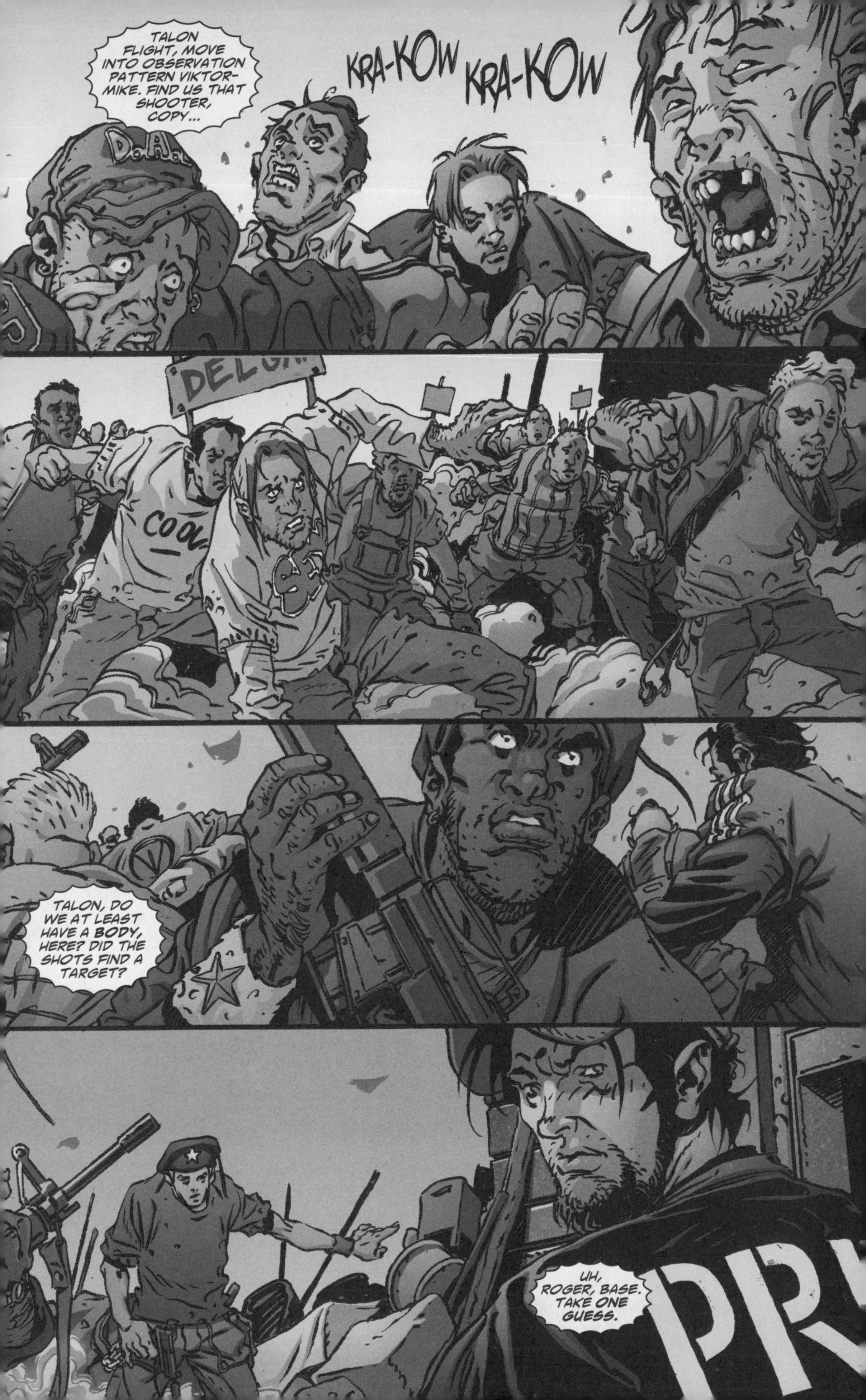
TALON FLIGHT, MOVE INTO OBSERVATION PATTERN VIKTOR-MIKE. FIND US THAT SHOOTER, COPY...
KRA-KOW KRA-KOW
TALON, DO WE AT LEAST HAVE A BODY, HERE? DID THE SHOTS FIND A TARGET?
UH, ROGER, BASE. TAKE ONE GUESS.

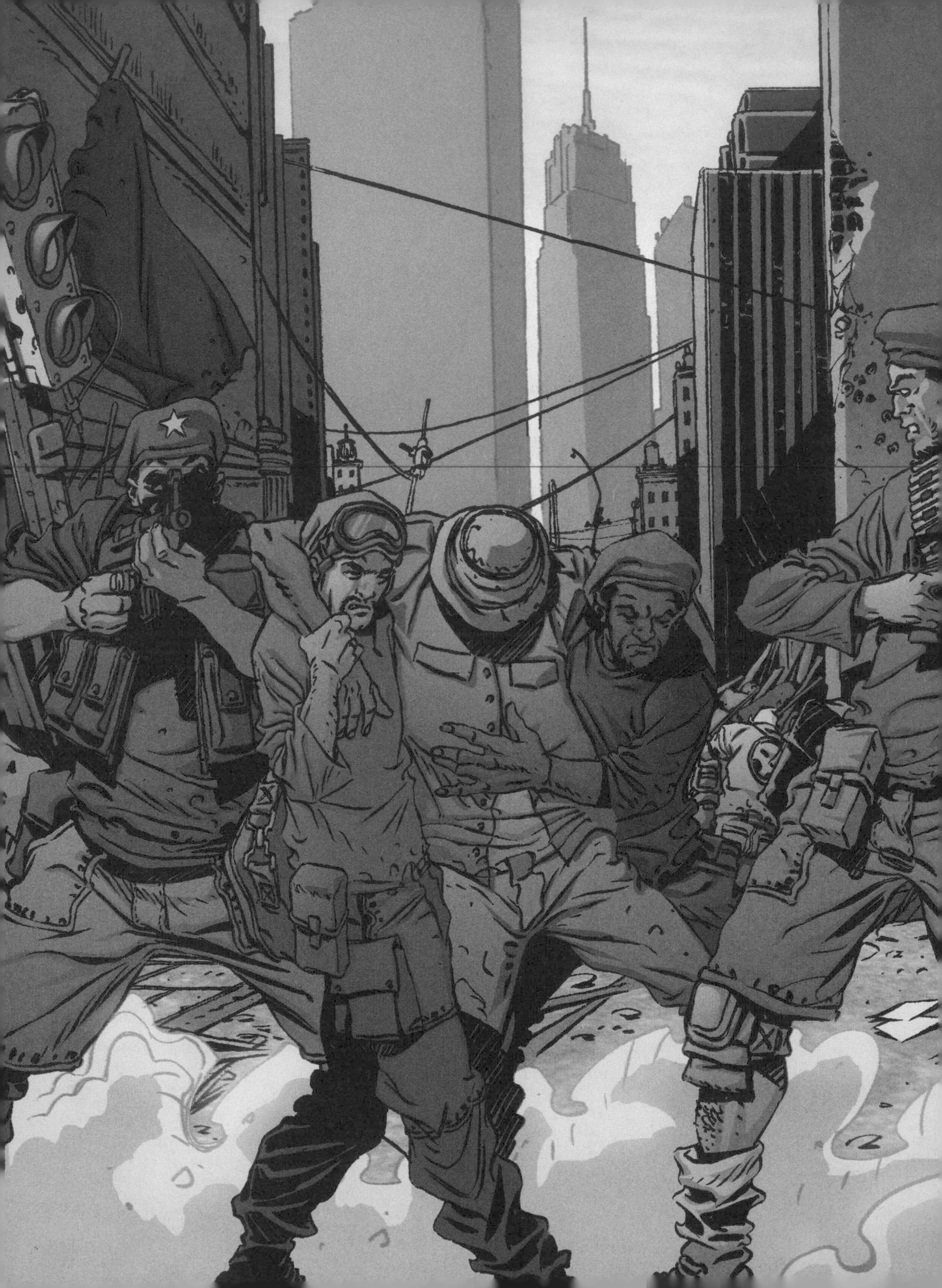

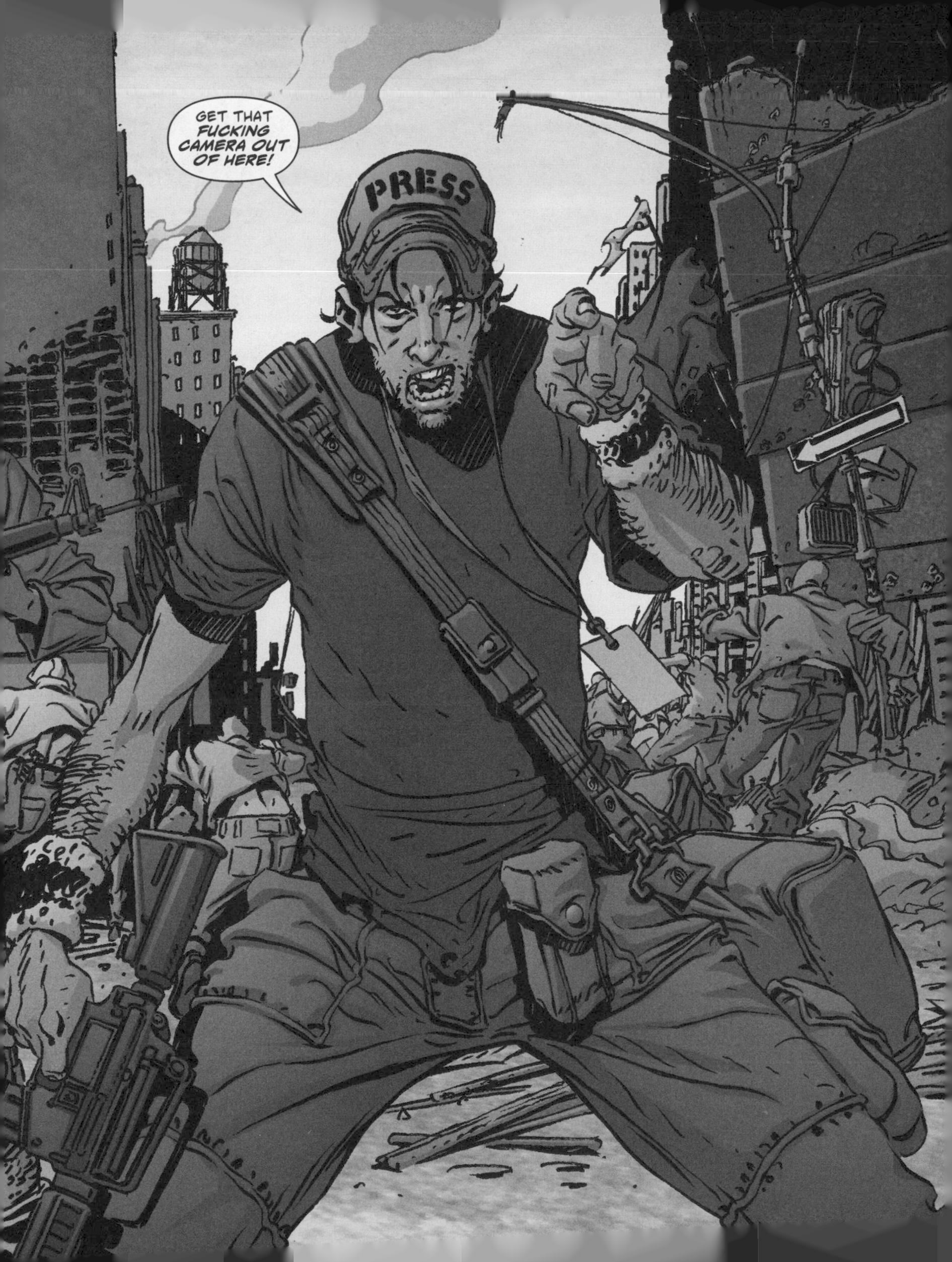
GET THAT FUCKING CAMERA OUT OF HERE!
PRESS

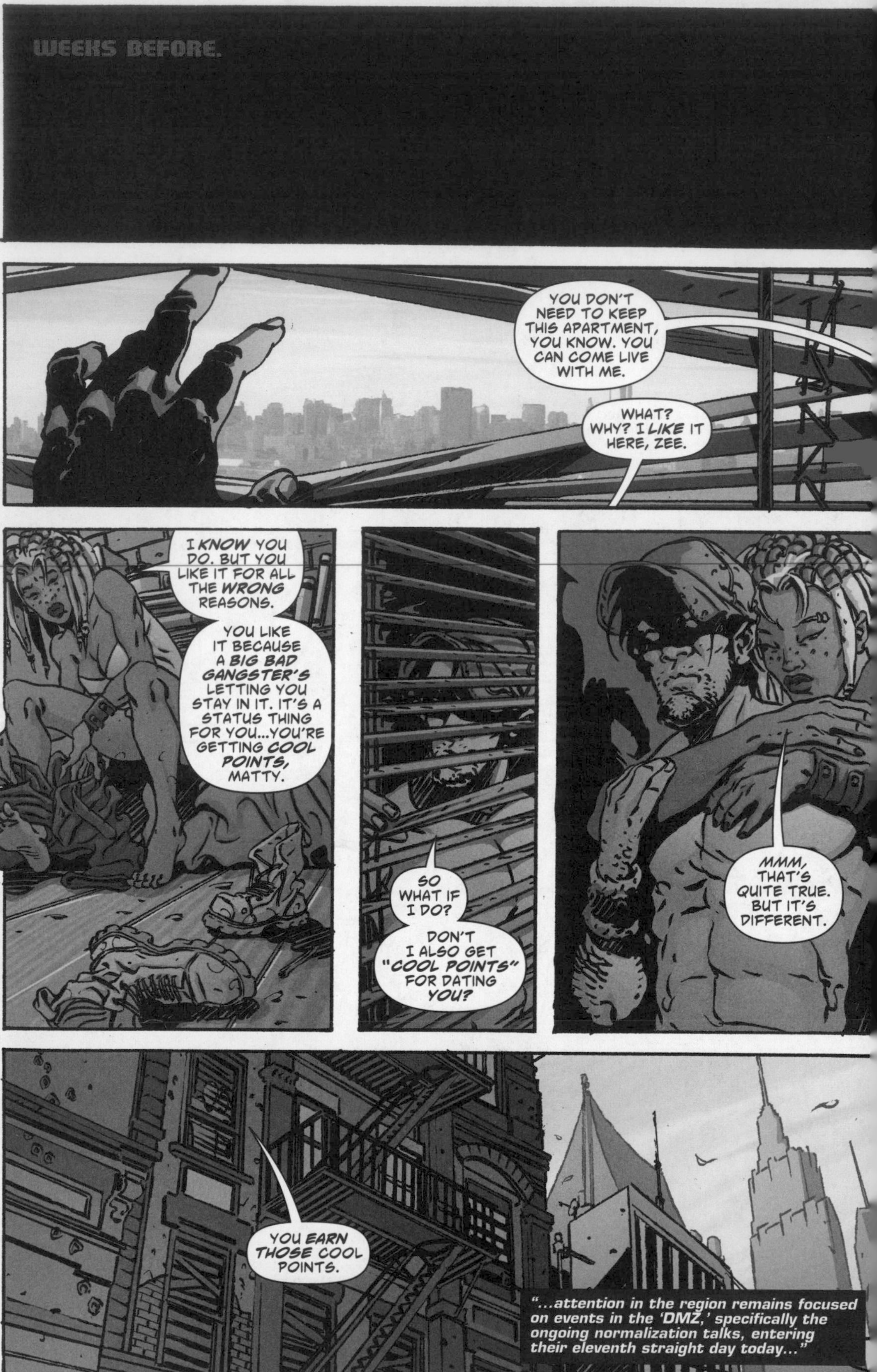
WEEKS BEFORE.
YOU DON'T NEED TO KEEP THIS APARTMENT, YOU KNOW. YOU CAN COME LIVE WITH ME.
WHAT? WHY? I LIKE IT HERE, ZEE.
I KNOW YOU DO. BUT YOU LIKE IT FOR ALL THE WRONG REASONS.
YOU LIKE IT BECAUSE A BIG BAD GANGSTER'S LETTING YOU STAY IN IT. IT'S A STATUS THING FOR YOU...YOU'RE GETTING COOL POINTS, MATTY.
SO WHAT IF I DO?
DON'T I ALSO GET "COOL POINTS" FOR DATING YOU?
MMM, THAT'S QUITE TRUE. BUT IT'S DIFFERENT.
YOU EARN THOSE COOL POINTS.
"...attention in the region remains focused on events in the 'DMZ,' specifically the ongoing normalization talks, entering their eleventh straight day today..."

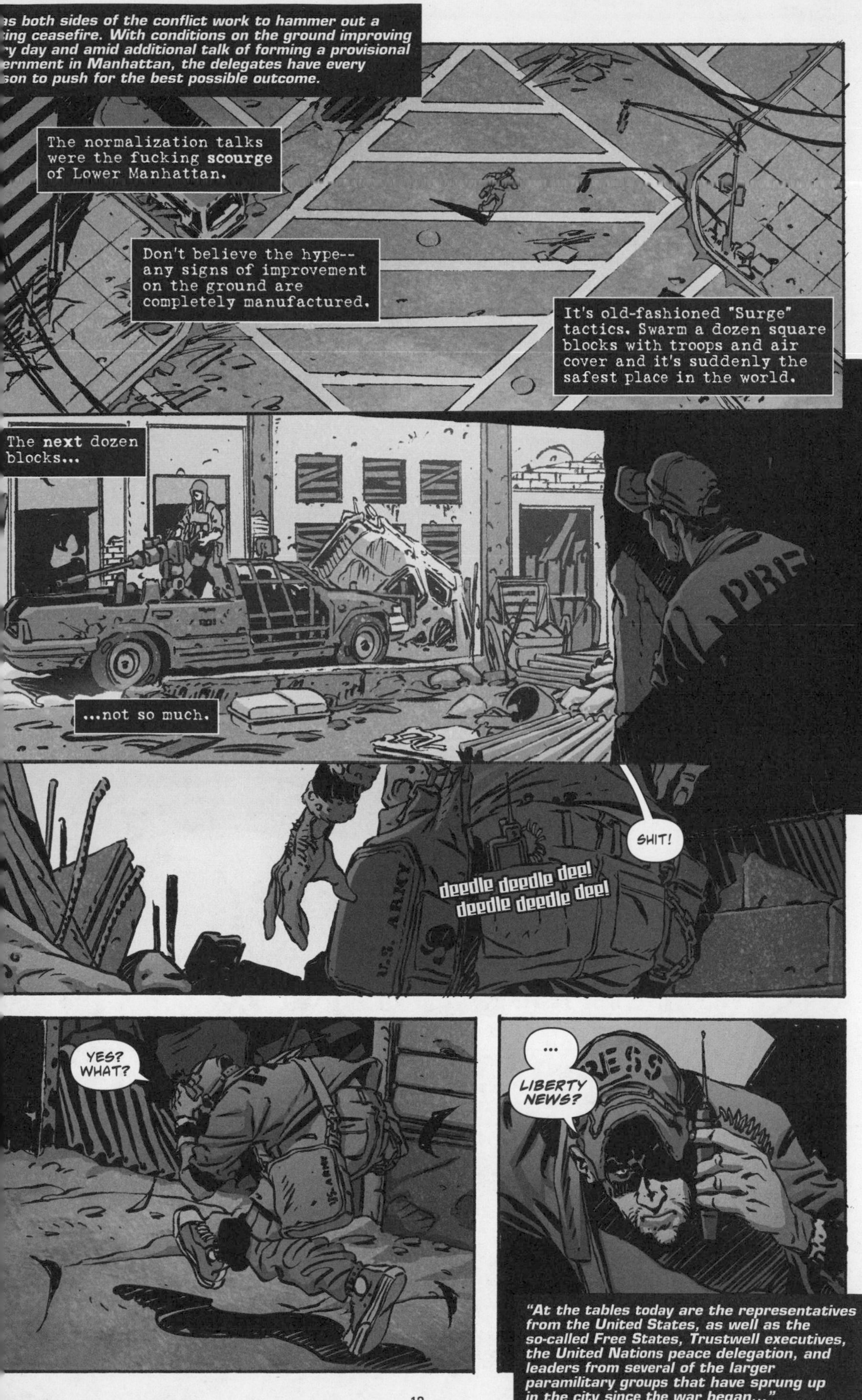

as both sides of the conflict work to hammer out a
ing ceasefire. With conditions on the ground improving
y day and amid additional talk of forming a provisional
ernment in Manhattan, the delegates have every
son to push for the best possible outcome.
The normalization talks were the fucking **scourge** of Lower Manhattan.
Don't believe the hype--any signs of improvement on the ground are completely manufactured.
It's old-fashioned "Surge" tactics. Swarm a dozen square blocks with troops and air cover and it's suddenly the safest place in the world.
The **next** dozen blocks...
...not so much.
SHIT!
deedle deedle dee! deedle deedle dee!
YES? WHAT?
...
LIBERTY NEWS?
"At the tables today are the representatives from the United States, as well as the so-called Free States, Trustwell executives, the United Nations peace delegation, and leaders from several of the larger paramilitary groups that have sprung up in the city since the war began..."

"...some question the inclusion of these leaders in the talks, but inside sources seem to indicate their presence is purely honorary-- a lasting peace solution will not include them as equal partners, or any sort of partner at all. They are expected to lay down arms and assimilate back into the civilian population."

"But for now, their strategic situation has earned them a minor place in the process, as they all gather to seek a way to end this war, once and for all."

ALL VERY STANDARD LANGUAGE, MR. ROTH...

ARE YOU *SERIOUS*? THE *LAST* CONTRACT I SIGNED FROM YOU GUYS, I ENDED UP OWING YOU FOR SHOT-UP EQUIPMENT.

SO HOLD ON, LET ME *READ* THE FUCKING THING, OK?

I signed their contract, yeah. Makes me a hypocrite, I know.

It also ge
me full pr
access to t
normalizat
talks and
conference
afterwards

I was heading up there anyway, so at least now I can be a **player** and not some loser behind a security cordon.

And what do they get?

My **soul**, of course.

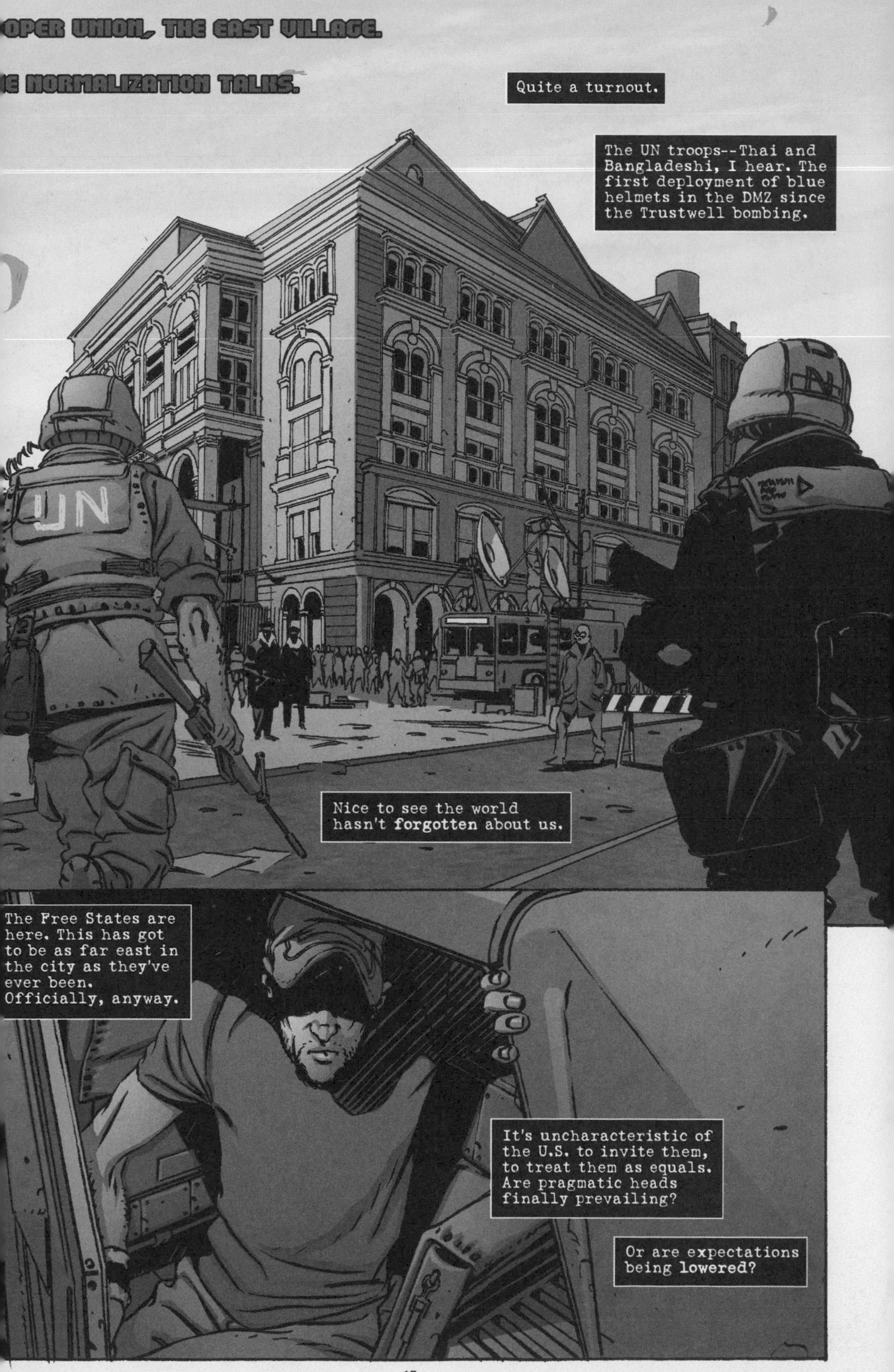
OPER UNION, THE EAST VILLAGE.
E NORMALIZATION TALKS.
Quite a turnout.
The UN troops--Thai and Bangladeshi, I hear. The first deployment of blue helmets in the DMZ since the Trustwell bombing.
UN
Nice to see the world hasn't **forgotten** about us.
The Free States are here. This has got to be as far east in the city as they've ever been. Officially, anyway.
It's uncharacteristic of the U.S. to invite them, to treat them as equals. Are pragmatic heads finally prevailing?
Or are expectations being **lowered**?

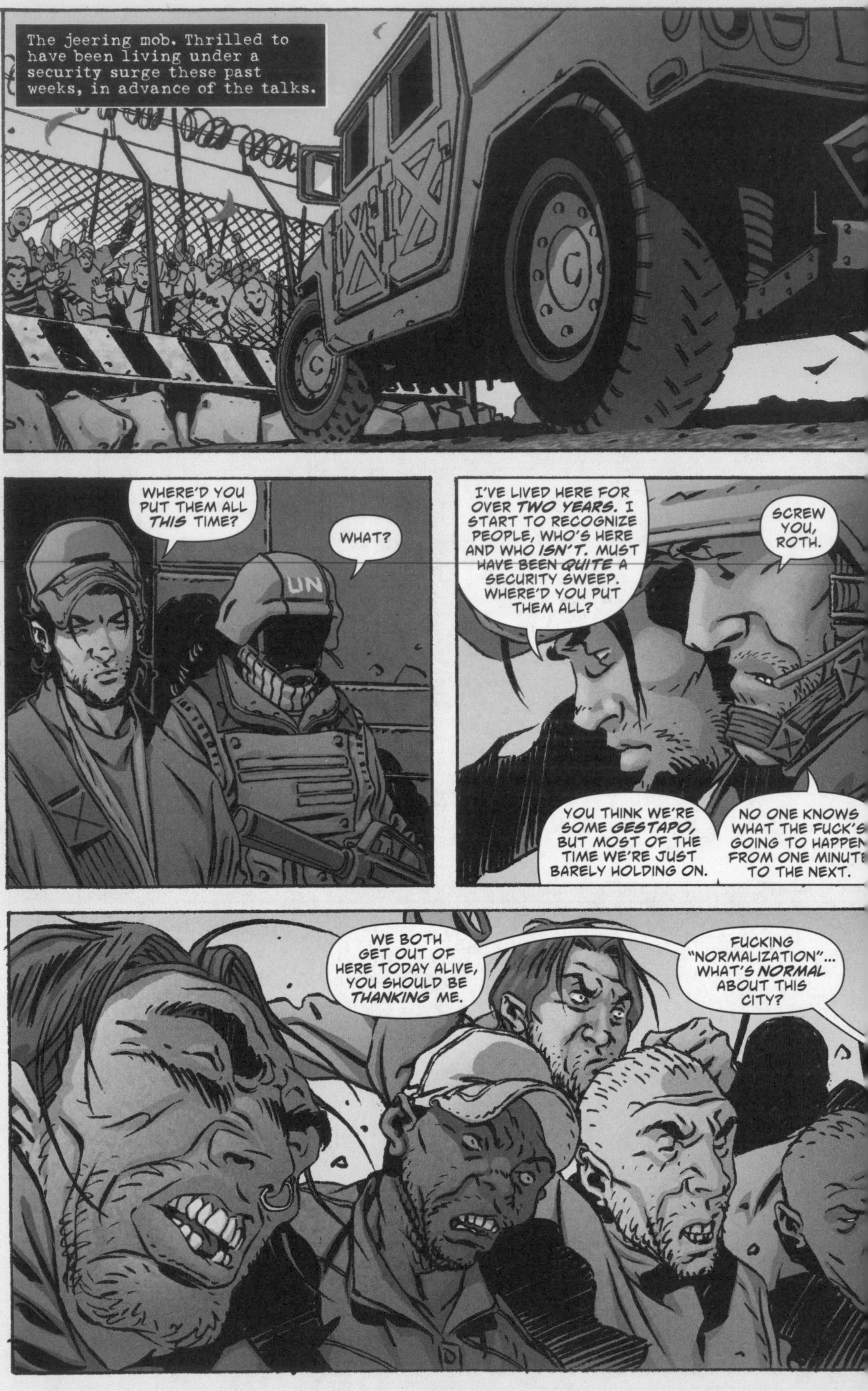
The jeering mob. Thrilled to have been living under a security surge these past weeks, in advance of the talks.
WHERE'D YOU PUT THEM ALL THIS TIME?
WHAT?
I'VE LIVED HERE FOR OVER TWO YEARS. I START TO RECOGNIZE PEOPLE, WHO'S HERE AND WHO ISN'T. MUST HAVE BEEN QUITE A SECURITY SWEEP. WHERE'D YOU PUT THEM ALL?
SCREW YOU, ROTH.
YOU THINK WE'RE SOME GESTAPO, BUT MOST OF THE TIME WE'RE JUST BARELY HOLDING ON.
NO ONE KNOWS WHAT THE FUCK'S GOING TO HAPPEN FROM ONE MINUTE TO THE NEXT.
WE BOTH GET OUT OF HERE TODAY ALIVE, YOU SHOULD BE THANKING ME.
FUCKING "NORMALIZATION"... WHAT'S NORMAL ABOUT THIS CITY?

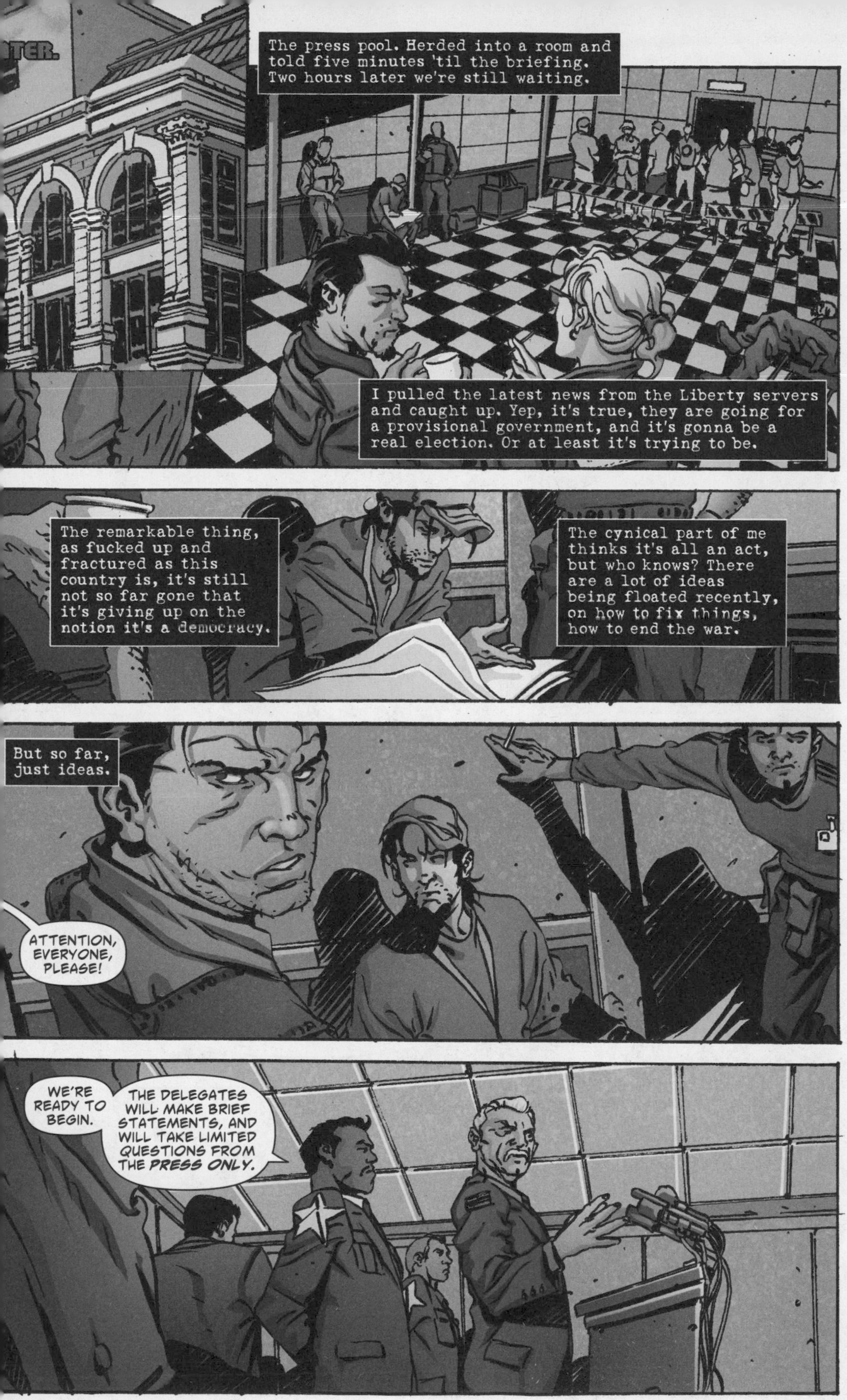
TER.
The press pool. Herded into a room and told five minutes 'til the briefing. Two hours later we're still waiting.
I pulled the latest news from the Liberty servers and caught up. Yep, it's true, they are going for a provisional government, and it's gonna be a real election. Or at least it's trying to be.
The remarkable thing, as fucked up and fractured as this country is, it's still not so far gone that it's giving up on the notion it's a democracy.
The cynical part of me thinks it's all an act, but who knows? There are a lot of ideas being floated recently, on how to fix things, how to end the war.
But so far, just ideas.
ATTENTION, EVERYONE, PLEASE!
WE'RE READY TO BEGIN.
THE DELEGATES WILL MAKE BRIEF STATEMENTS, AND WILL TAKE LIMITED QUESTIONS FROM THE PRESS ONLY.

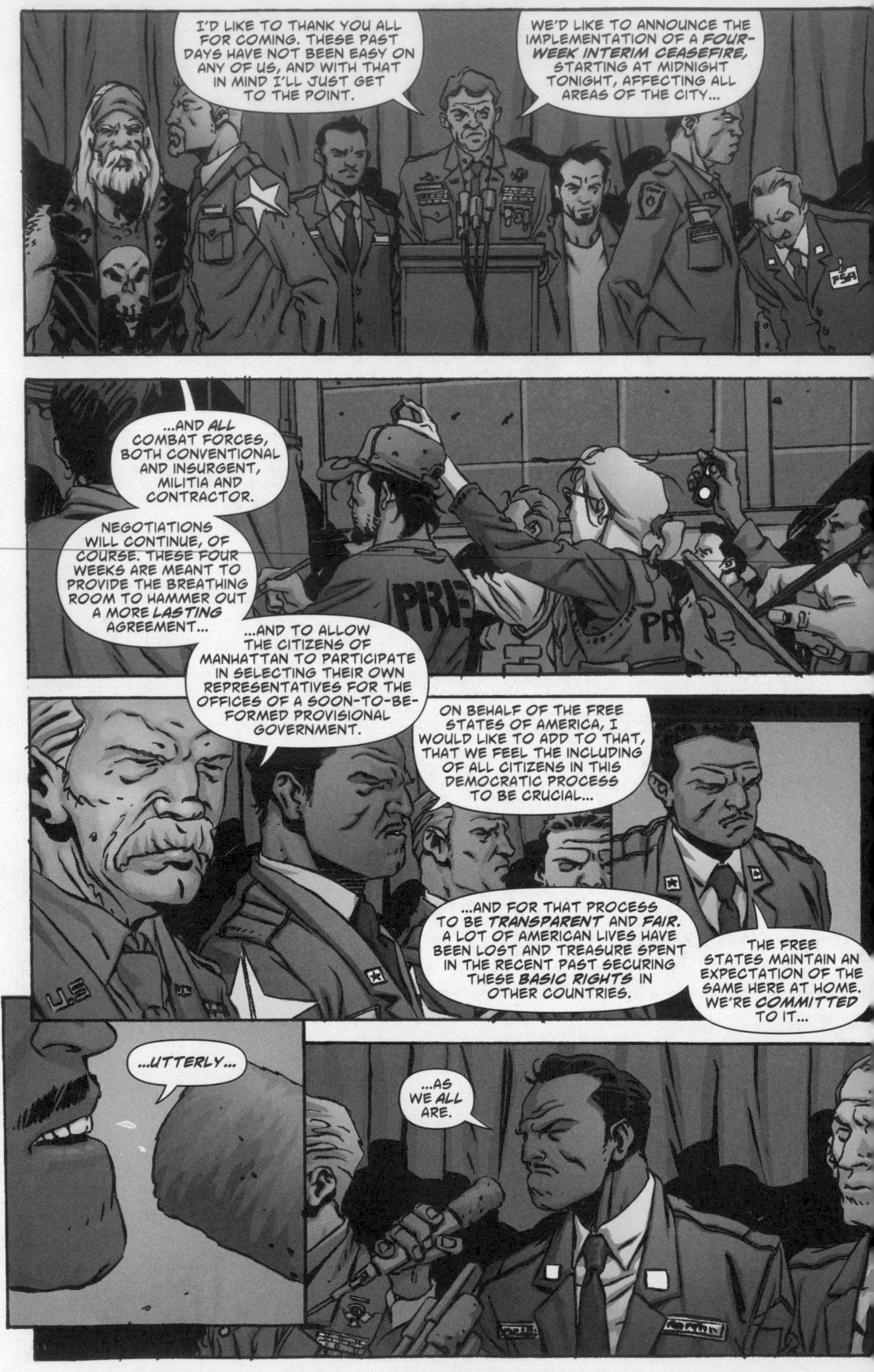

I'D LIKE TO THANK YOU ALL FOR COMING. THESE PAST DAYS HAVE NOT BEEN EASY ON ANY OF US, AND WITH THAT IN MIND I'LL JUST GET TO THE POINT.
WE'D LIKE TO ANNOUNCE THE IMPLEMENTATION OF A *FOUR-WEEK INTERIM CEASEFIRE,* STARTING AT MIDNIGHT TONIGHT, AFFECTING ALL AREAS OF THE CITY...
...AND *ALL* COMBAT FORCES, BOTH CONVENTIONAL AND INSURGENT, MILITIA AND CONTRACTOR.
NEGOTIATIONS WILL CONTINUE, OF COURSE. THESE FOUR WEEKS ARE MEANT TO PROVIDE THE BREATHING ROOM TO HAMMER OUT A MORE *LASTING* AGREEMENT...
...AND TO ALLOW THE CITIZENS OF MANHATTAN TO PARTICIPATE IN SELECTING THEIR OWN REPRESENTATIVES FOR THE OFFICES OF A SOON-TO-BE-FORMED PROVISIONAL GOVERNMENT.
ON BEHALF OF THE FREE STATES OF AMERICA, I WOULD LIKE TO ADD TO THAT, THAT WE FEEL THE INCLUDING OF ALL CITIZENS IN THIS DEMOCRATIC PROCESS TO BE CRUCIAL...
...AND FOR THAT PROCESS TO BE *TRANSPARENT* AND *FAIR.* A LOT OF AMERICAN LIVES HAVE BEEN LOST AND TREASURE SPENT IN THE RECENT PAST SECURING THESE *BASIC RIGHTS* IN OTHER COUNTRIES.
THE FREE STATES MAINTAIN AN EXPECTATION OF THE SAME HERE AT HOME. WE'RE *COMMITTED* TO IT...
...UTTERLY...
...AS WE *ALL* ARE.

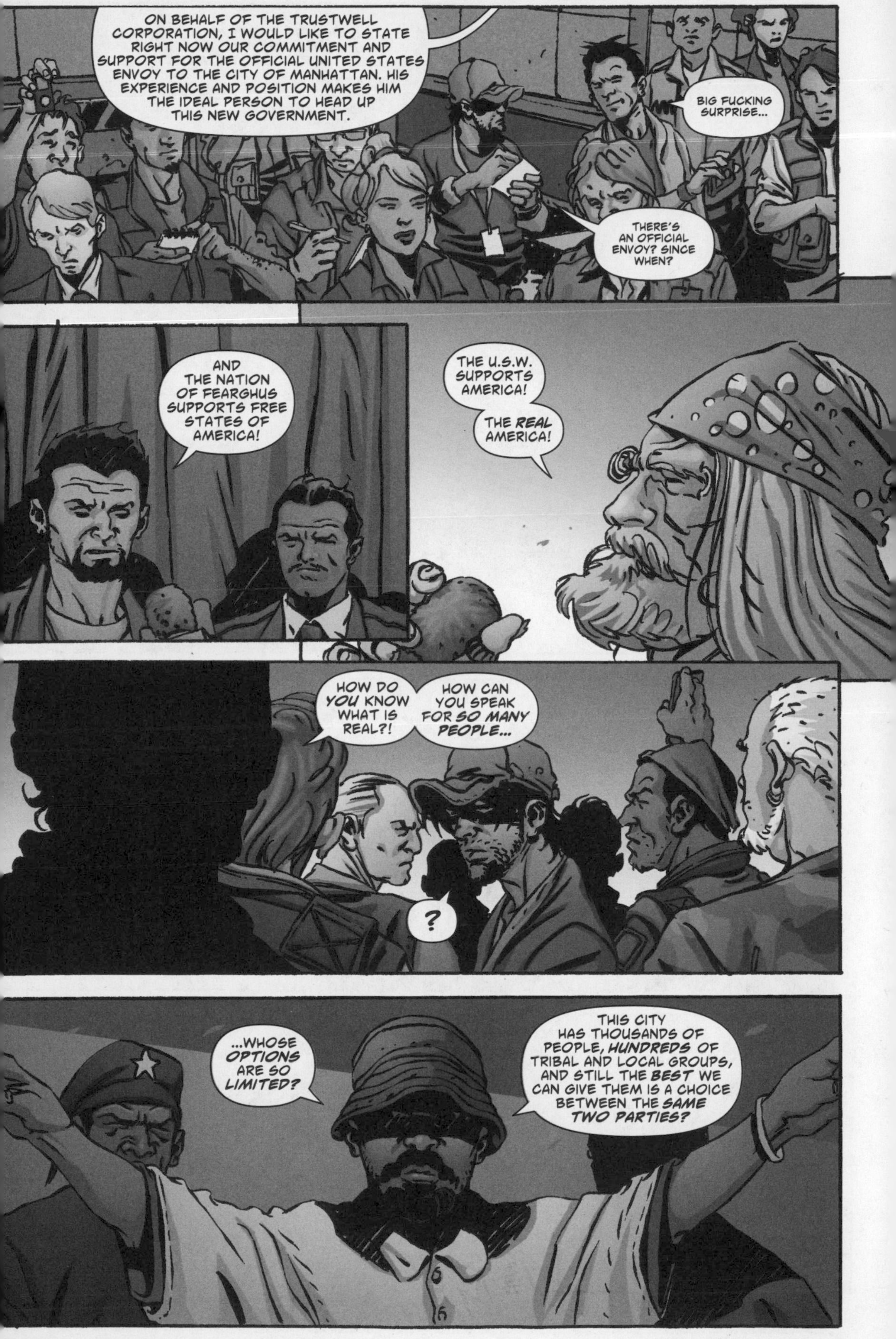
ON BEHALF OF THE TRUSTWELL CORPORATION, I WOULD LIKE TO STATE RIGHT NOW OUR COMMITMENT AND SUPPORT FOR THE OFFICIAL UNITED STATES ENVOY TO THE CITY OF MANHATTAN. HIS EXPERIENCE AND POSITION MAKES HIM THE IDEAL PERSON TO HEAD UP THIS NEW GOVERNMENT.
BIG FUCKING SURPRISE...
THERE'S AN OFFICIAL ENVOY? SINCE WHEN?
AND THE NATION OF FEARGHUS SUPPORTS FREE STATES OF AMERICA!
THE U.S.W. SUPPORTS AMERICA!
THE REAL AMERICA!
HOW DO YOU KNOW WHAT IS REAL?!
HOW CAN YOU SPEAK FOR SO MANY PEOPLE...
?
...WHOSE OPTIONS ARE SO LIMITED?
THIS CITY HAS THOUSANDS OF PEOPLE, HUNDREDS OF TRIBAL AND LOCAL GROUPS, AND STILL THE BEST WE CAN GIVE THEM IS A CHOICE BETWEEN THE SAME TWO PARTIES?

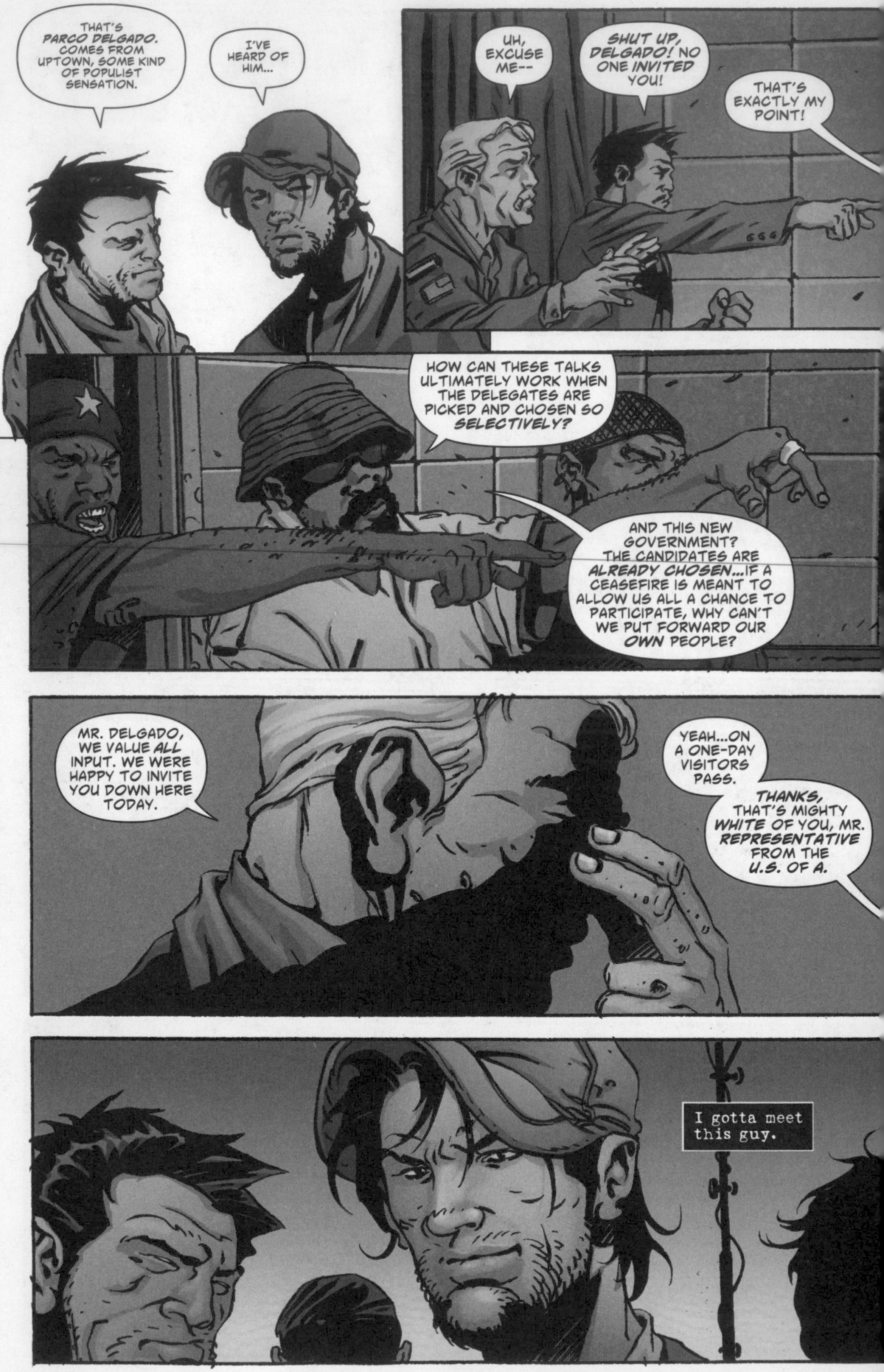
THAT'S PARCO DELGADO. COMES FROM UPTOWN, SOME KIND OF POPULIST SENSATION.
I'VE HEARD OF HIM...
UH, EXCUSE ME--
SHUT UP, DELGADO! NO ONE INVITED YOU!
THAT'S EXACTLY MY POINT!
HOW CAN THESE TALKS ULTIMATELY WORK WHEN THE DELEGATES ARE PICKED AND CHOSEN SO SELECTIVELY?
AND THIS NEW GOVERNMENT? THE CANDIDATES ARE ALREADY CHOSEN...IF A CEASEFIRE IS MEANT TO ALLOW US ALL A CHANCE TO PARTICIPATE, WHY CAN'T WE PUT FORWARD OUR OWN PEOPLE?
MR. DELGADO, WE VALUE ALL INPUT. WE WERE HAPPY TO INVITE YOU DOWN HERE TODAY.
YEAH...ON A ONE-DAY VISITORS PASS.
THANKS, THAT'S MIGHTY WHITE OF YOU, MR. REPRESENTATIVE FROM THE U.S. OF A.
I gotta meet this guy.

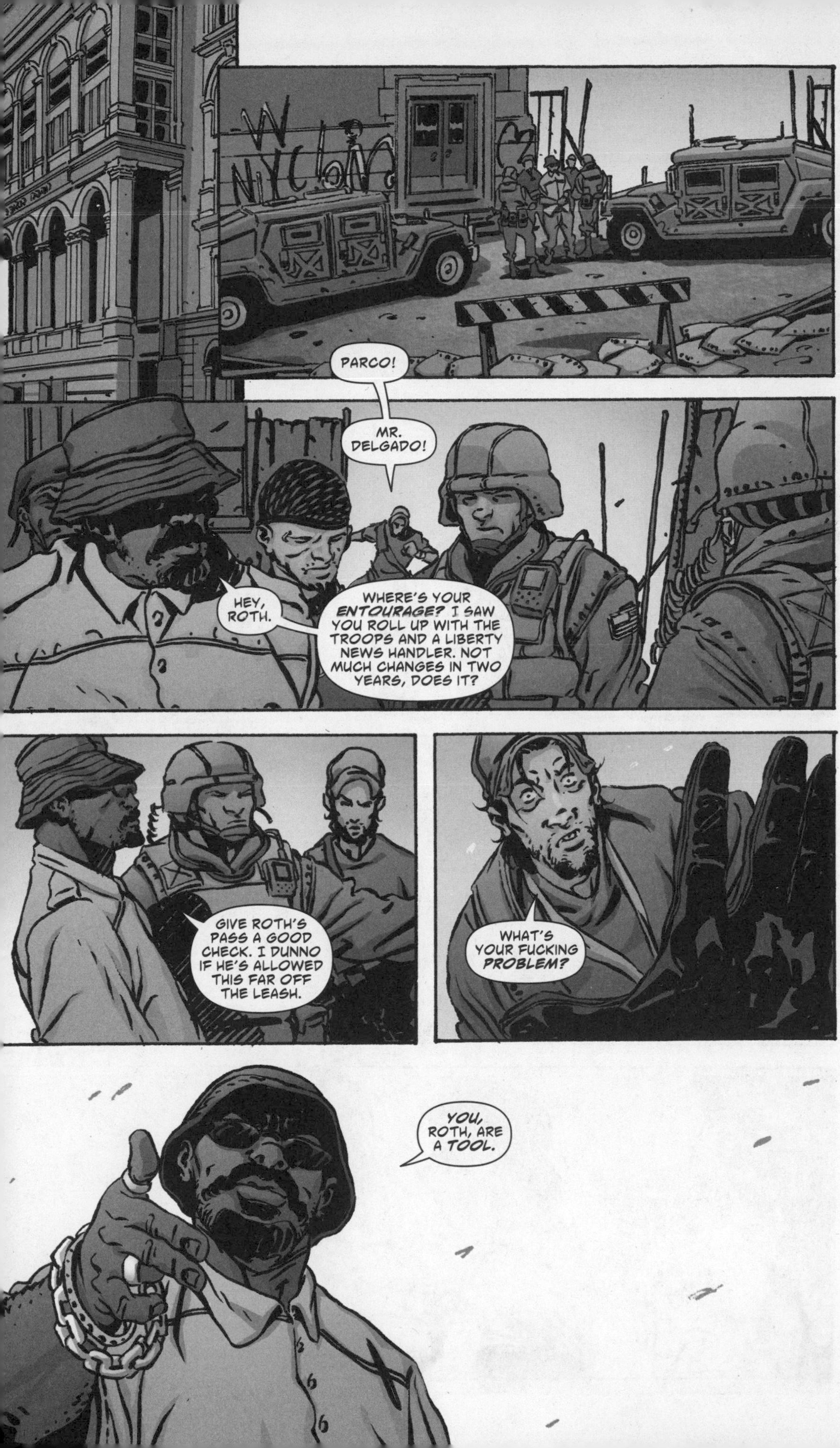
PARCO!
MR. DELGADO!
HEY, ROTH.
WHERE'S YOUR *ENTOURAGE?* I SAW YOU ROLL UP WITH THE TROOPS AND A LIBERTY NEWS HANDLER. NOT MUCH CHANGES IN TWO YEARS, DOES IT?
GIVE ROTH'S PASS A GOOD CHECK. I DUNNO IF HE'S ALLOWED THIS FAR OFF THE LEASH.
WHAT'S YOUR FUCKING *PROBLEM?*
YOU, ROTH, ARE A *TOOL.*

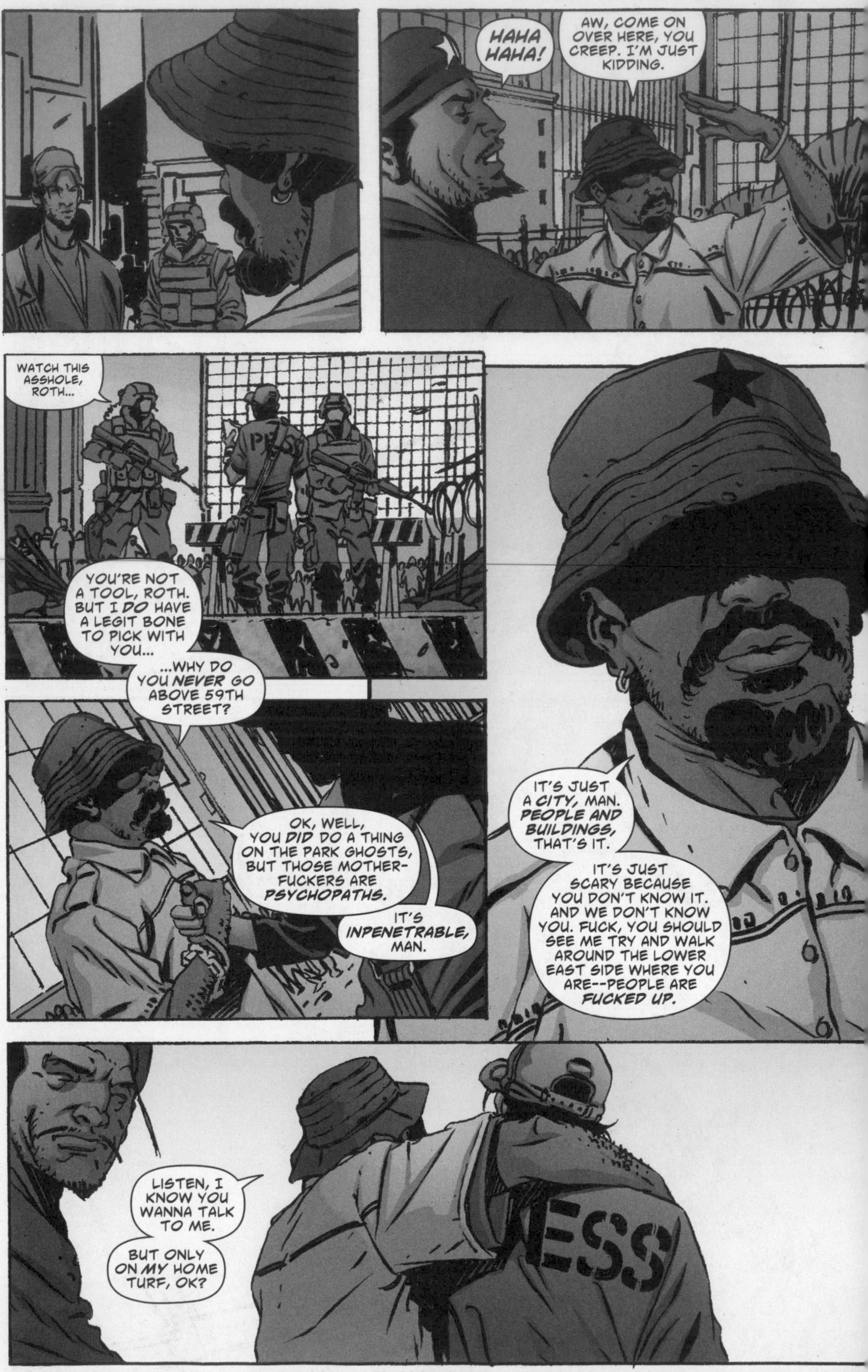
HAHA HAHA!
AW, COME ON OVER HERE, YOU CREEP. I'M JUST KIDDING.
WATCH THIS ASSHOLE, ROTH...
YOU'RE NOT A TOOL, ROTH. BUT I DO HAVE A LEGIT BONE TO PICK WITH YOU...
...WHY DO YOU NEVER GO ABOVE 59TH STREET?
OK, WELL, YOU DID DO A THING ON THE PARK GHOSTS, BUT THOSE MOTHER-FUCKERS ARE PSYCHOPATHS.
IT'S INPENETRABLE, MAN.
IT'S JUST A CITY, MAN. PEOPLE AND BUILDINGS, THAT'S IT.
IT'S JUST SCARY BECAUSE YOU DON'T KNOW IT. AND WE DON'T KNOW YOU. FUCK, YOU SHOULD SEE ME TRY AND WALK AROUND THE LOWER EAST SIDE WHERE YOU ARE--PEOPLE ARE FUCKED UP.
LISTEN, I KNOW YOU WANNA TALK TO ME.
BUT ONLY ON MY HOME TURF, OK?

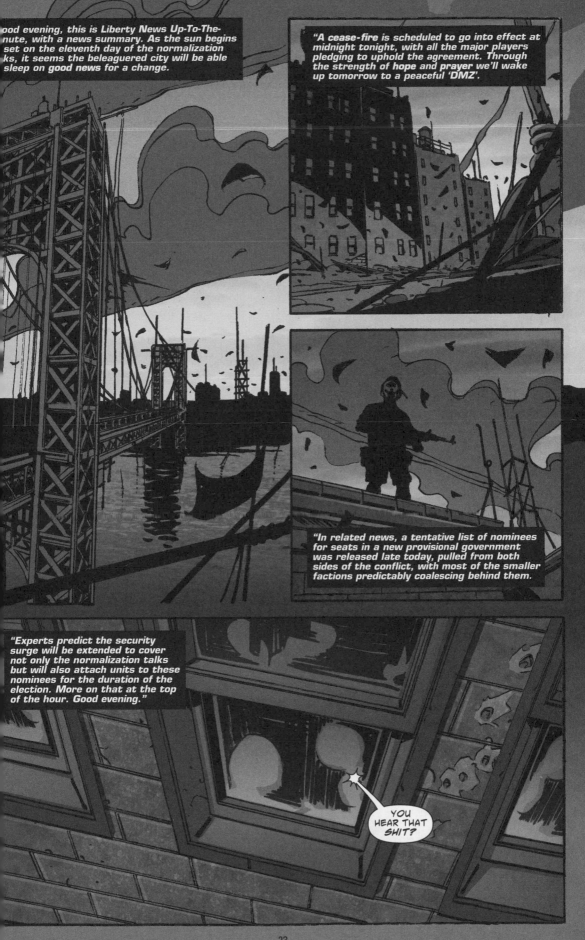

"ood evening, this is Liberty News Up-To-The-nute, with a news summary. As the sun begins set on the eleventh day of the normalization ks, it seems the beleaguered city will be able sleep on *good news* for a change.

"A cease-fire is scheduled to go into effect at midnight tonight, with all the major players pledging to uphold the agreement. Through the strength of *hope* and *prayer* we'll wake up tomorrow to a peaceful 'DMZ'.

"In related news, a tentative list of nominees for seats in a new provisional government was released late today, pulled from both sides of the conflict, with most of the smaller factions predictably coalescing behind them.

"Experts predict the security surge will be extended to cover not only the normalization talks but will also attach units to these nominees for the duration of the election. More on that at the top of the hour. Good evening."

YOU HEAR THAT SHIT?

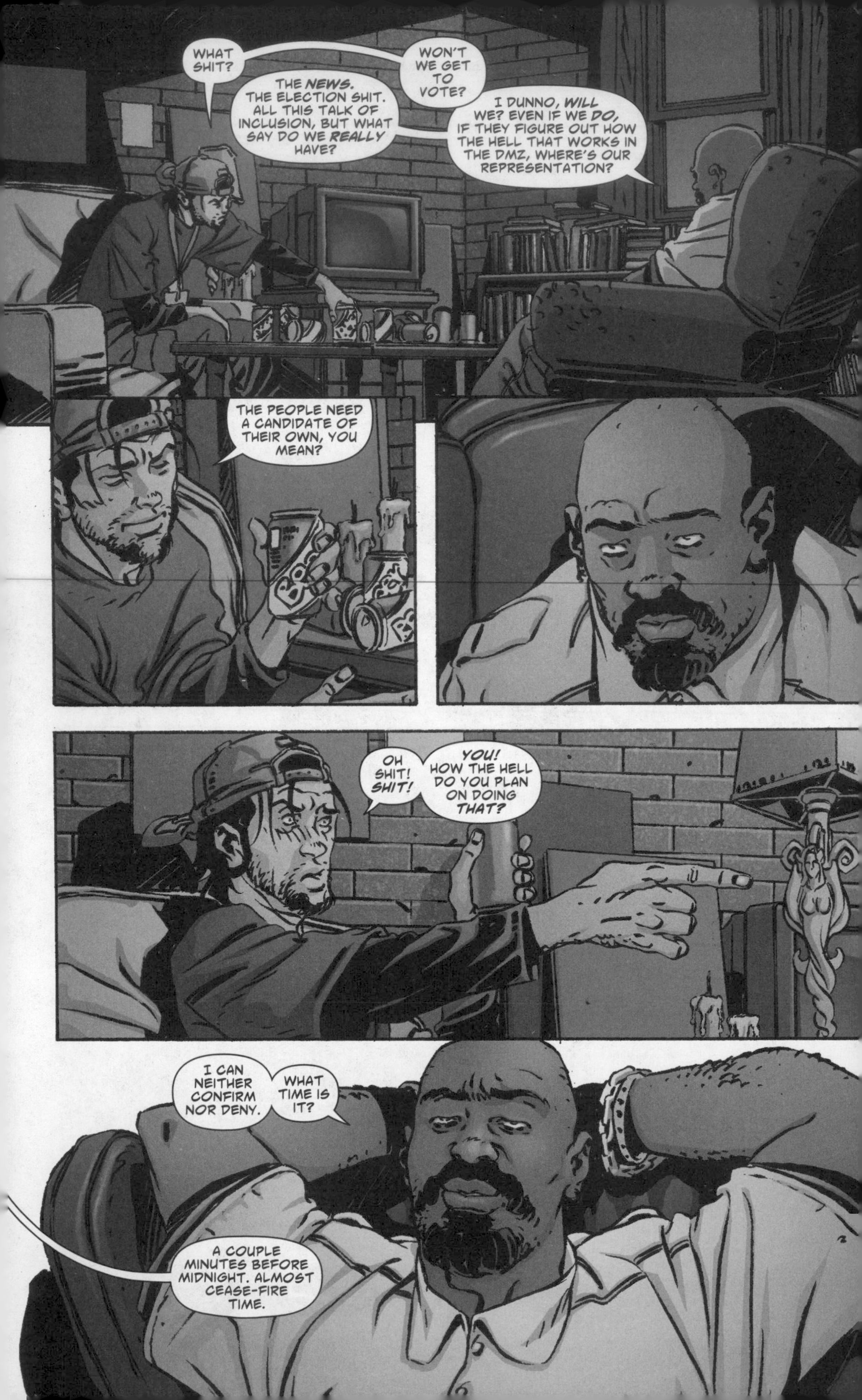
WHAT SHIT?
THE NEWS. THE ELECTION SHIT. ALL THIS TALK OF INCLUSION, BUT WHAT SAY DO WE REALLY HAVE?
WON'T WE GET TO VOTE?
I DUNNO, WILL WE? EVEN IF WE DO, IF THEY FIGURE OUT HOW THE HELL THAT WORKS IN THE DMZ, WHERE'S OUR REPRESENTATION?
THE PEOPLE NEED A CANDIDATE OF THEIR OWN, YOU MEAN?
OH SHIT! SHIT!
YOU! HOW THE HELL DO YOU PLAN ON DOING THAT?
I CAN NEITHER CONFIRM NOR DENY.
WHAT TIME IS IT?
A COUPLE MINUTES BEFORE MIDNIGHT. ALMOST CEASE-FIRE TIME.

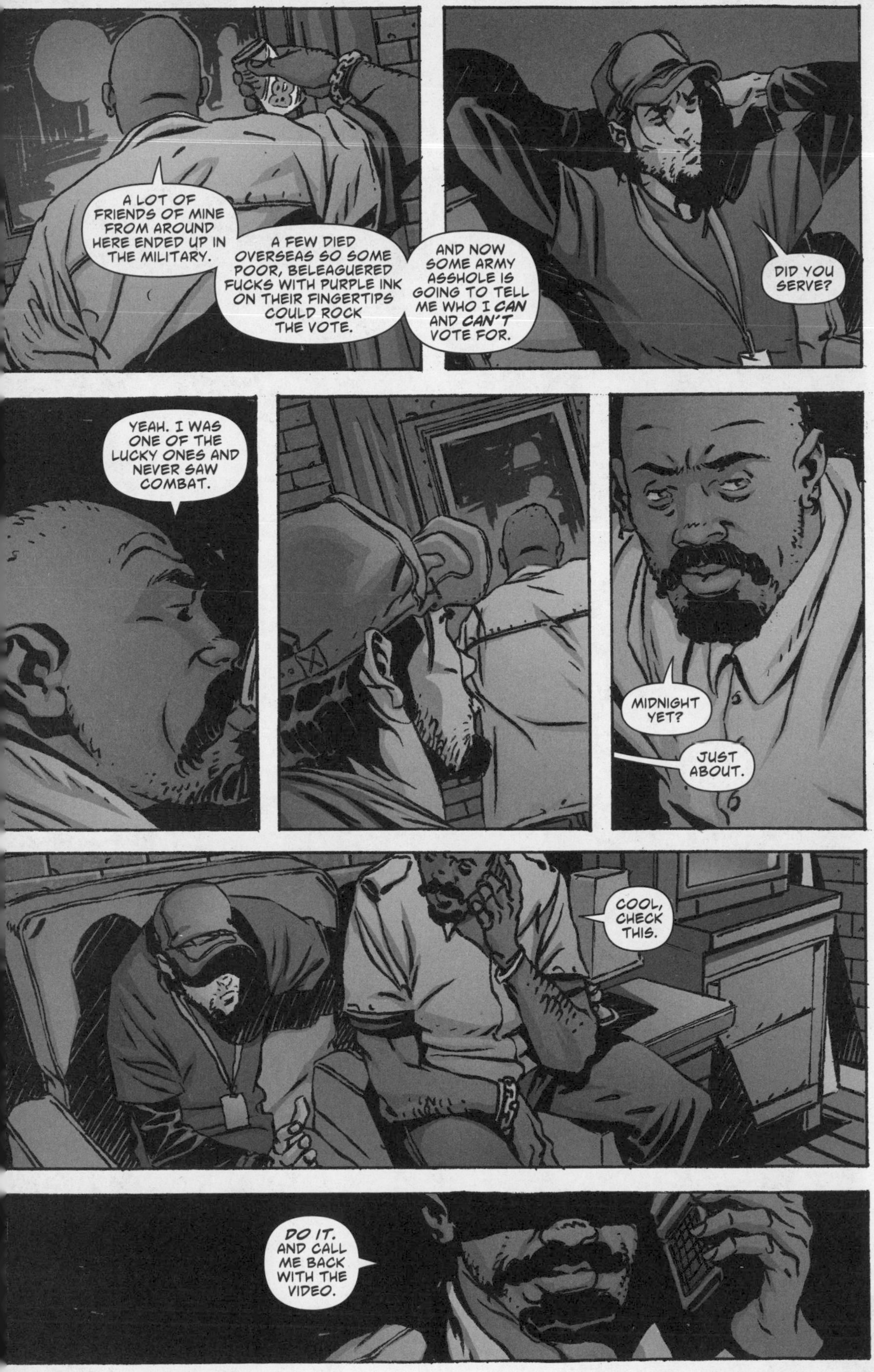
A LOT OF FRIENDS OF MINE FROM AROUND HERE ENDED UP IN THE MILITARY.
A FEW DIED OVERSEAS SO SOME POOR, BELEAGUERED FUCKS WITH PURPLE INK ON THEIR FINGERTIPS COULD ROCK THE VOTE.
AND NOW SOME ARMY ASSHOLE IS GOING TO TELL ME WHO I *CAN* AND *CAN'T* VOTE FOR.
DID YOU SERVE?
YEAH. I WAS ONE OF THE LUCKY ONES AND NEVER SAW COMBAT.
MIDNIGHT YET?
JUST ABOUT.
COOL, CHECK THIS.
DO IT. AND CALL ME BACK WITH THE VIDEO.

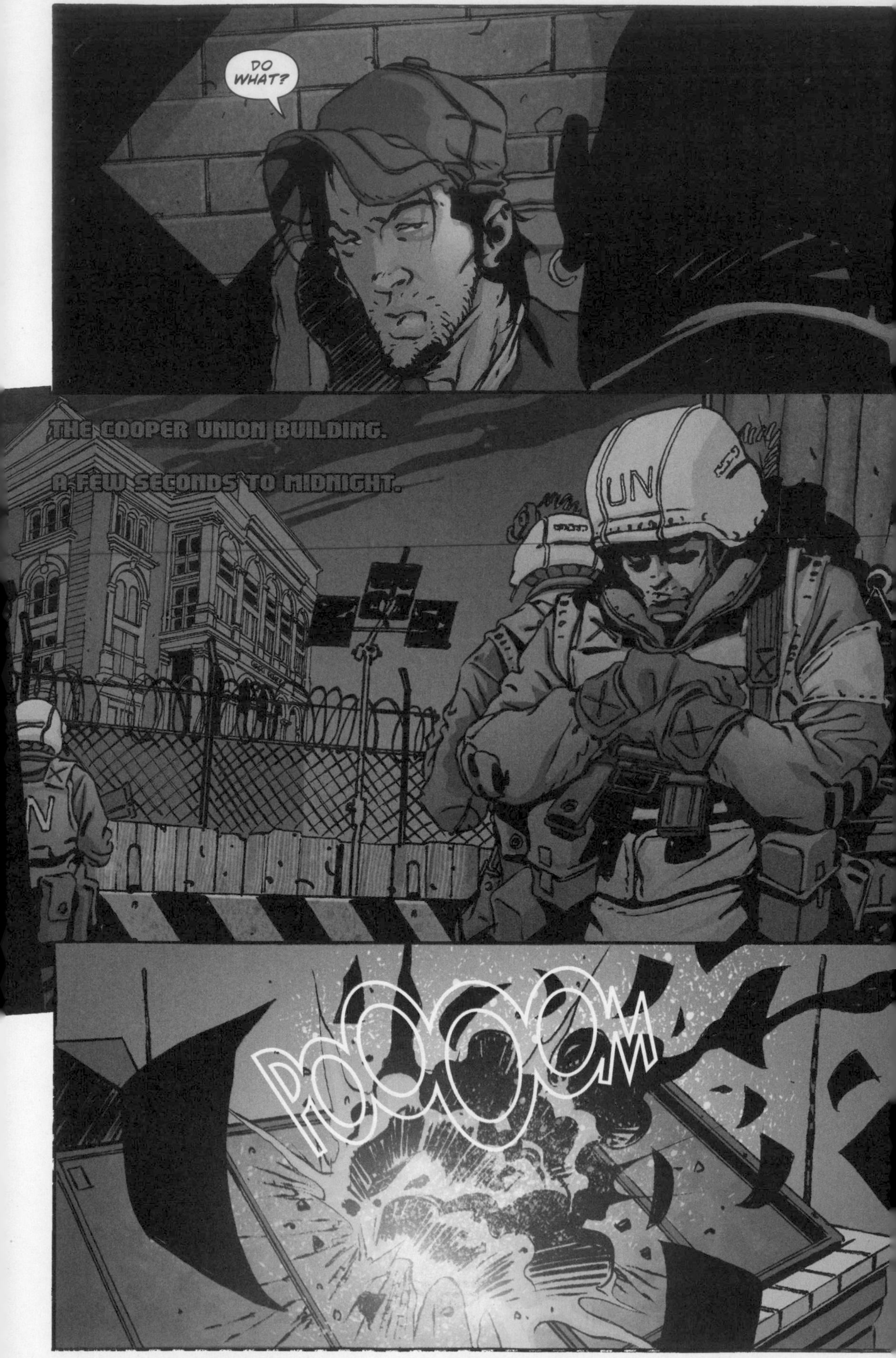
DO WHAT?
THE COOPER UNION BUILDING.
A FEW SECONDS TO MIDNIGHT.
POOOOOM

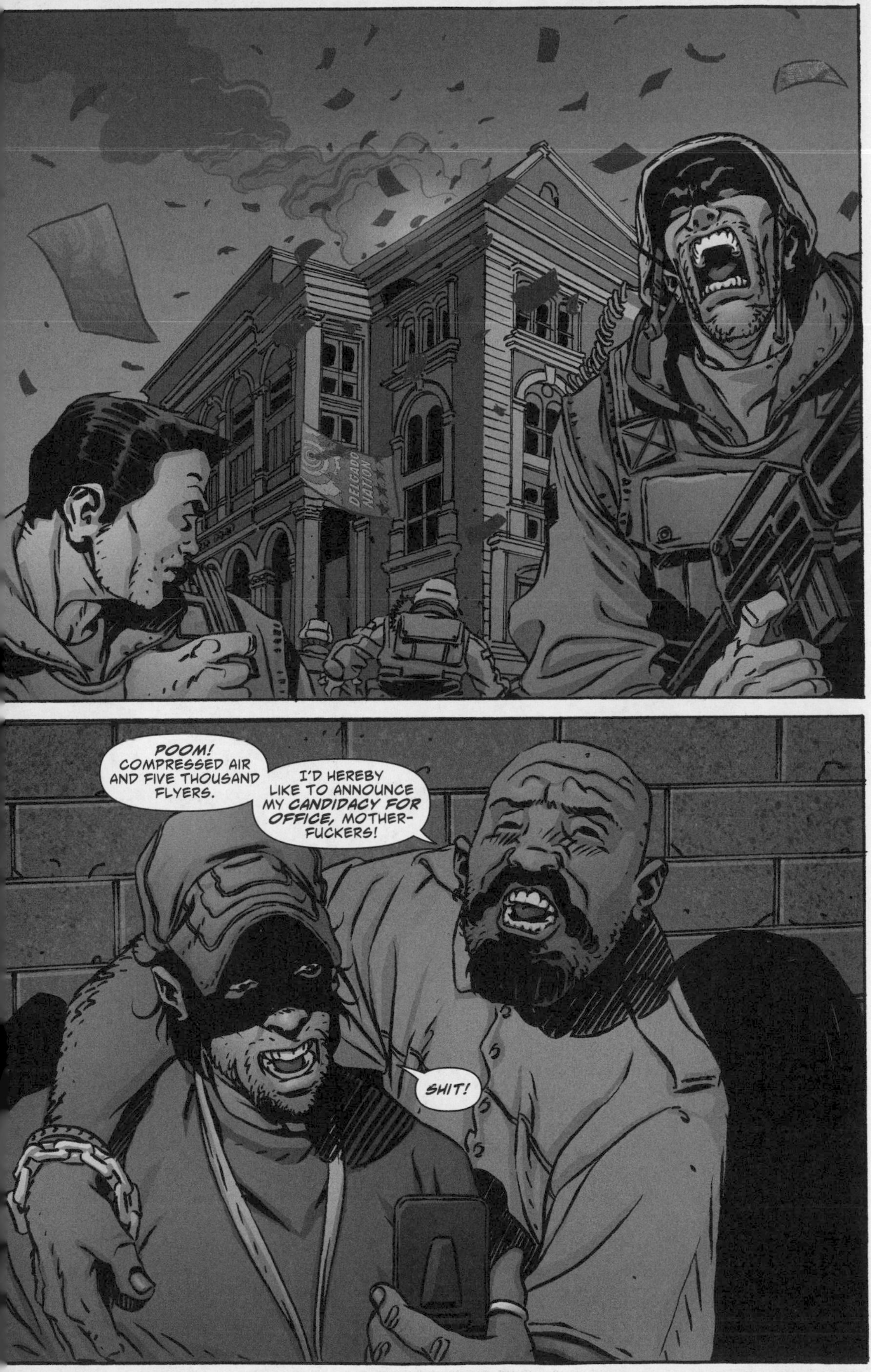
DELGADO NATION
POOM! COMPRESSED AIR AND FIVE THOUSAND FLYERS.
I'D HEREBY LIKE TO ANNOUNCE MY CANDIDACY FOR OFFICE, MOTHER-FUCKERS!
SHIT!

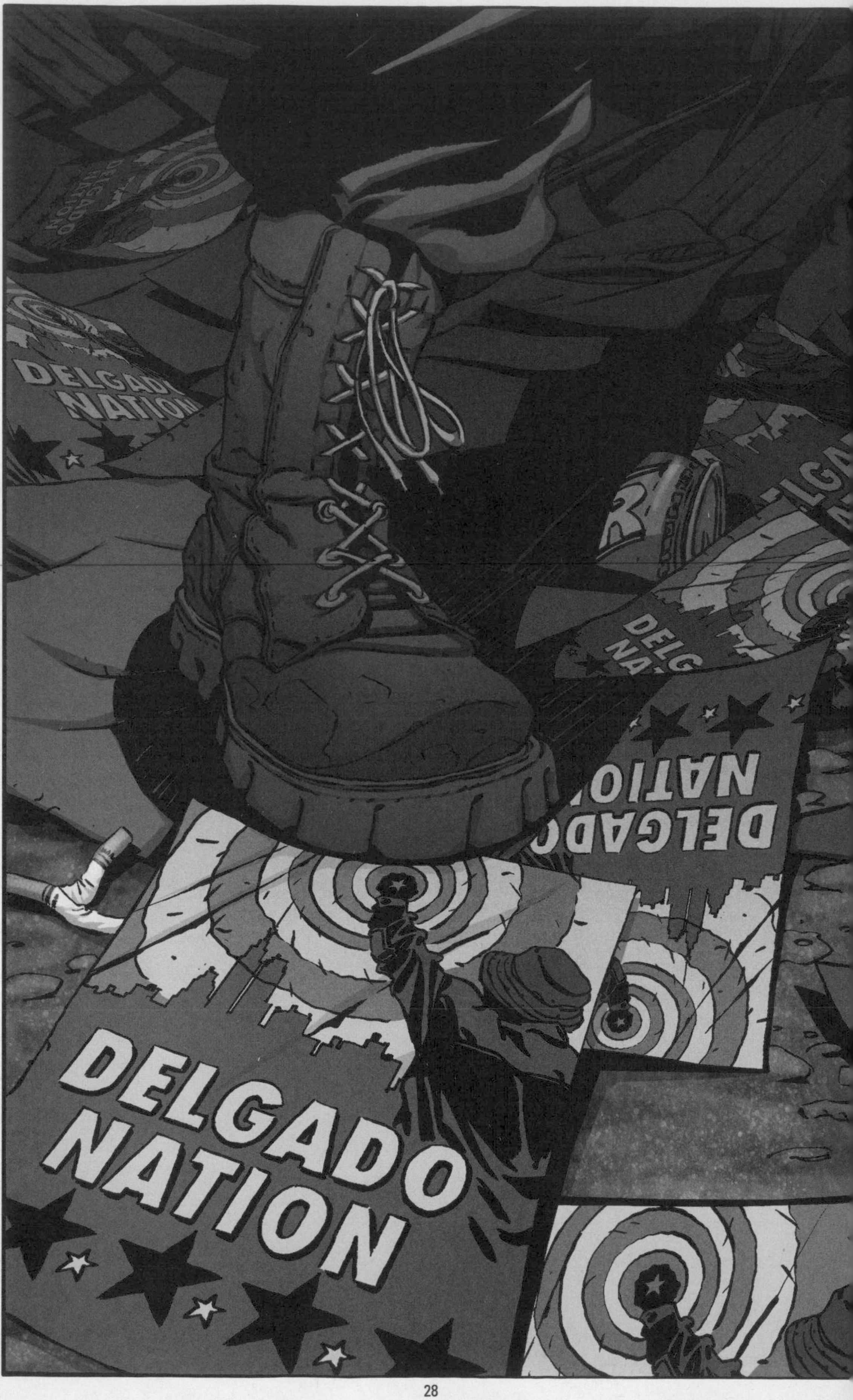
DELGADO
NATION

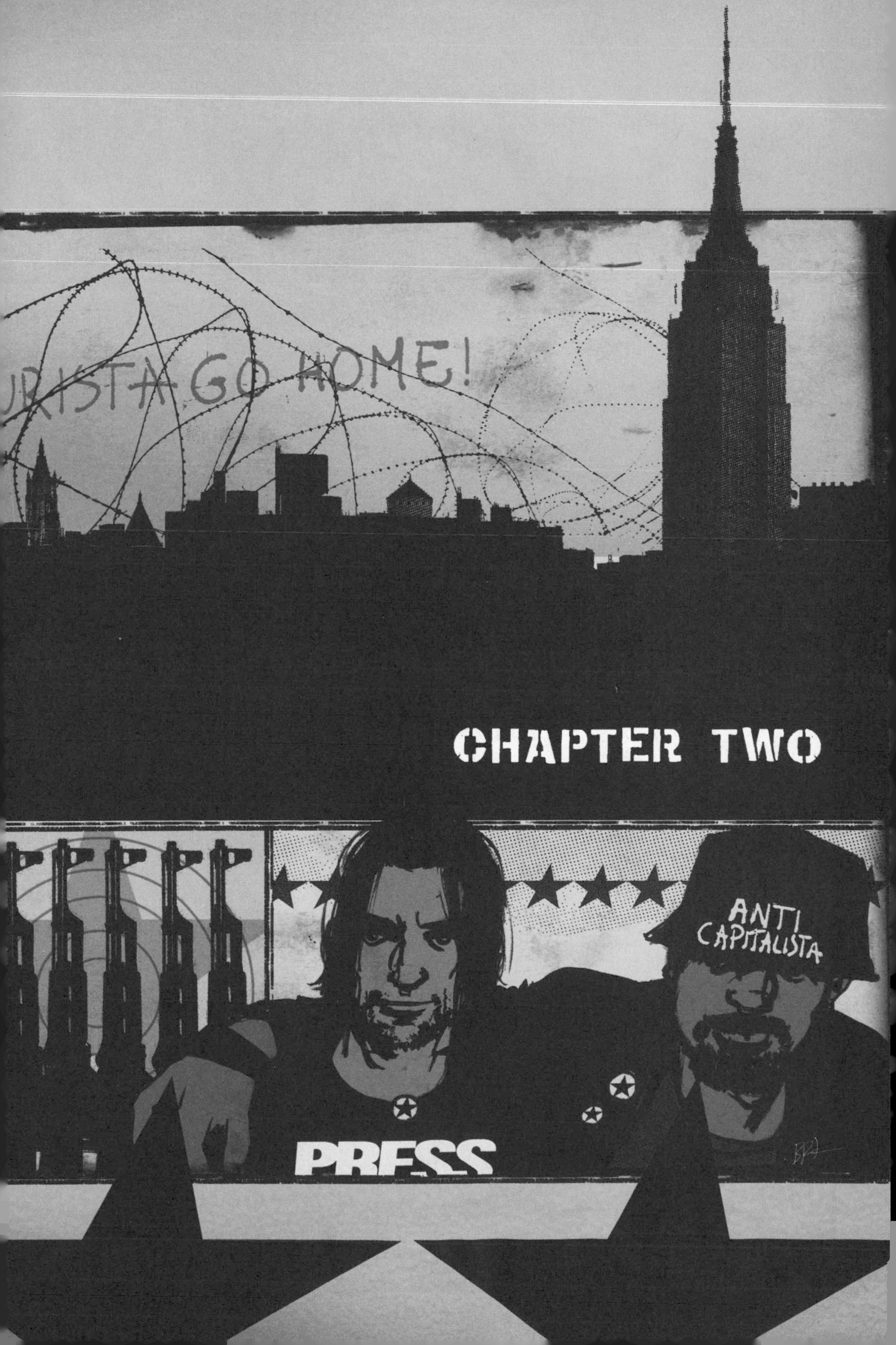
URISTA GO HOME!
ANTI CAPITALISTA
PRESS

CHAPTER TWO

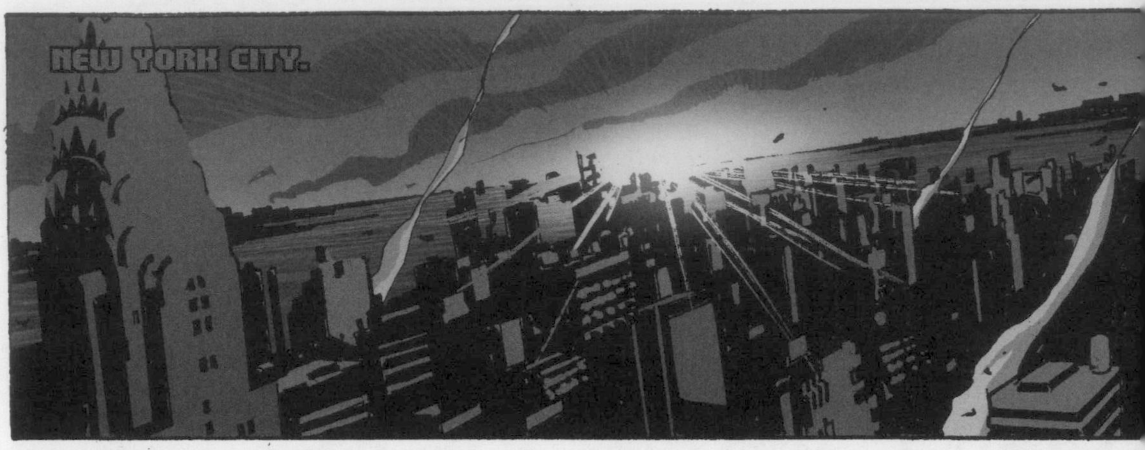
NEW YORK CITY.

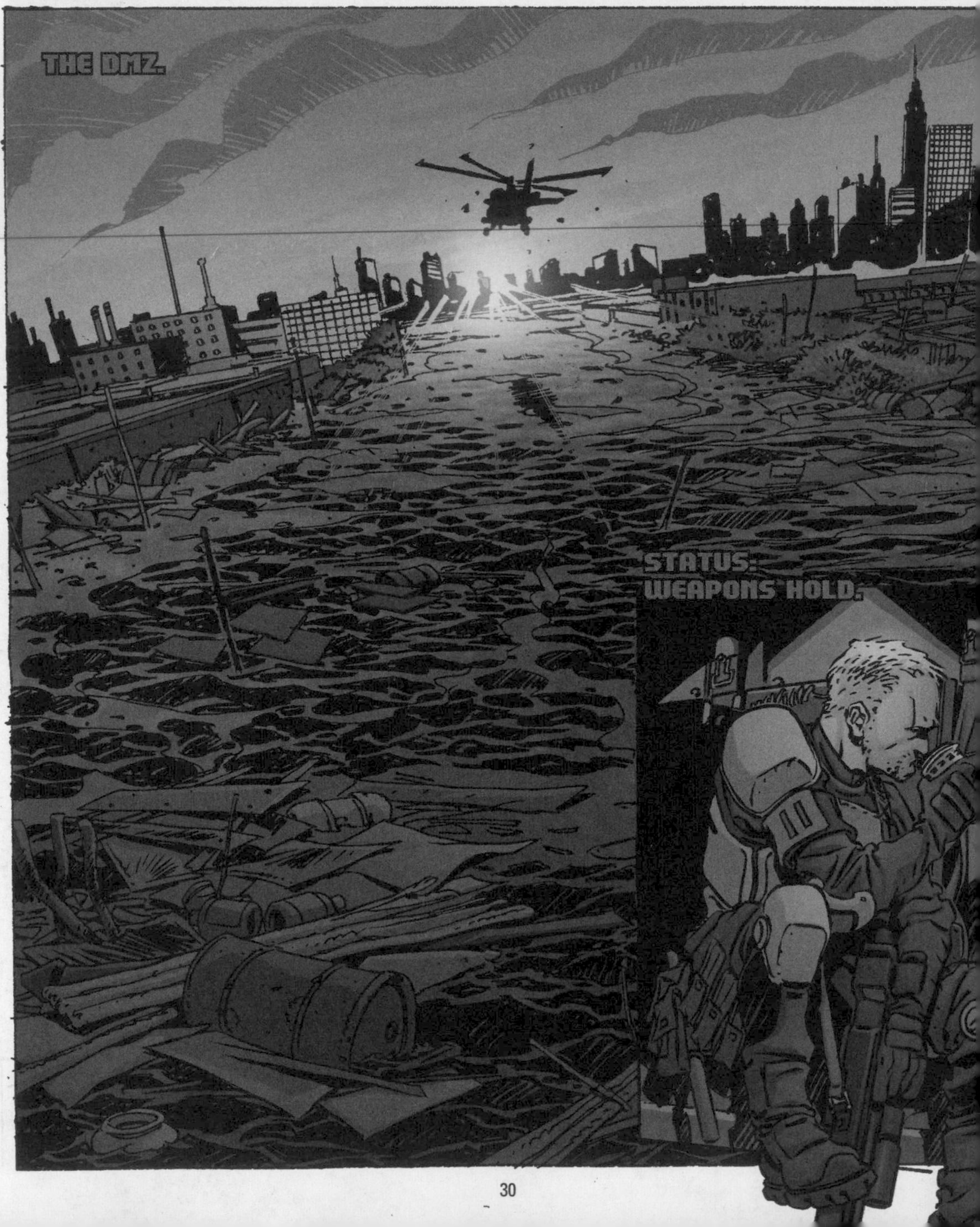
THE DMZ.
STATUS:
WEAPONS HOLD.

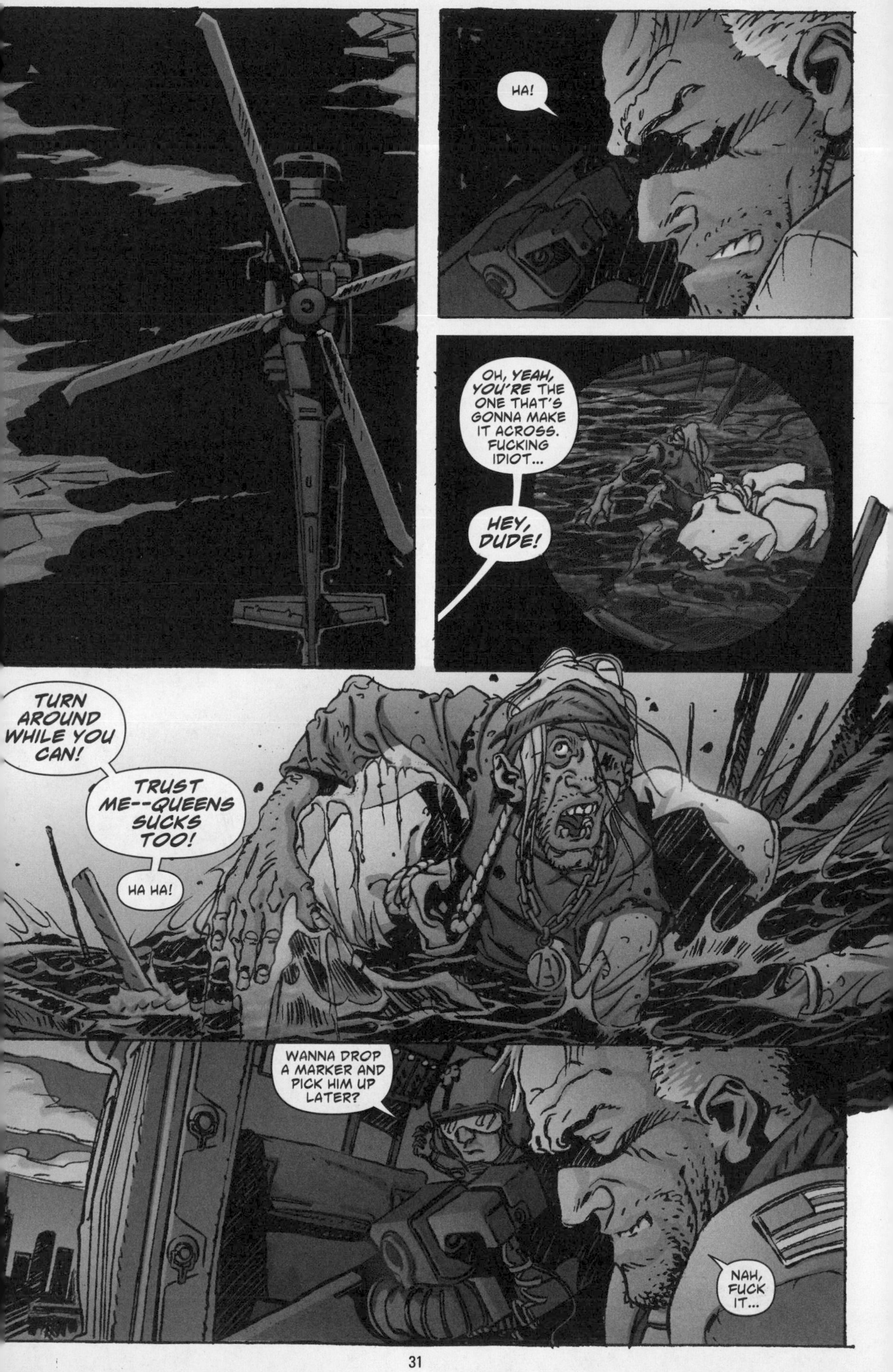
HA!
OH, YEAH, YOU'RE THE ONE THAT'S GONNA MAKE IT ACROSS. FUCKING IDIOT...
HEY, DUDE!
TURN AROUND WHILE YOU CAN!
TRUST ME--QUEENS SUCKS TOO!
HA HA!
WANNA DROP A MARKER AND PICK HIM UP LATER?
NAH, FUCK IT...

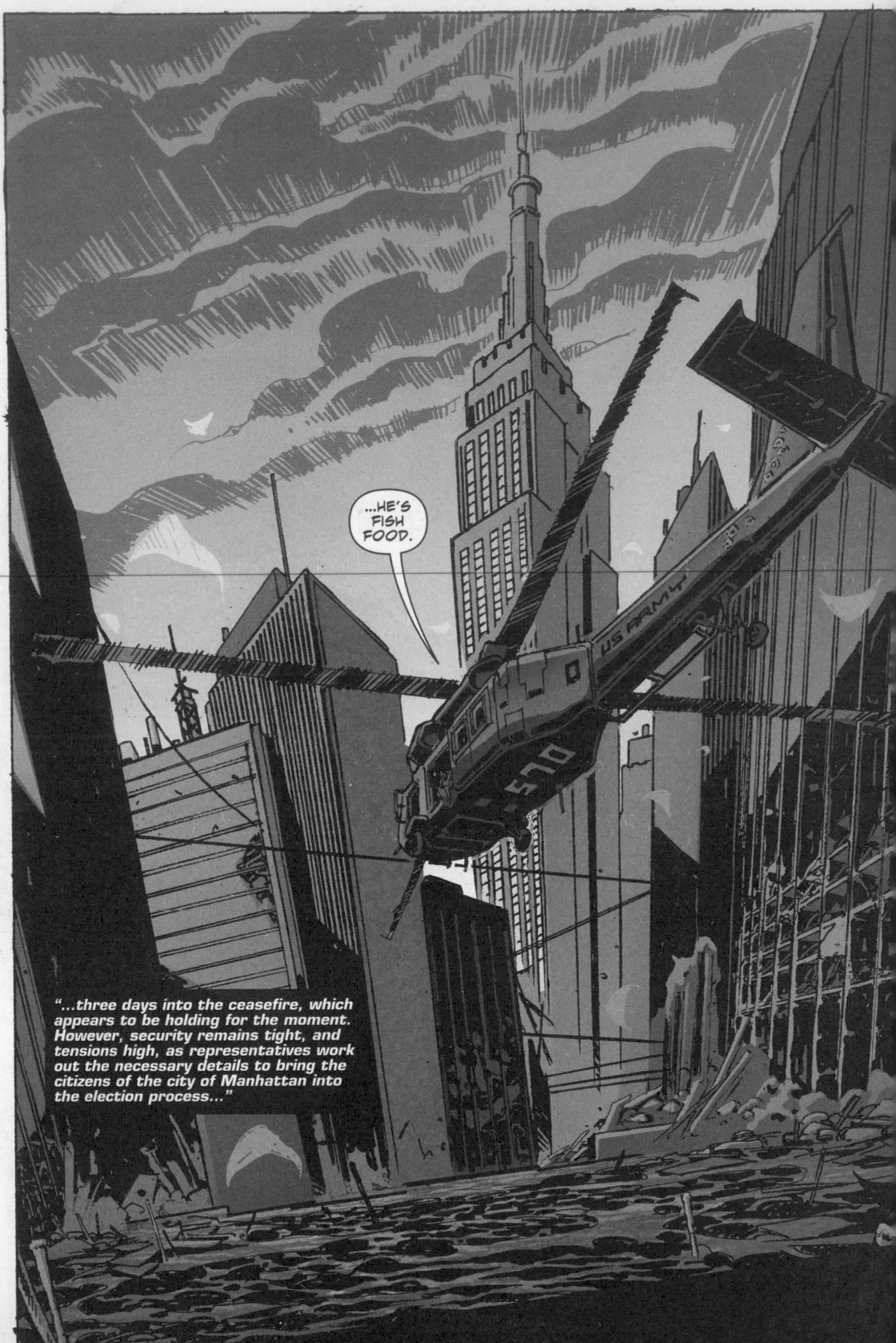
...HE'S FISH FOOD.
"...three days into the ceasefire, which appears to be holding for the moment. However, security remains tight, and tensions high, as representatives work out the necessary details to bring the citizens of the city of Manhattan into the election process..."
US ARMY
DL5

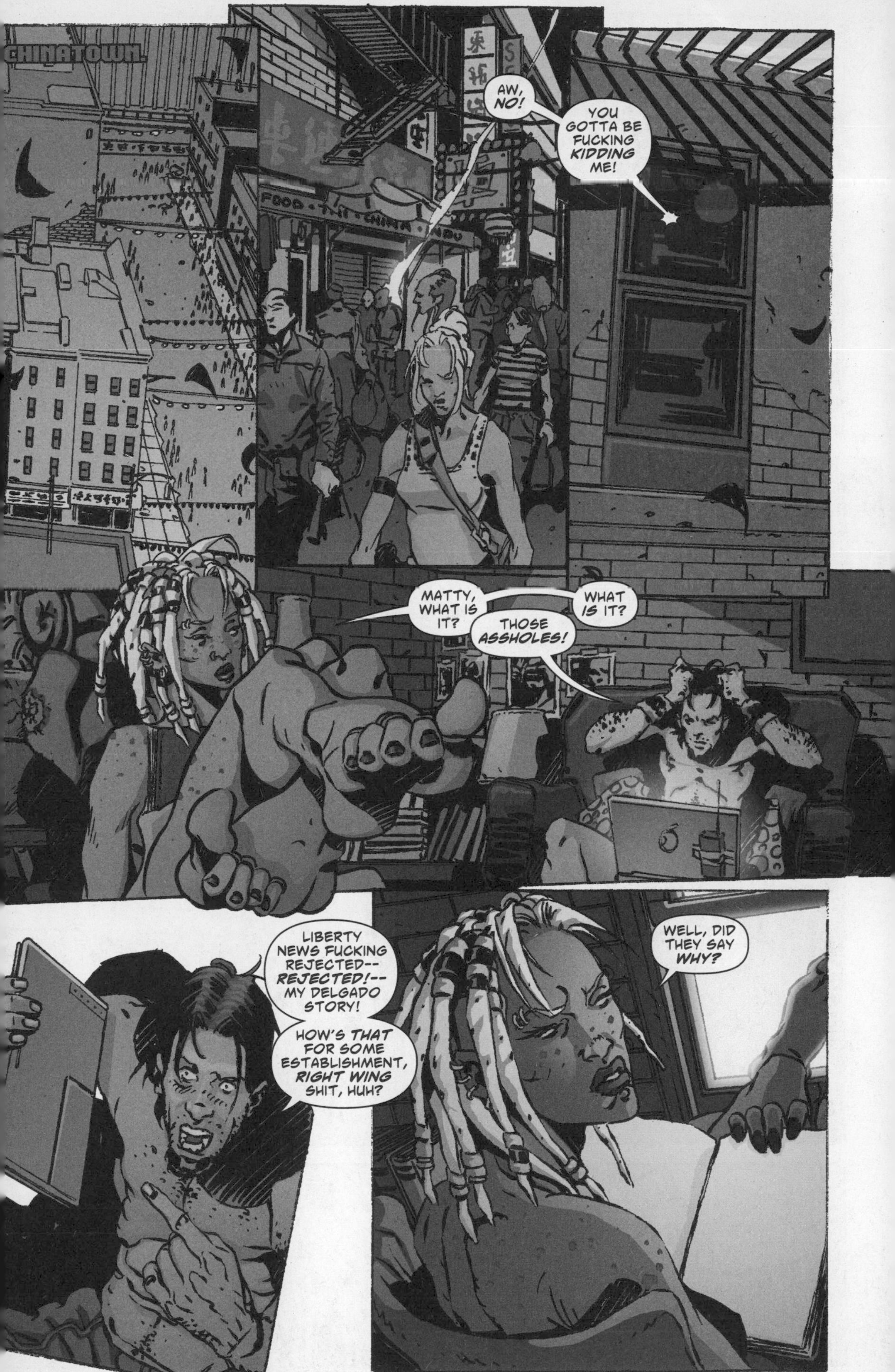
CHINATOWN.
AW, NO!
YOU GOTTA BE FUCKING KIDDING ME!
MATTY, WHAT IS IT?
WHAT IS IT?
THOSE ASSHOLES!
LIBERTY NEWS FUCKING REJECTED-- REJECTED!-- MY DELGADO STORY!
HOW'S THAT FOR SOME ESTABLISHMENT, RIGHT WING SHIT, HUH?
WELL, DID THEY SAY WHY?

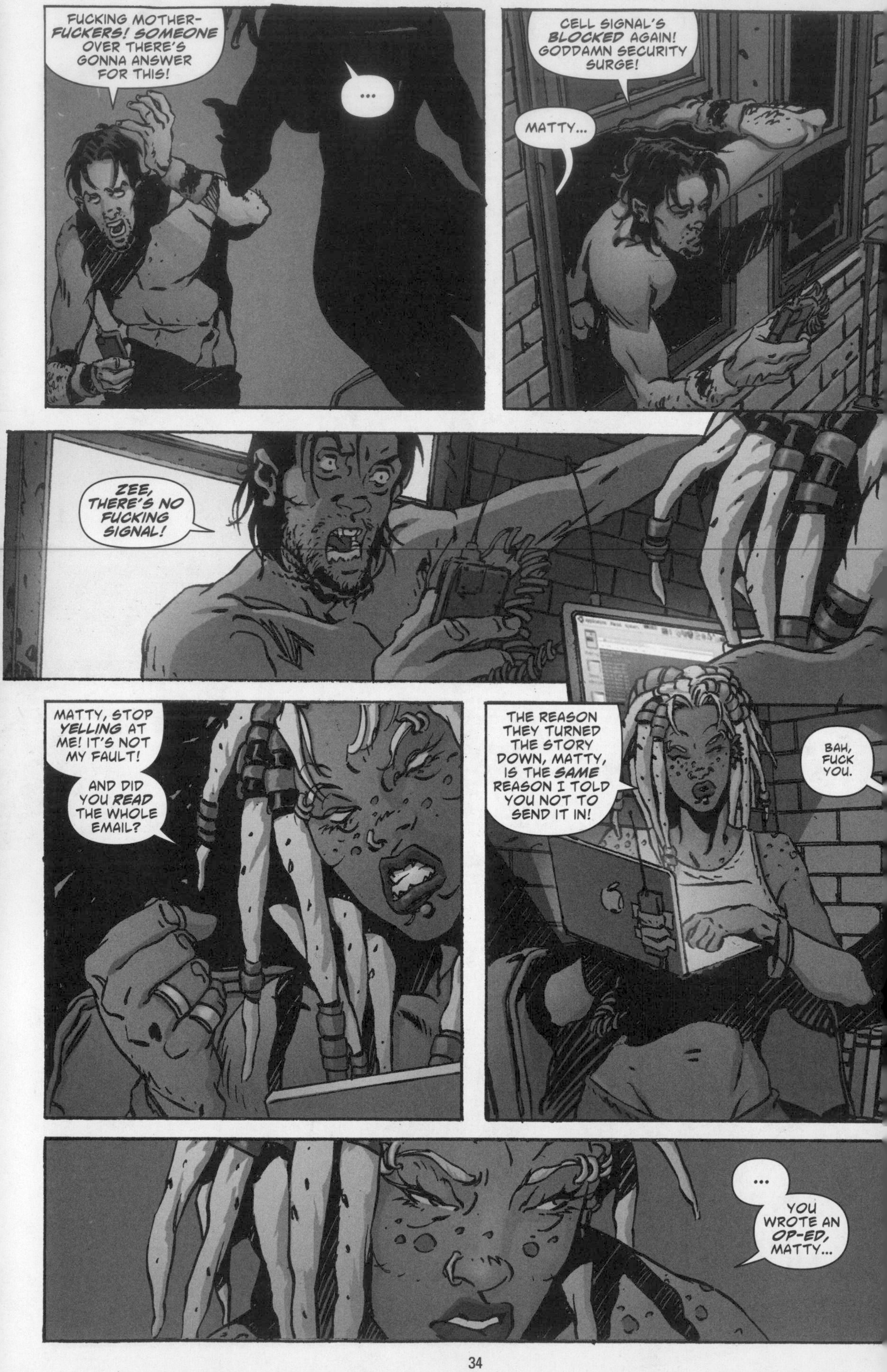
FUCKING MOTHER-FUCKERS! SOMEONE OVER THERE'S GONNA ANSWER FOR THIS!
...
CELL SIGNAL'S BLOCKED AGAIN! GODDAMN SECURITY SURGE!
MATTY...
ZEE, THERE'S NO FUCKING SIGNAL!
MATTY, STOP YELLING AT ME! IT'S NOT MY FAULT!
AND DID YOU READ THE WHOLE EMAIL?
THE REASON THEY TURNED THE STORY DOWN, MATTY, IS THE SAME REASON I TOLD YOU NOT TO SEND IT IN!
BAH, FUCK YOU.
...
YOU WROTE AN OP-ED, MATTY...

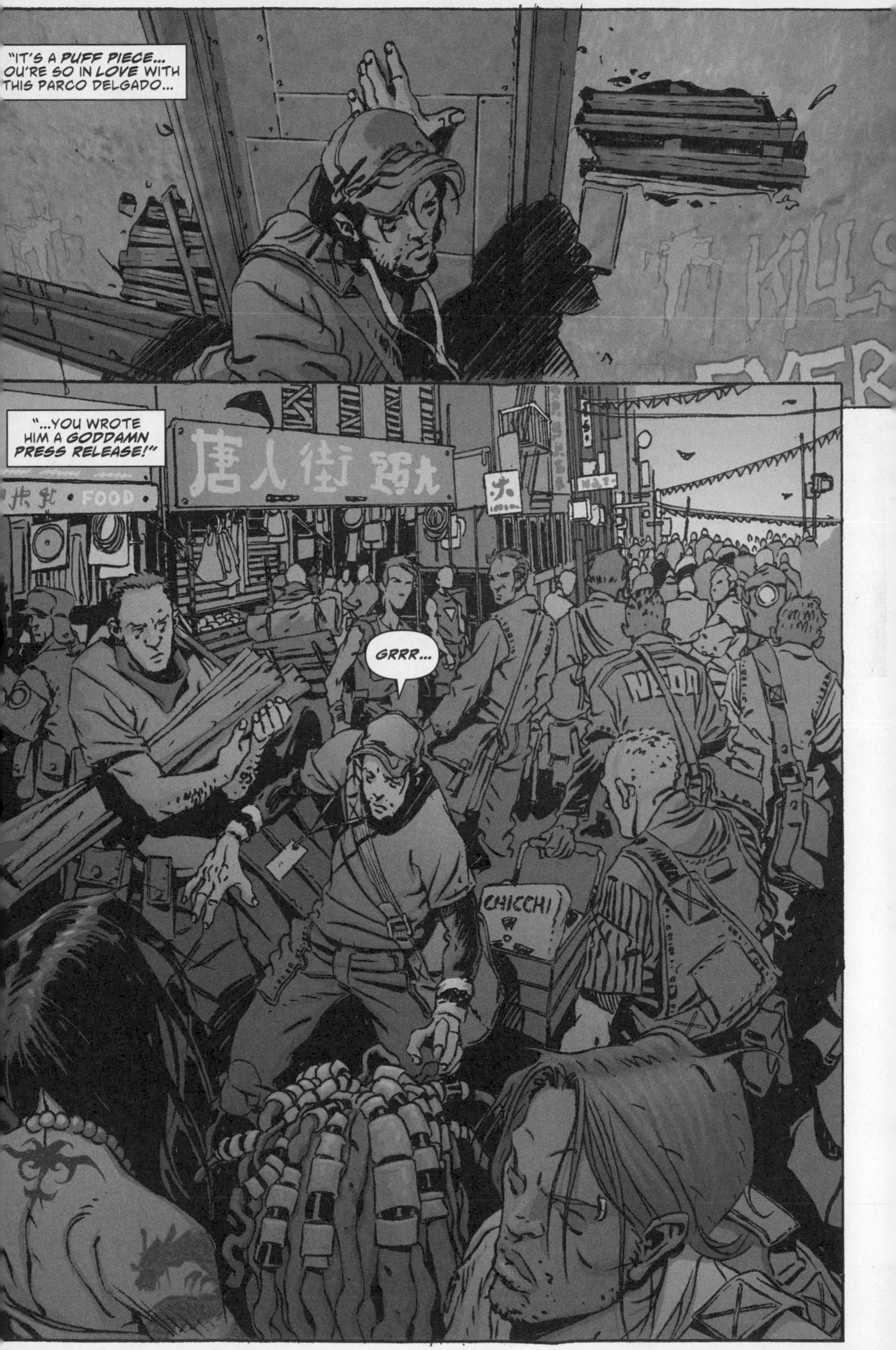
"IT'S A PUFF PIECE... OU'RE SO IN LOVE WITH THIS PARCO DELGADO...
"...YOU WROTE HIM A GODDAMN PRESS RELEASE!"
FOOD
GRRR...
CHICCHI

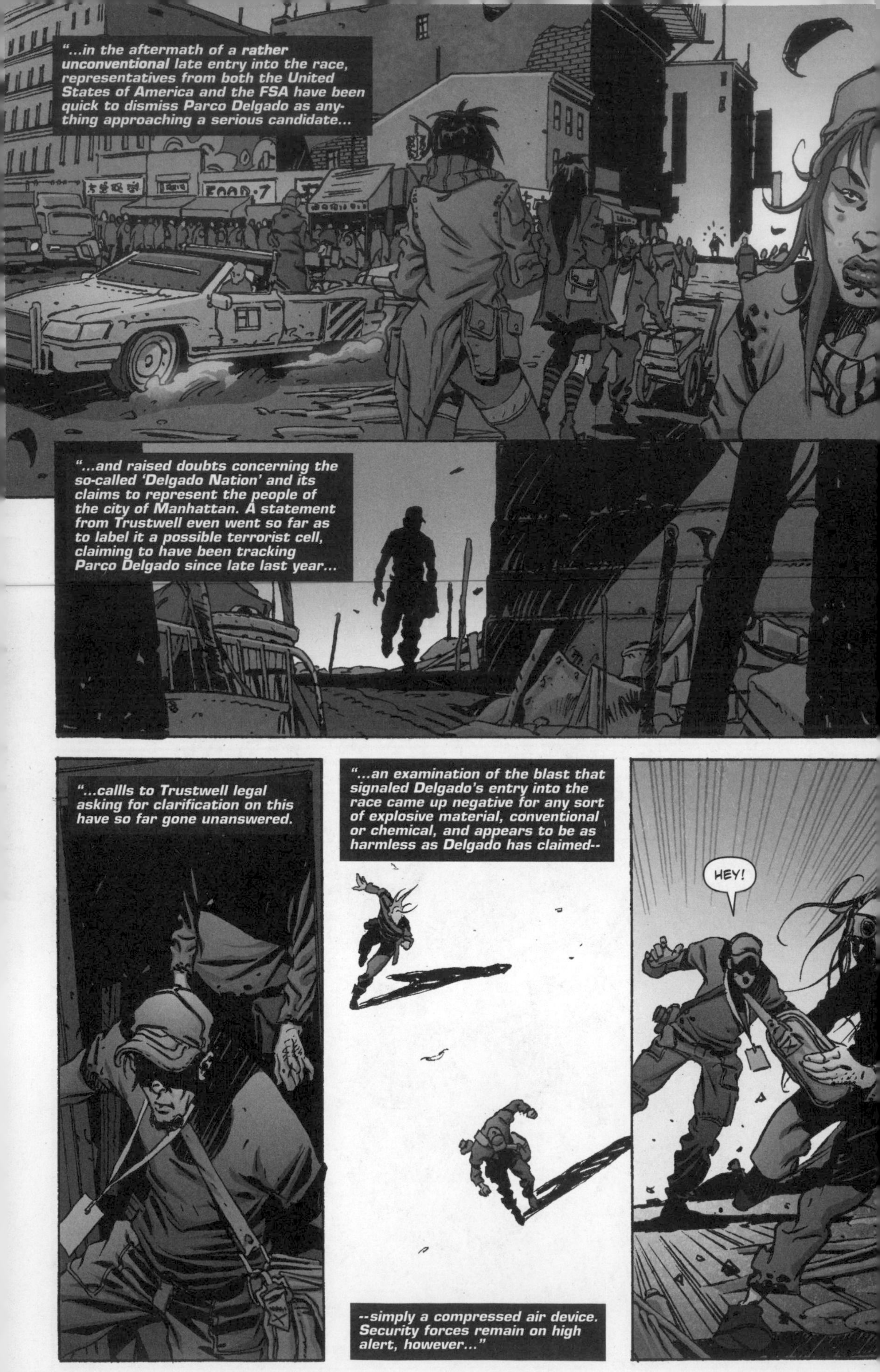
"...in the aftermath of a rather unconventional late entry into the race, representatives from both the United States of America and the FSA have been quick to dismiss Parco Delgado as anything approaching a serious candidate...
"...and raised doubts concerning the so-called 'Delgado Nation' and its claims to represent the people of the city of Manhattan. A statement from Trustwell even went so far as to label it a possible terrorist cell, claiming to have been tracking Parco Delgado since late last year...
"...callls to Trustwell legal asking for clarification on this have so far gone unanswered.
"...an examination of the blast that signaled Delgado's entry into the race came up negative for any sort of explosive material, conventional or chemical, and appears to be as harmless as Delgado has claimed--
--simply a compressed air device. Security forces remain on high alert, however..."
HEY!

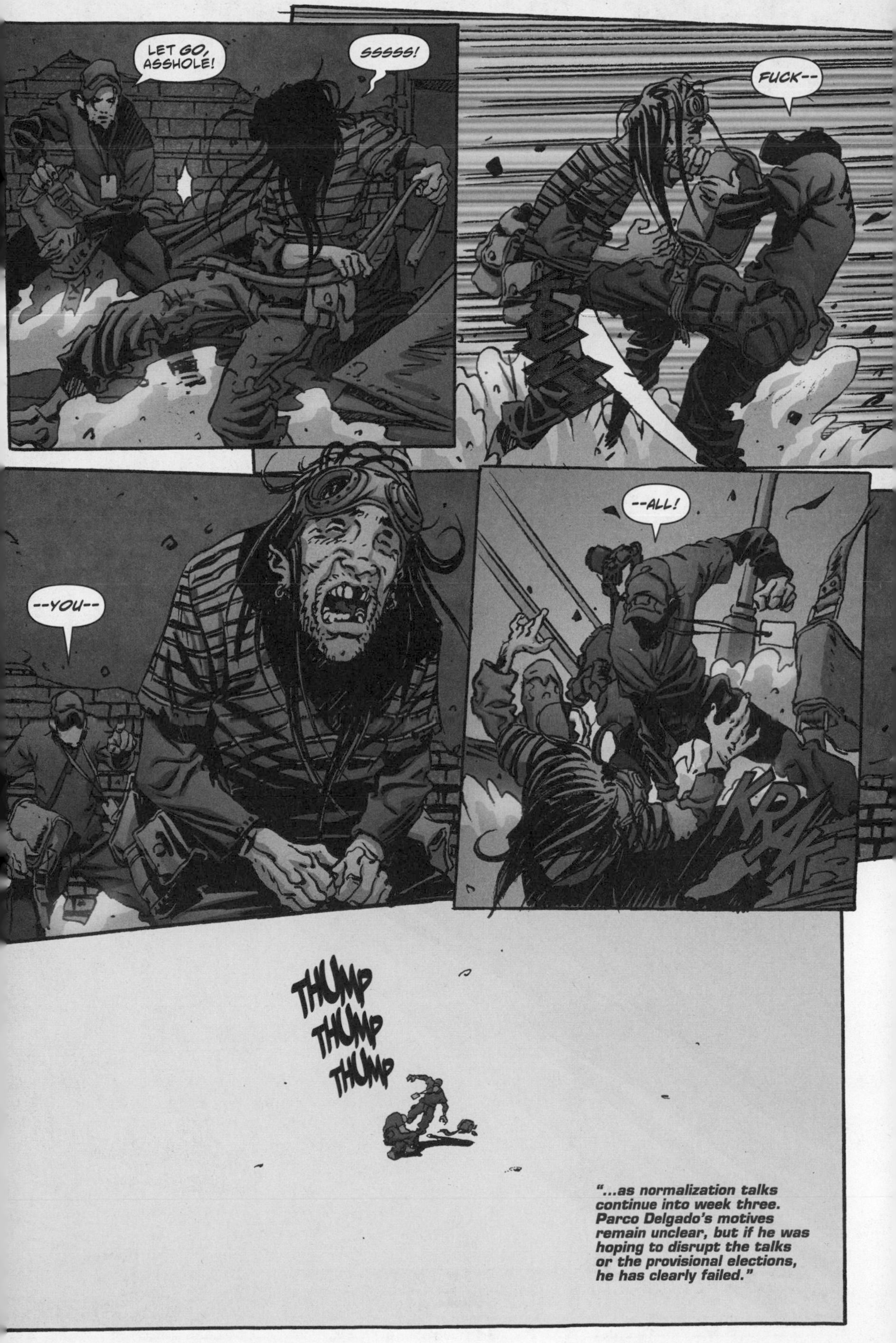
LET GO, ASSHOLE!
SSSSS!
FUCK--
--YOU--
--ALL!
KRAK
THUMP
THUMP
THUMP
"...as normalization talks continue into week three. Parco Delgado's motives remain unclear, but if he was hoping to disrupt the talks or the provisional elections, he has clearly failed."

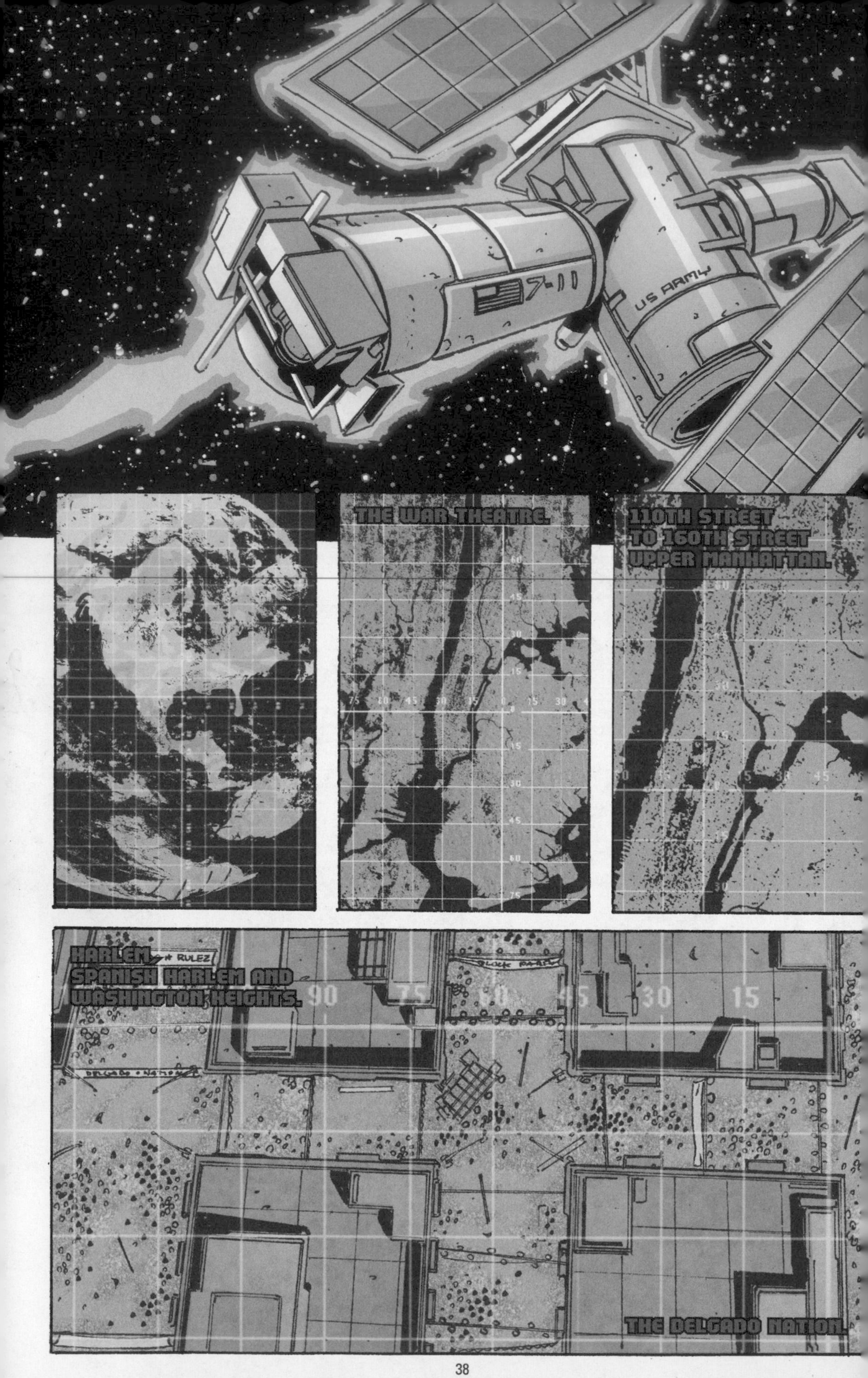
7-11
US ARMY
THE WAR THEATRE.
110TH STREET
TO 160TH STREET
UPPER MANHATTAN.
HARLEM,
SPANISH HARLEM AND
WASHINGTON HEIGHTS.
RULEZ
THE DELGADO NATION.

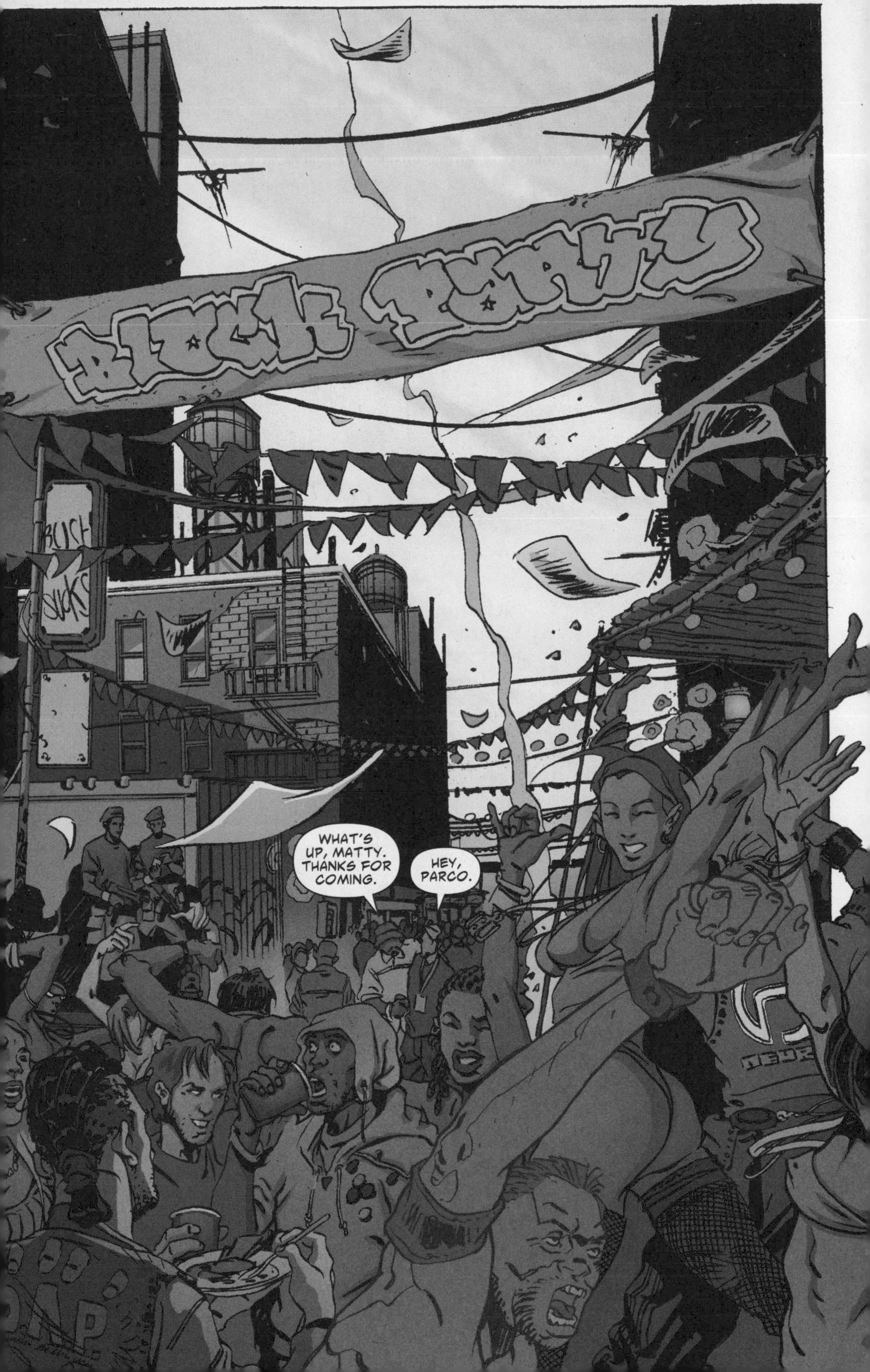
WHAT'S UP, MATTY. THANKS FOR COMING.
HEY, PARCO.

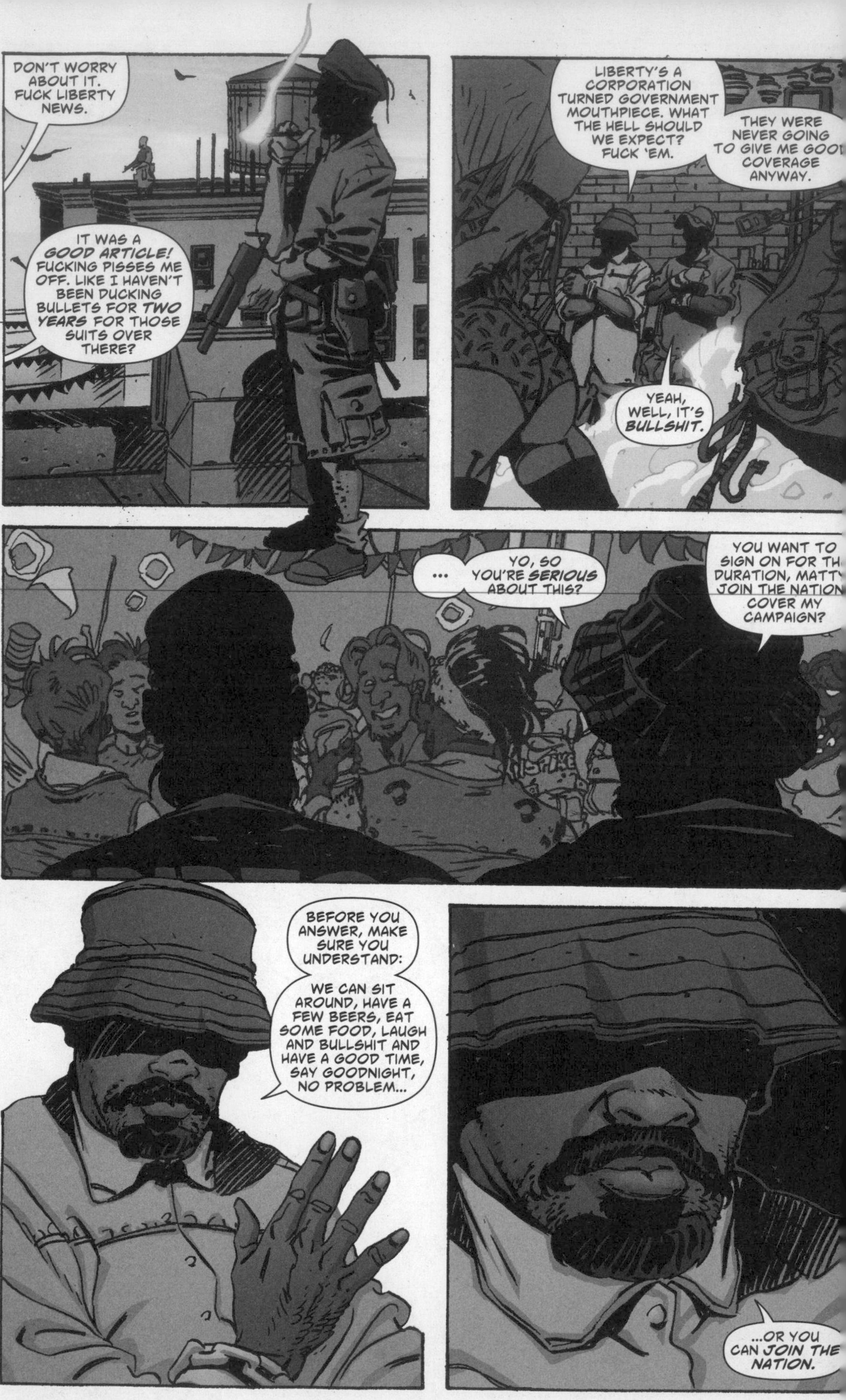

DON'T WORRY ABOUT IT. FUCK LIBERTY NEWS.
IT WAS A GOOD ARTICLE! FUCKING PISSES ME OFF. LIKE I HAVEN'T BEEN DUCKING BULLETS FOR TWO YEARS FOR THOSE SUITS OVER THERE?
LIBERTY'S A CORPORATION TURNED GOVERNMENT MOUTHPIECE. WHAT THE HELL SHOULD WE EXPECT? FUCK 'EM.
THEY WERE NEVER GOING TO GIVE ME GOO COVERAGE ANYWAY.
YEAH, WELL, IT'S BULLSHIT.
...
YO, SO YOU'RE SERIOUS ABOUT THIS?
YOU WANT TO SIGN ON FOR TH DURATION, MATTY JOIN THE NATION COVER MY CAMPAIGN?
BEFORE YOU ANSWER, MAKE SURE YOU UNDERSTAND:
WE CAN SIT AROUND, HAVE A FEW BEERS, EAT SOME FOOD, LAUGH AND BULLSHIT AND HAVE A GOOD TIME, SAY GOODNIGHT, NO PROBLEM...
...OR YOU CAN JOIN THE NATION.

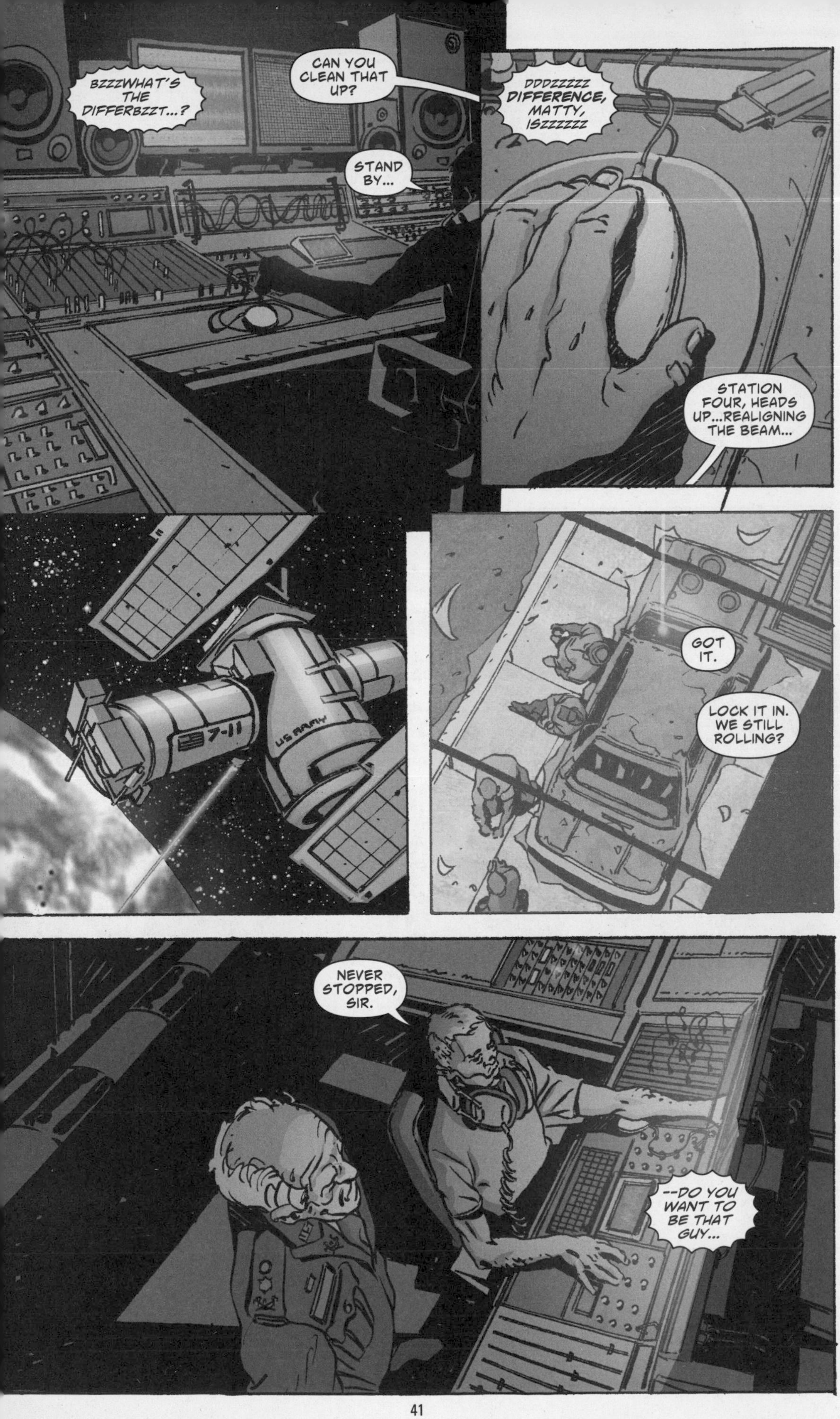
BZZZWHAT'S THE DIFFERBZZT...?
CAN YOU CLEAN THAT UP?
DDDZZZZZ DIFFERENCE, MATTY, ISZZZZZZ
STAND BY...
STATION FOUR, HEADS UP...REALIGNING THE BEAM...
US ARMY
7-11
GOT IT.
LOCK IT IN. WE STILL ROLLING?
NEVER STOPPED, SIR.
--DO YOU WANT TO BE THAT GUY...

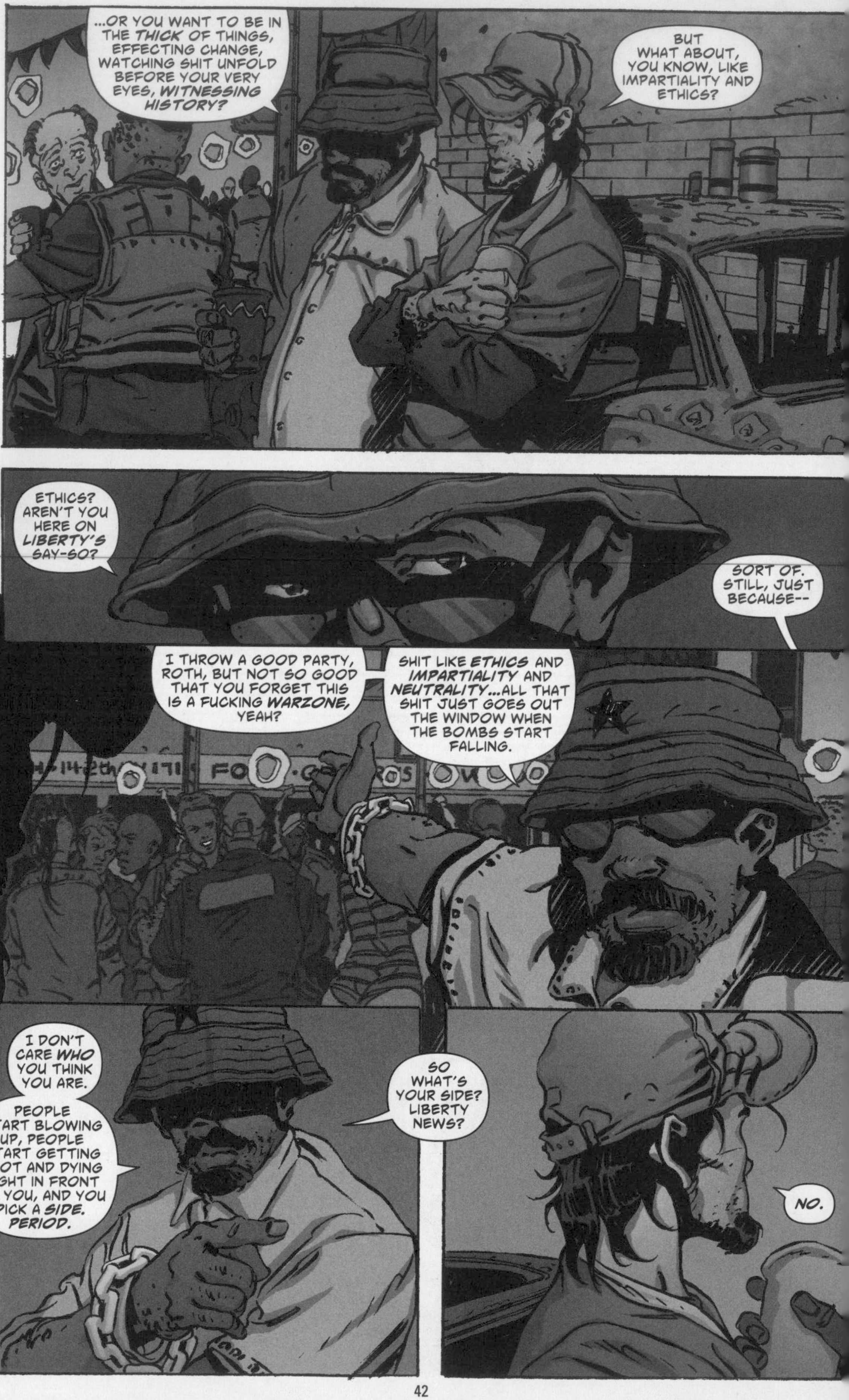

...OR YOU WANT TO BE IN THE *THICK* OF THINGS, EFFECTING CHANGE, WATCHING SHIT UNFOLD BEFORE YOUR VERY EYES, *WITNESSING HISTORY?*
BUT WHAT ABOUT, YOU KNOW, LIKE IMPARTIALITY AND ETHICS?
ETHICS? AREN'T YOU HERE ON *LIBERTY'S* SAY-SO?
SORT OF. STILL, JUST BECAUSE--
I THROW A GOOD PARTY, ROTH, BUT NOT SO GOOD THAT YOU FORGET THIS IS A FUCKING *WARZONE,* YEAH?
SHIT LIKE *ETHICS* AND *IMPARTIALITY* AND *NEUTRALITY*...ALL THAT SHIT JUST GOES OUT THE WINDOW WHEN THE BOMBS START FALLING.
I DON'T CARE *WHO* YOU THINK YOU ARE.
PEOPLE START BLOWING UP, PEOPLE START GETTING SHOT AND DYING RIGHT IN FRONT OF YOU, AND YOU PICK A *SIDE. PERIOD.*
SO WHAT'S YOUR SIDE? LIBERTY NEWS?
NO.

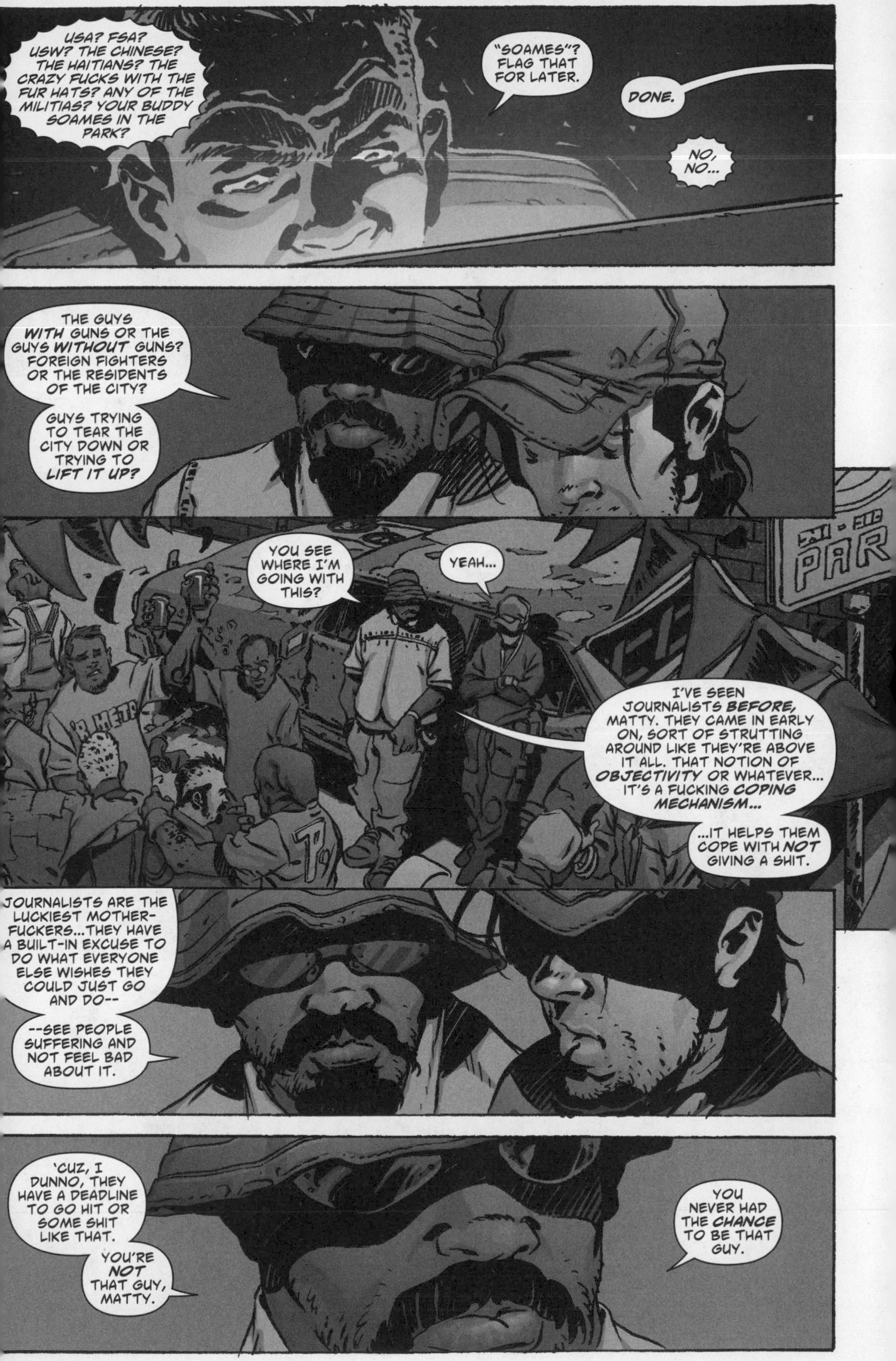
USA? FSA? USW? THE CHINESE? THE HAITIANS? THE CRAZY FUCKS WITH THE FUR HATS? ANY OF THE MILITIAS? YOUR BUDDY SOAMES IN THE PARK?
"SOAMES"? FLAG THAT FOR LATER.
DONE.
NO, NO...
THE GUYS WITH GUNS OR THE GUYS WITHOUT GUNS? FOREIGN FIGHTERS OR THE RESIDENTS OF THE CITY?
GUYS TRYING TO TEAR THE CITY DOWN OR TRYING TO LIFT IT UP?
YOU SEE WHERE I'M GOING WITH THIS?
YEAH...
PAR
I'VE SEEN JOURNALISTS BEFORE, MATTY. THEY CAME IN EARLY ON, SORT OF STRUTTING AROUND LIKE THEY'RE ABOVE IT ALL. THAT NOTION OF OBJECTIVITY OR WHATEVER... IT'S A FUCKING COPING MECHANISM...
...IT HELPS THEM COPE WITH NOT GIVING A SHIT.
JOURNALISTS ARE THE LUCKIEST MOTHER-FUCKERS...THEY HAVE A BUILT-IN EXCUSE TO DO WHAT EVERYONE ELSE WISHES THEY COULD JUST GO AND DO--
--SEE PEOPLE SUFFERING AND NOT FEEL BAD ABOUT IT.
'CUZ, I DUNNO, THEY HAVE A DEADLINE TO GO HIT OR SOME SHIT LIKE THAT.
YOU'RE NOT THAT GUY, MATTY.
YOU NEVER HAD THE CHANCE TO BE THAT GUY.

I KNOW YOUR STORY, PEOPLE TALK ABOUT IT.

DAY FUCKING ONE, YOUR BOYS FROM LIBERTY TRIED TO LEAVE YOU BEHIND? *BOOM*, YOU CUT TIES. YOU CUT THE EMOTIONAL CORD. YOU WERE NEVER GONNA BE THE GUY THEY WANT YOU TO BE... A GODDAMN *JOURNALIST*.

THEN THE FREE STATES MOTHERFUCKERS WANT YOU TO BE THEIR GUY... HALLELUJAH, RIGHT?

...WHO TRIES TO PLAY YOU BACK. THEN YOU MAKE THE FIRST TRULY *HUMAN* DECISION SINCE YOU CRASH-LANDED.

A FUCKING WHITE FACE IN THE CITY, WE CAN USE THAT! THEY SAY. TWISTING YOU ALL AROUND, PLAYING YOU OFF THE OTHER SIDE...

YOU PUT THE PEOPLE FIRST. YOU STICK YOUR NECK OUT FOR THE CITY. THE *REAL* CITY, THE PEOPLE WHO LIVE HERE.

EVEN WHEN OTHERS DIDN'T.

THAT'S WHEN I KNEW YOU WERE ALL RIGHT, MAN. YOU'D MAKE IT. I HAD THAT *FAITH*, YA KNOW?

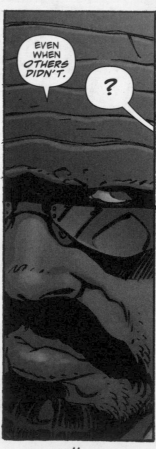

?

WHAT? DO YOU MEAN *ZEE*? YOU MEAN ZEE, *RIGHT*?

SHUT THE *FUCK* UP, OK? WHAT THE *HELL* DO YOU KNOW ABOUT IT?

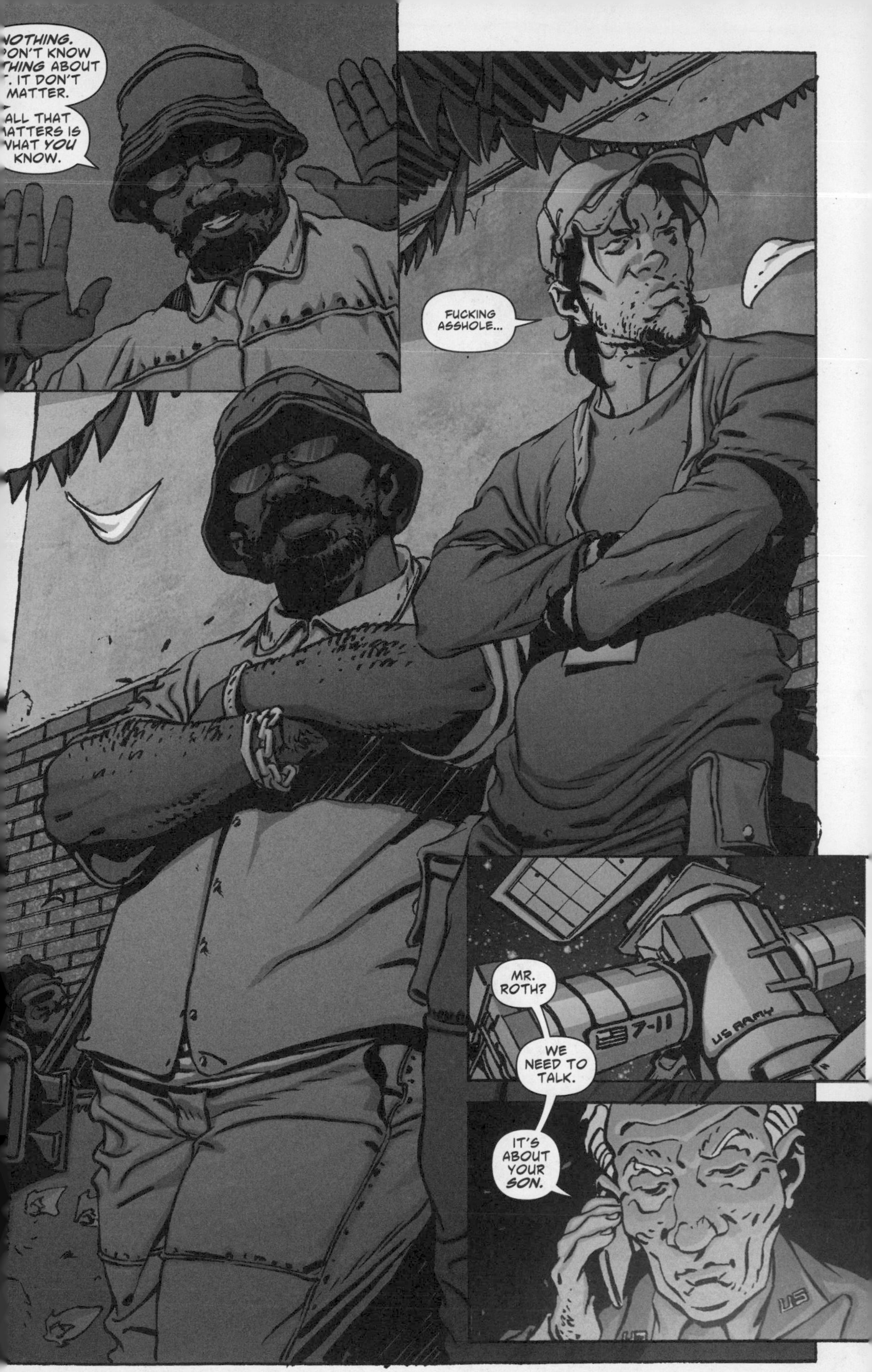
NOTHING. ON'T KNOW THING ABOUT . IT DON'T MATTER.
ALL THAT ATTERS IS WHAT YOU KNOW.
FUCKING ASSHOLE...
MR. ROTH?
WE NEED TO TALK.
IT'S ABOUT YOUR SON.
7-11
US ARMY
US

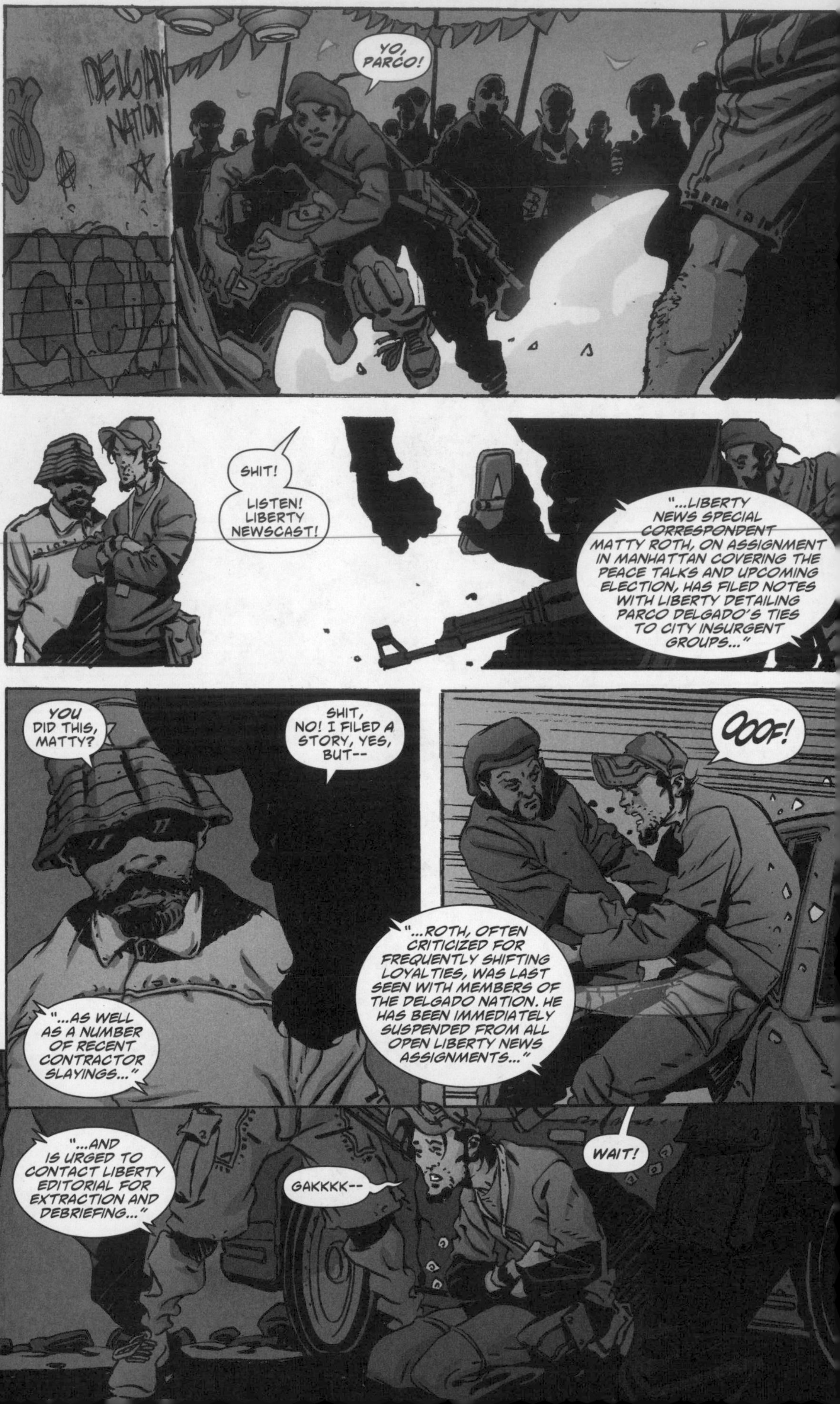

DELGADO NATION
YO, PARCO!
SHIT!
LISTEN! LIBERTY NEWSCAST!
"...LIBERTY NEWS SPECIAL CORRESPONDENT MATTY ROTH, ON ASSIGNMENT IN MANHATTAN COVERING THE PEACE TALKS AND UPCOMING ELECTION, HAS FILED NOTES WITH LIBERTY DETAILING PARCO DELGADO'S TIES TO CITY INSURGENT GROUPS..."
YOU DID THIS, MATTY?
SHIT, NO! I FILED A STORY, YES, BUT--
"...AS WELL AS A NUMBER OF RECENT CONTRACTOR SLAYINGS..."
OOOF!
"...ROTH, OFTEN CRITICIZED FOR FREQUENTLY SHIFTING LOYALTIES, WAS LAST SEEN WITH MEMBERS OF THE DELGADO NATION. HE HAS BEEN IMMEDIATELY SUSPENDED FROM ALL OPEN LIBERTY NEWS ASSIGNMENTS..."
"...AND IS URGED TO CONTACT LIBERTY EDITORIAL FOR EXTRACTION AND DEBRIEFING..."
GAKKKK--
WAIT!

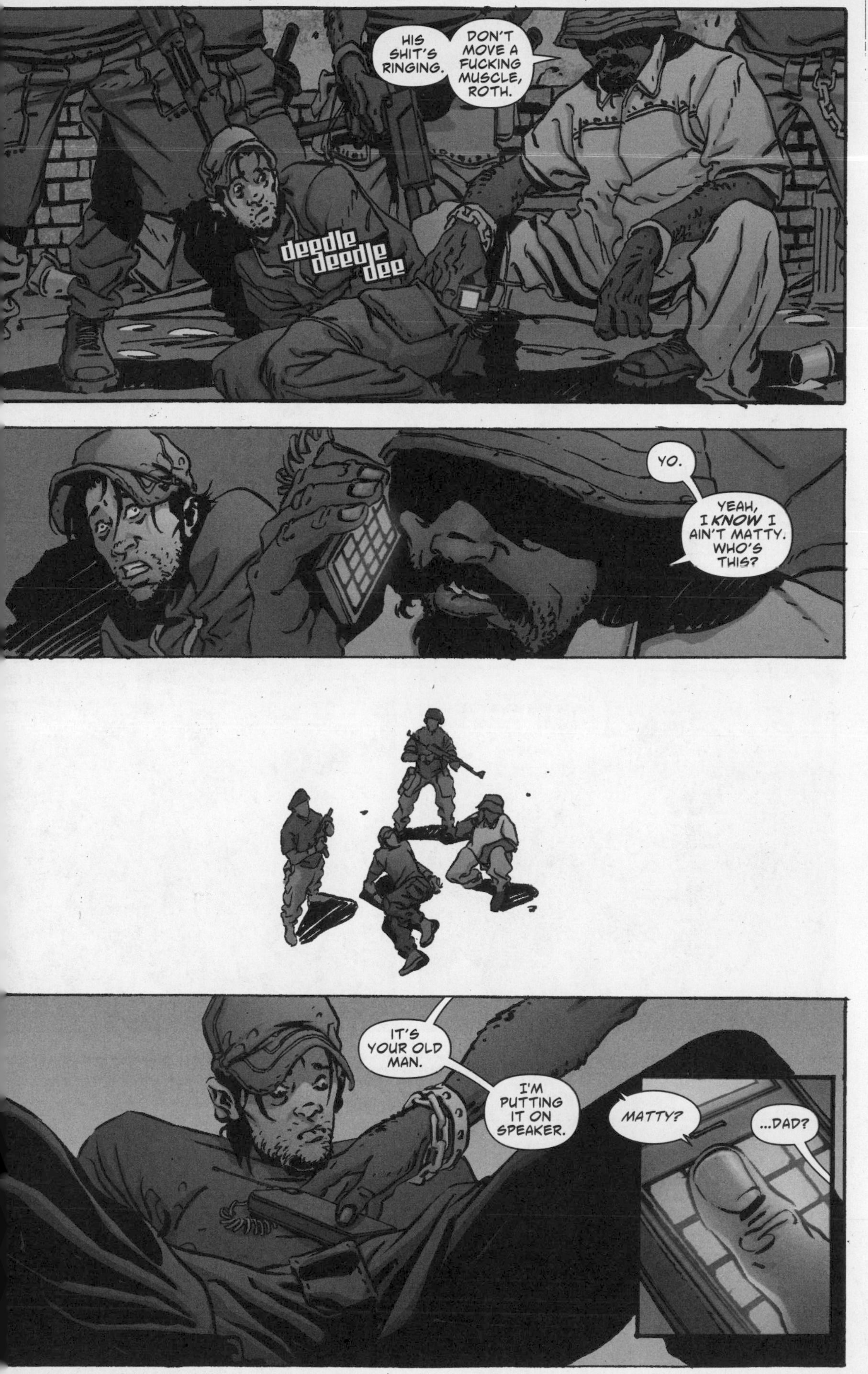
HIS SHIT'S RINGING.
DON'T MOVE A FUCKING MUSCLE, ROTH.
deedle deedle dee
YO.
YEAH, I KNOW I AIN'T MATTY. WHO'S THIS?
IT'S YOUR OLD MAN.
I'M PUTTING IT ON SPEAKER.
MATTY?
...DAD?

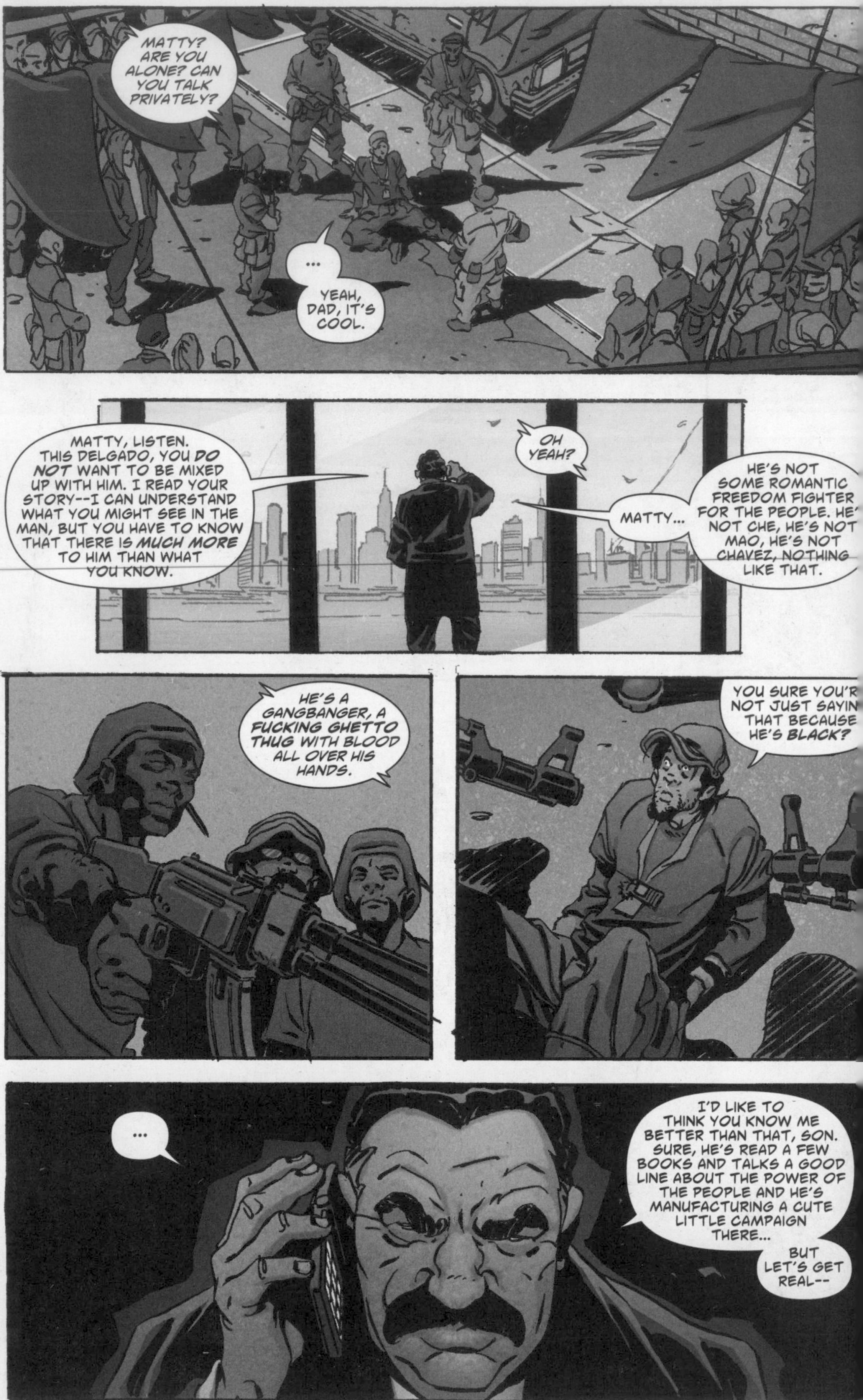
MATTY? ARE YOU ALONE? CAN YOU TALK PRIVATELY?
...
YEAH, DAD, IT'S COOL.
MATTY, LISTEN. THIS DELGADO, YOU DO NOT WANT TO BE MIXED UP WITH HIM. I READ YOUR STORY--I CAN UNDERSTAND WHAT YOU MIGHT SEE IN THE MAN, BUT YOU HAVE TO KNOW THAT THERE IS MUCH MORE TO HIM THAN WHAT YOU KNOW.
OH YEAH?
MATTY...
HE'S NOT SOME ROMANTIC FREEDOM FIGHTER FOR THE PEOPLE. HE' NOT CHE, HE'S NOT MAO, HE'S NOT CHAVEZ, NOTHING LIKE THAT.
HE'S A GANGBANGER, A FUCKING GHETTO THUG WITH BLOOD ALL OVER HIS HANDS.
YOU SURE YOU'R NOT JUST SAYIN THAT BECAUSE HE'S BLACK?
...
I'D LIKE TO THINK YOU KNOW ME BETTER THAN THAT, SON. SURE, HE'S READ A FEW BOOKS AND TALKS A GOOD LINE ABOUT THE POWER OF THE PEOPLE AND HE'S MANUFACTURING A CUTE LITTLE CAMPAIGN THERE...
BUT LET'S GET REAL--

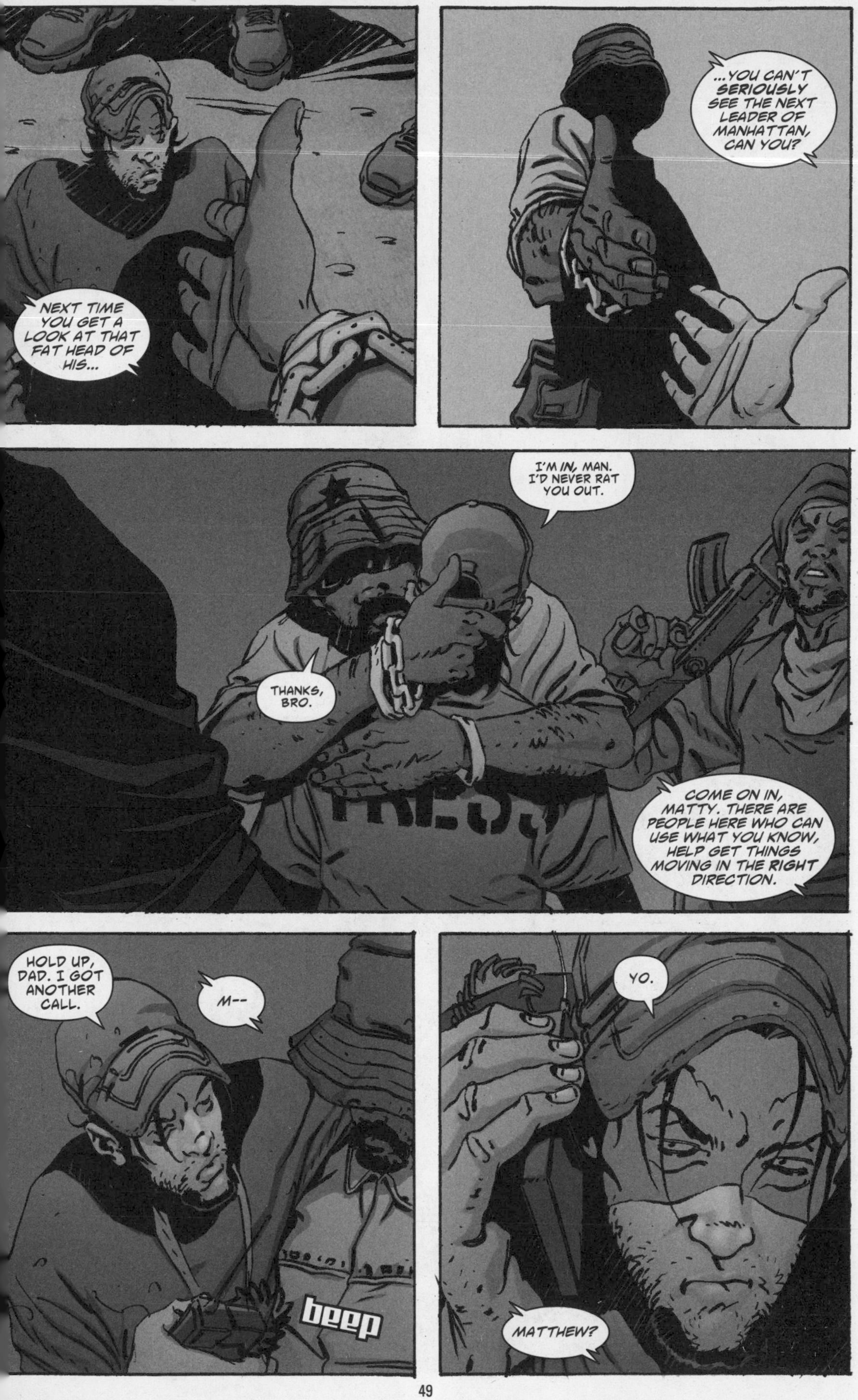
NEXT TIME YOU GET A LOOK AT THAT FAT HEAD OF HIS...
...YOU CAN'T SERIOUSLY SEE THE NEXT LEADER OF MANHATTAN, CAN YOU?
I'M IN, MAN. I'D NEVER RAT YOU OUT.
THANKS, BRO.
COME ON IN, MATTY. THERE ARE PEOPLE HERE WHO CAN USE WHAT YOU KNOW, HELP GET THINGS MOVING IN THE RIGHT DIRECTION.
HOLD UP, DAD. I GOT ANOTHER CALL.
M--
beep
YO.
MATTHEW?

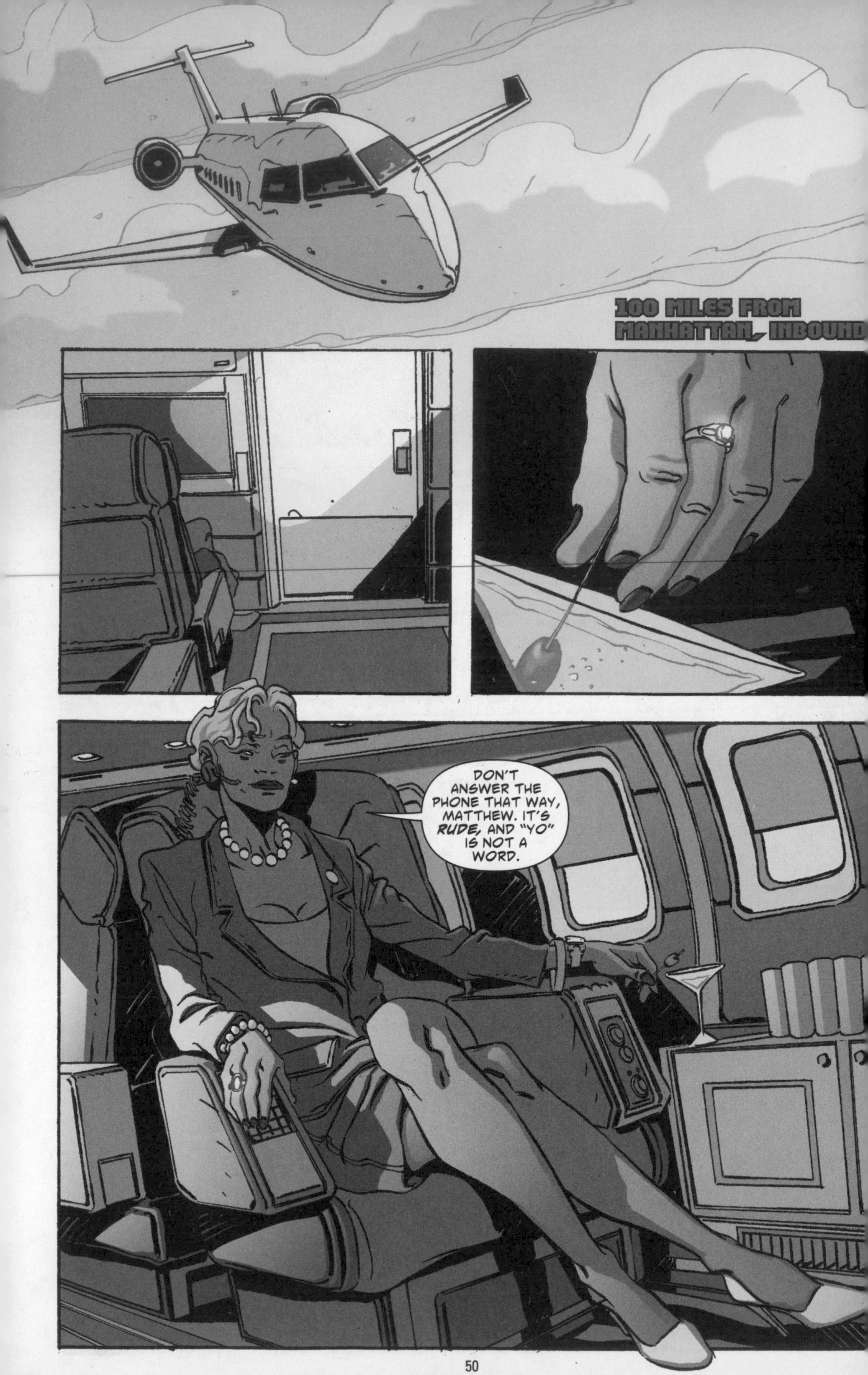
100 MILES FROM
MANHATTAN, INBOUND
DON'T ANSWER THE PHONE THAT WAY, MATTHEW. IT'S *RUDE,* AND "YO" IS NOT A WORD.

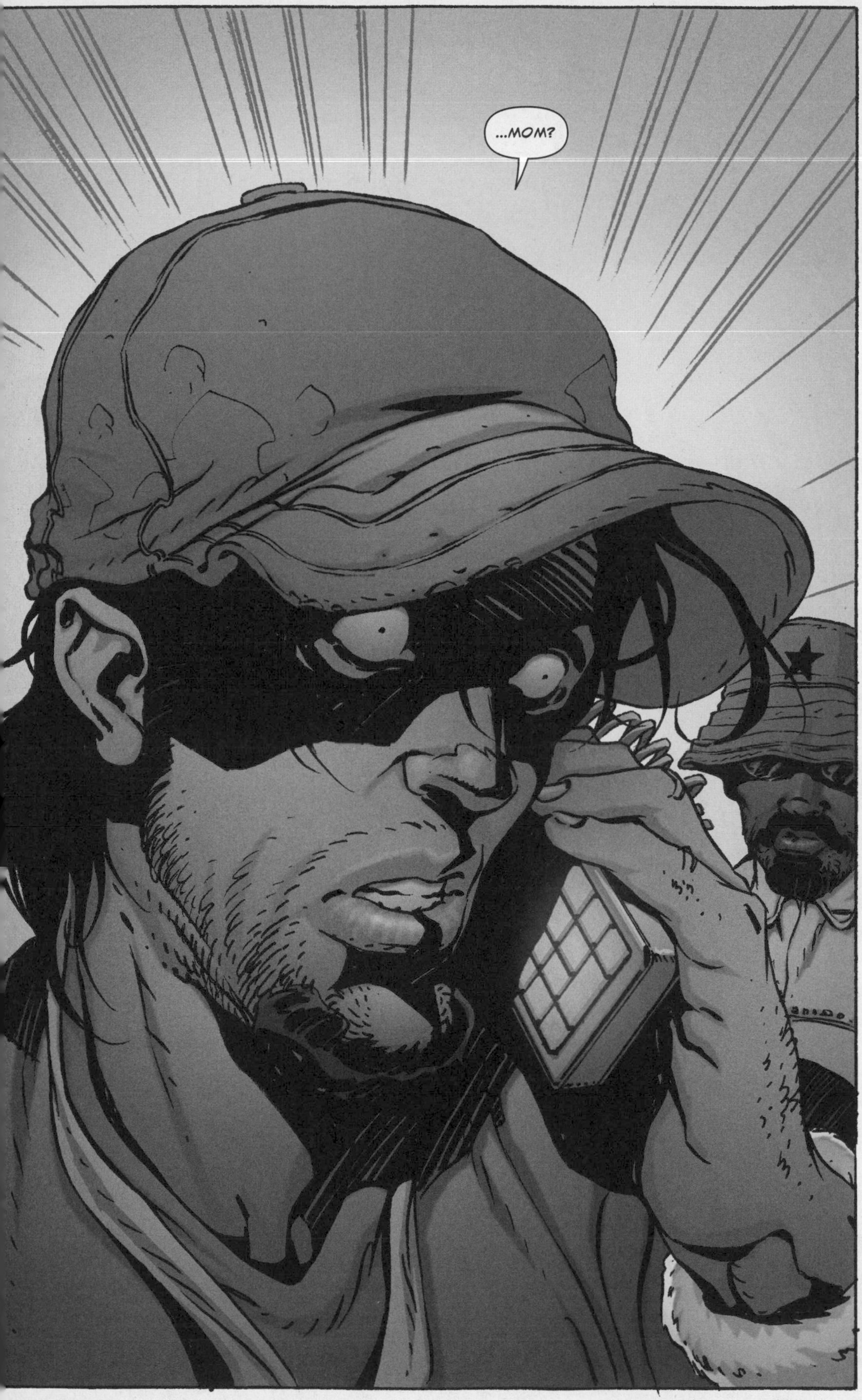
...MOM?

CHAPTER THREE

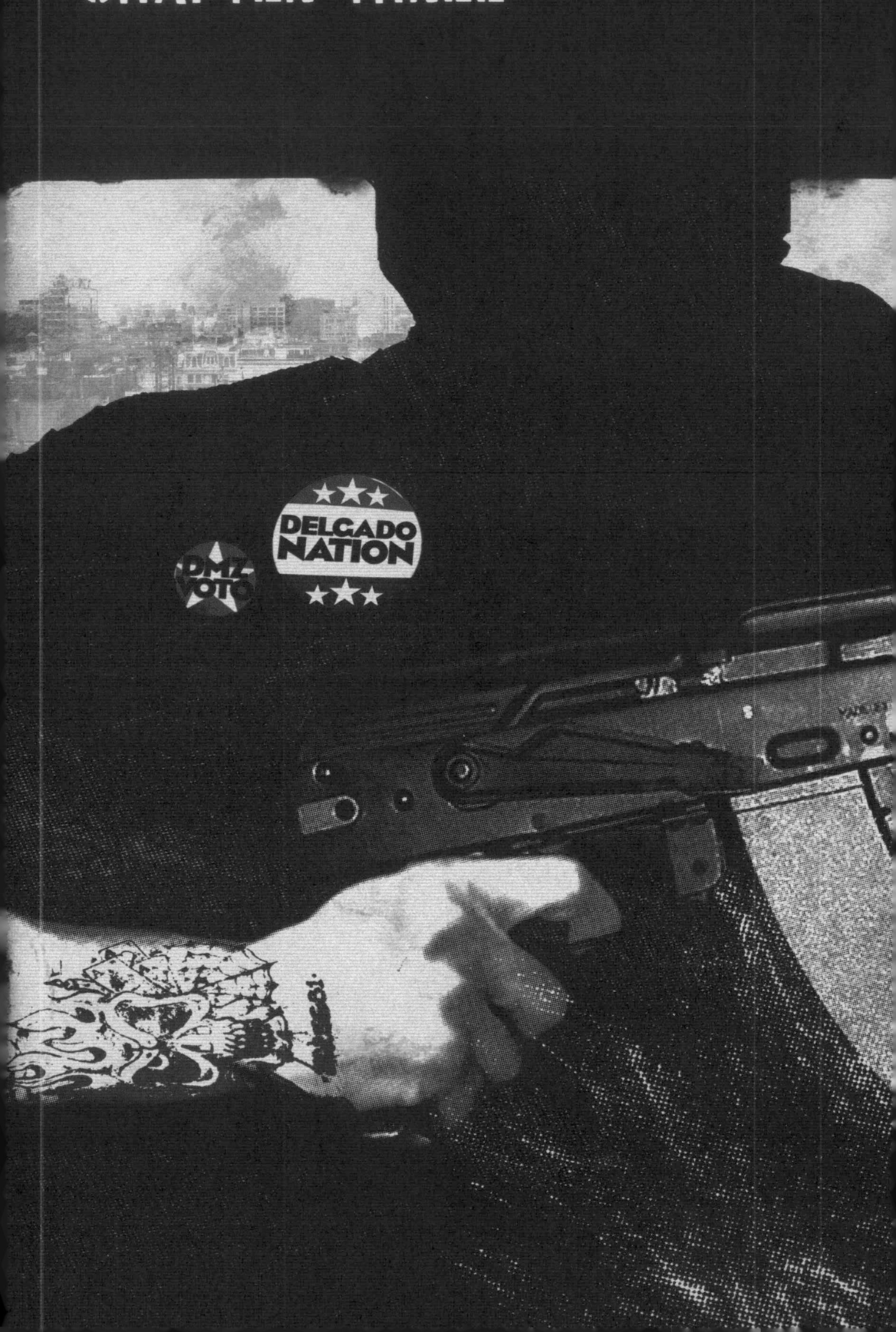
DELGADO
NATION
DMZ
VOTO

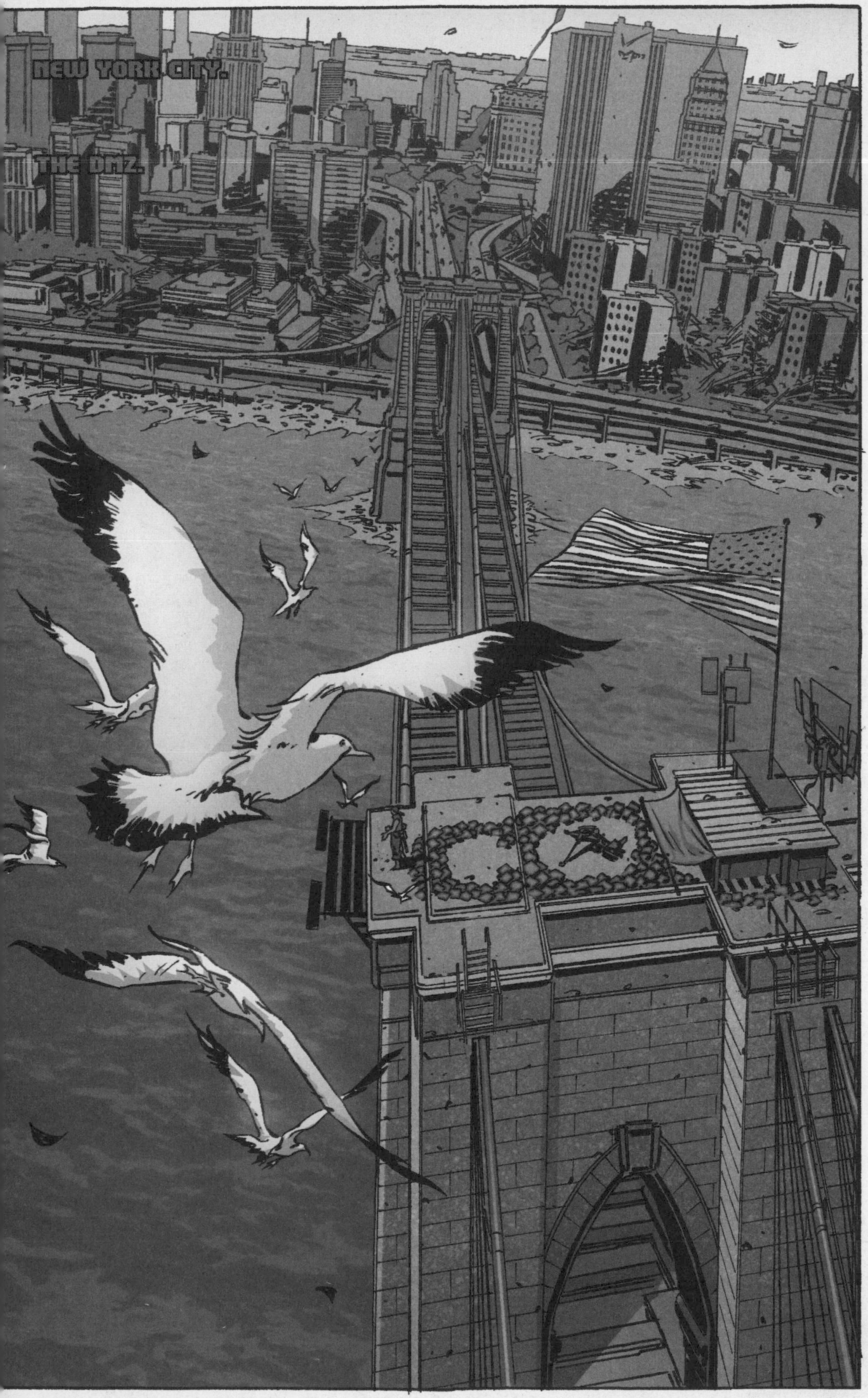
NEW YORK CITY.
THE DMZ.

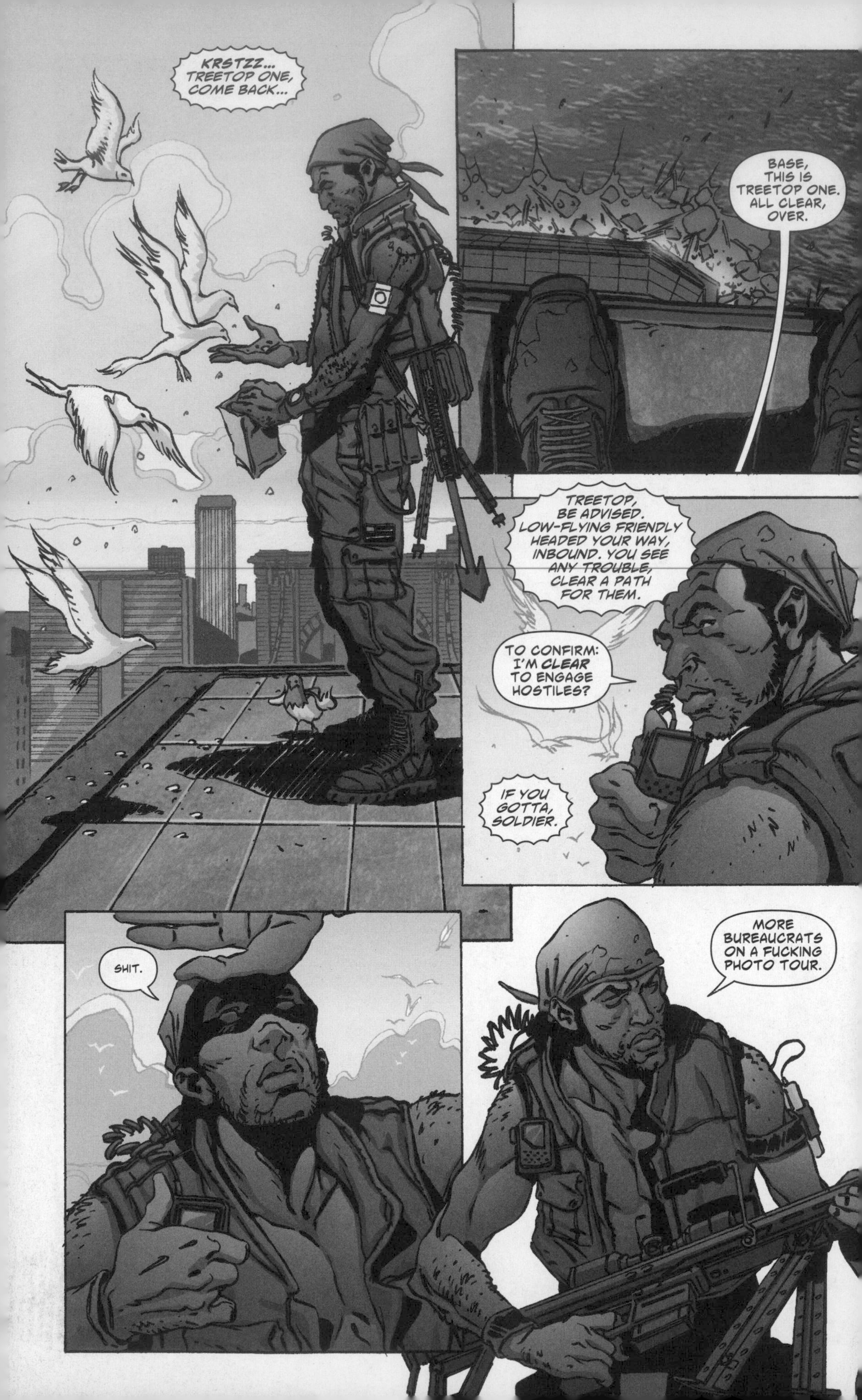
KRSTZZ... TREETOP ONE, COME BACK...
BASE, THIS IS TREETOP ONE. ALL CLEAR, OVER.
TREETOP, BE ADVISED. LOW-FLYING FRIENDLY HEADED YOUR WAY, INBOUND. YOU SEE ANY TROUBLE, CLEAR A PATH FOR THEM.
TO CONFIRM: I'M *CLEAR* TO ENGAGE HOSTILES?
IF YOU GOTTA, SOLDIER.
SHIT.
MORE BUREAUCRATS ON A FUCKING PHOTO TOUR.

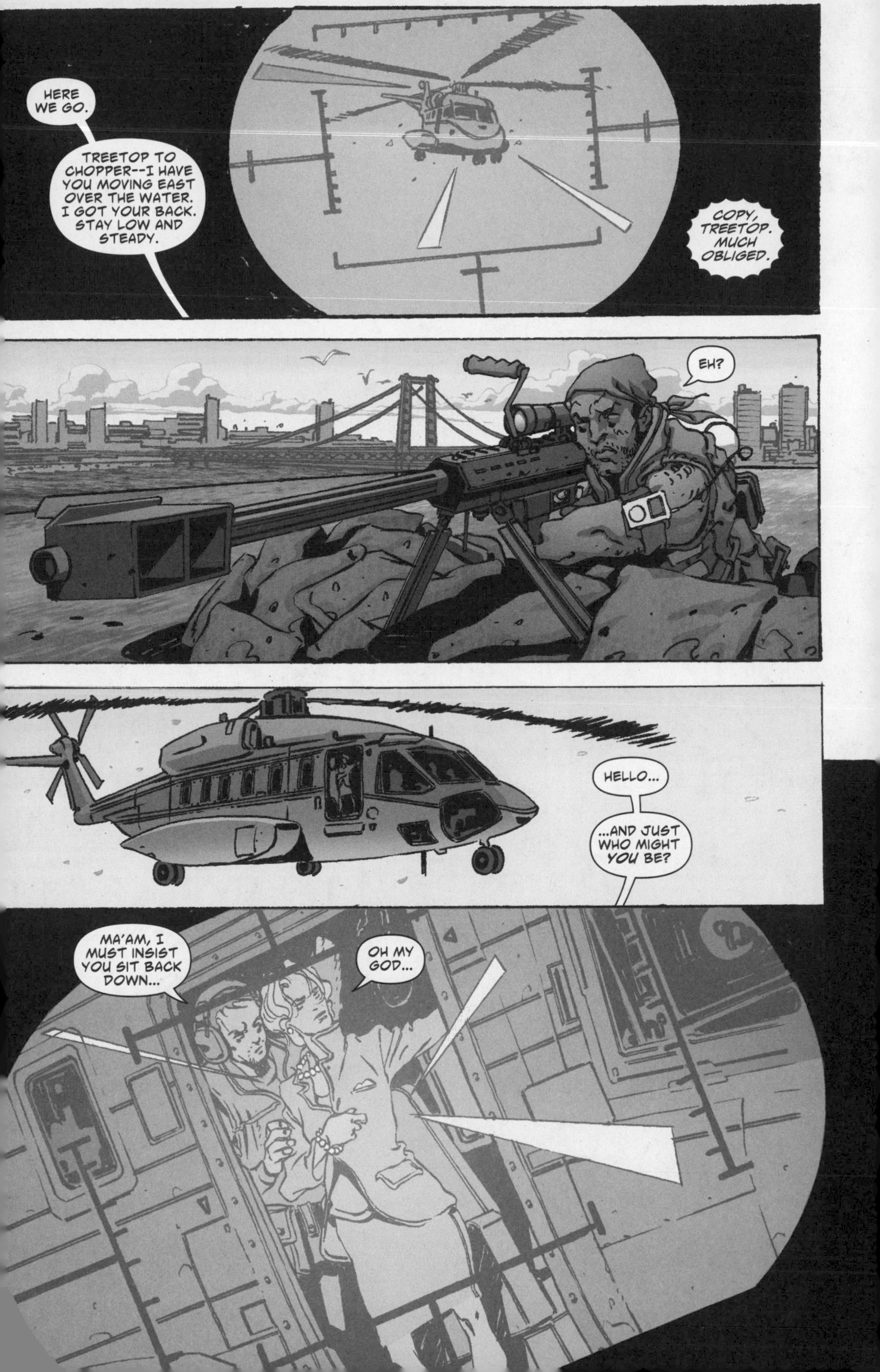
HERE WE GO.
TREETOP TO CHOPPER--I HAVE YOU MOVING EAST OVER THE WATER. I GOT YOUR BACK. STAY LOW AND STEADY.
COPY, TREETOP. MUCH OBLIGED.
EH?
HELLO...
...AND JUST WHO MIGHT *YOU* BE?
MA'AM, I MUST INSIST YOU SIT BACK DOWN...
OH MY GOD...

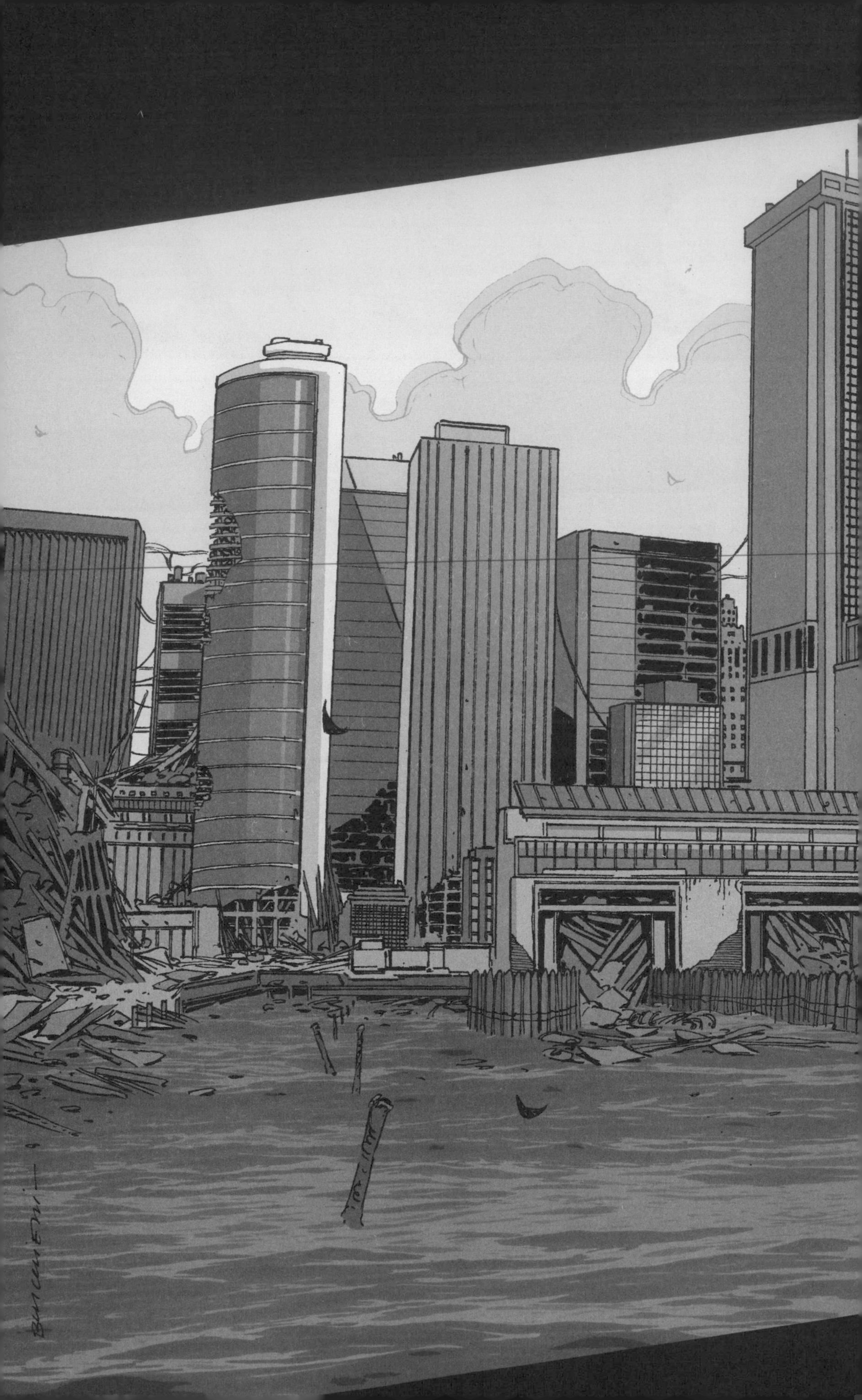

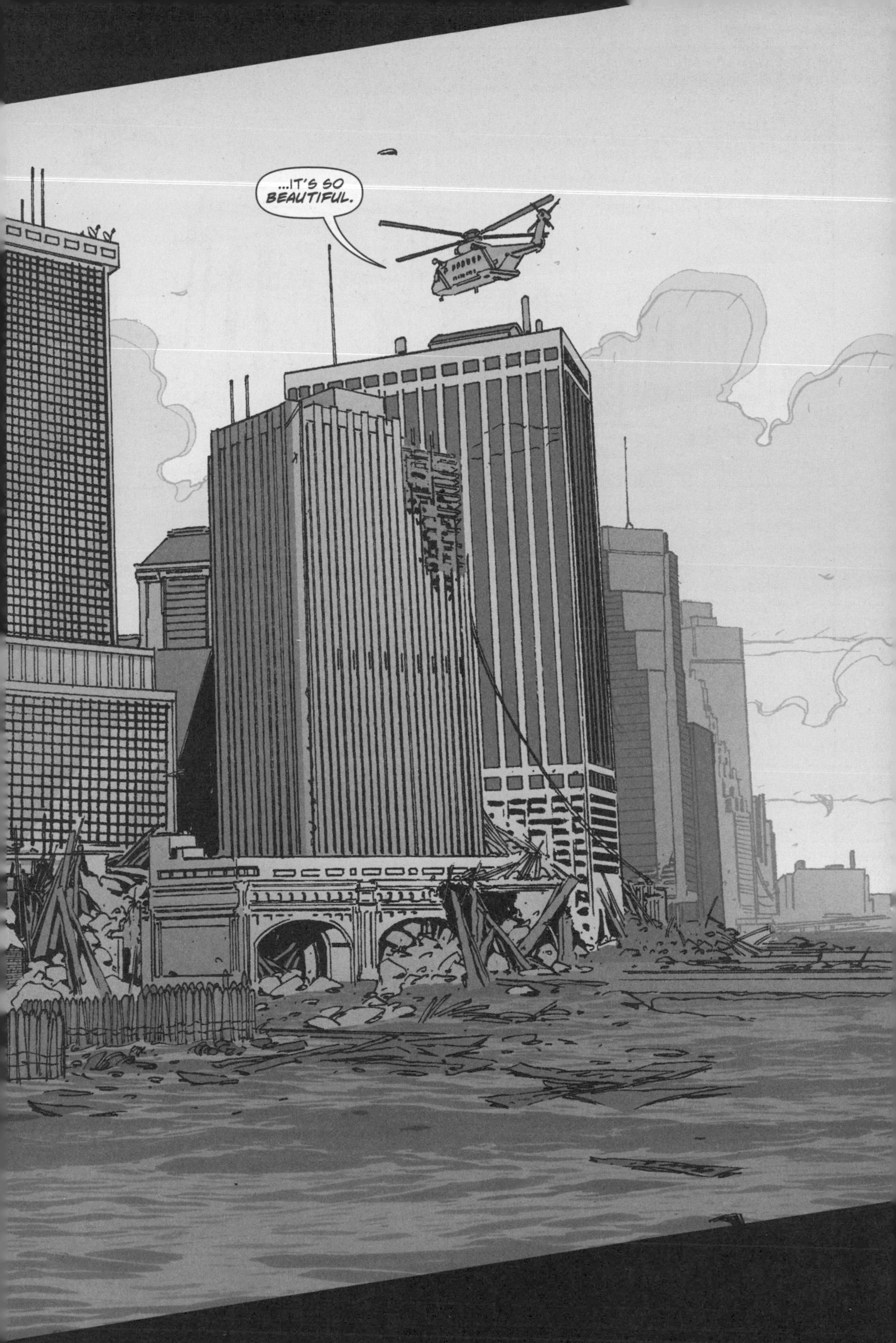
...IT'S SO BEAUTIFUL.

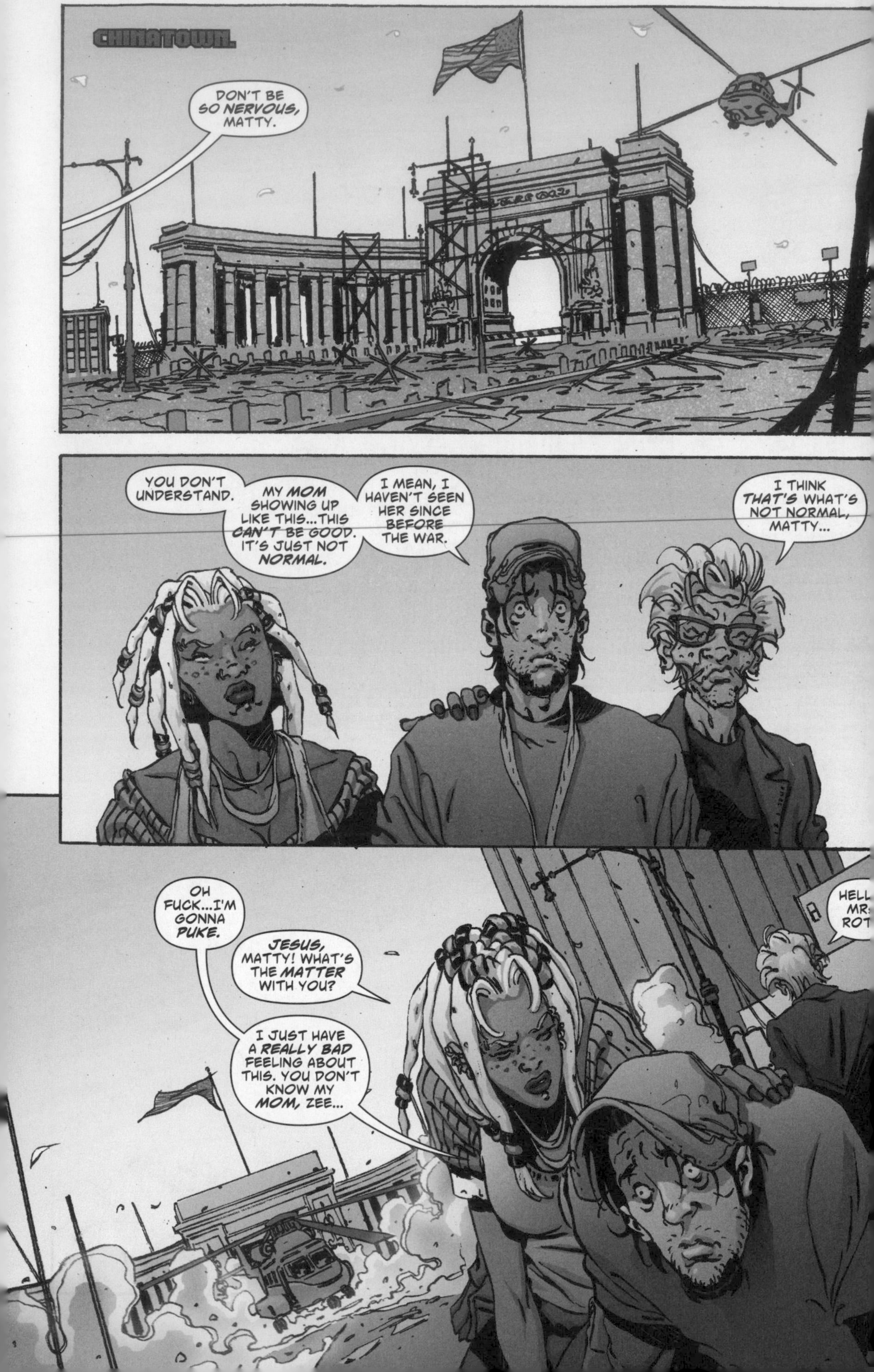
CHINATOWN.
DON'T BE SO NERVOUS, MATTY.
YOU DON'T UNDERSTAND.
MY MOM SHOWING UP LIKE THIS...THIS CAN'T BE GOOD. IT'S JUST NOT NORMAL.
I MEAN, I HAVEN'T SEEN HER SINCE BEFORE THE WAR.
I THINK THAT'S WHAT'S NOT NORMAL, MATTY...
OH FUCK...I'M GONNA PUKE.
JESUS, MATTY! WHAT'S THE MATTER WITH YOU?
I JUST HAVE A REALLY BAD FEELING ABOUT THIS. YOU DON'T KNOW MY MOM, ZEE...

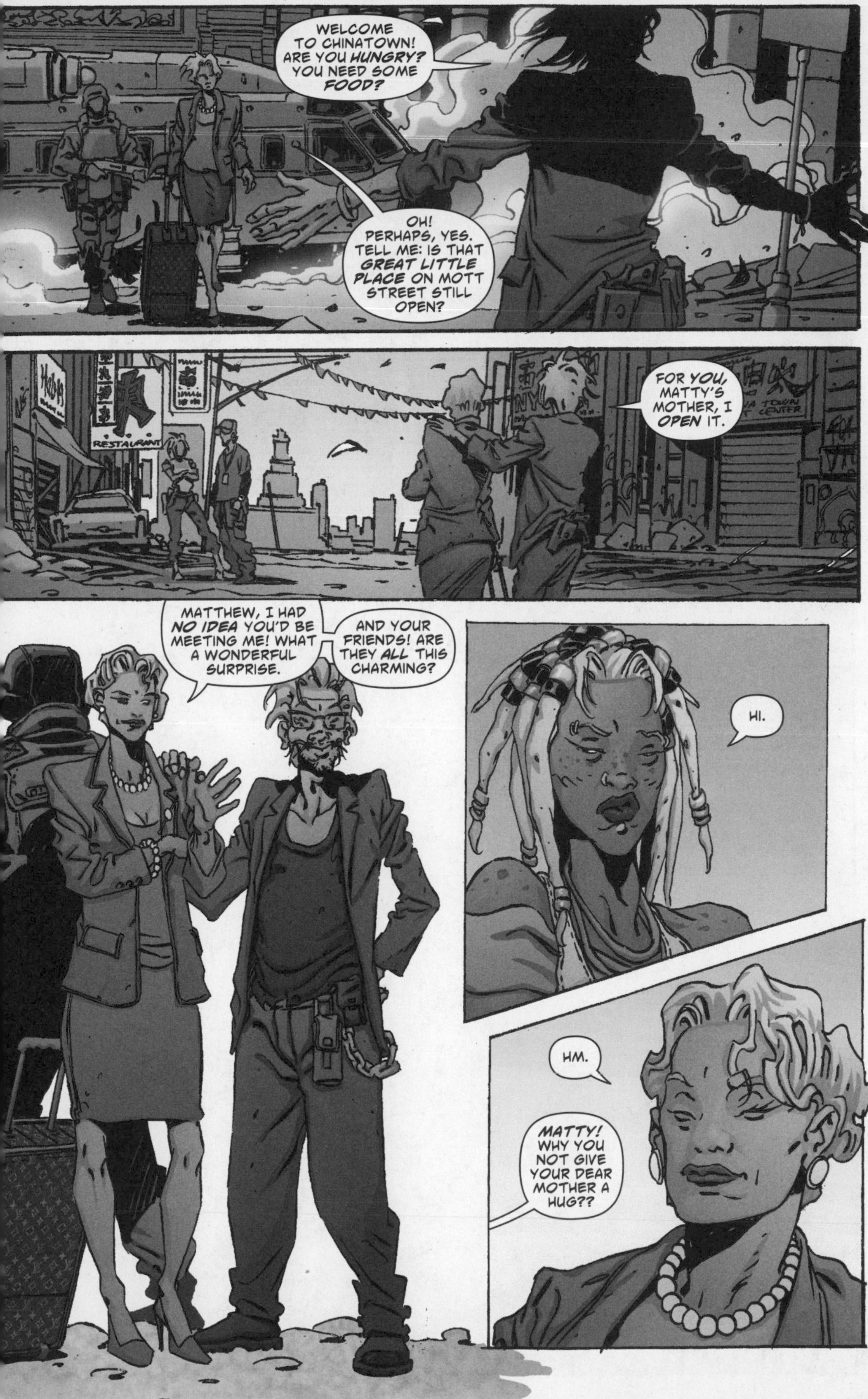
WELCOME TO CHINATOWN! ARE YOU HUNGRY? YOU NEED SOME FOOD?
OH! PERHAPS, YES. TELL ME: IS THAT GREAT LITTLE PLACE ON MOTT STREET STILL OPEN?
RESTAURANT
FOR YOU, MATTY'S MOTHER, I OPEN IT.
MATTHEW, I HAD NO IDEA YOU'D BE MEETING ME! WHAT A WONDERFUL SURPRISE.
AND YOUR FRIENDS! ARE THEY ALL THIS CHARMING?
HI.
HM.
MATTY! WHY YOU NOT GIVE YOUR DEAR MOTHER A HUG??

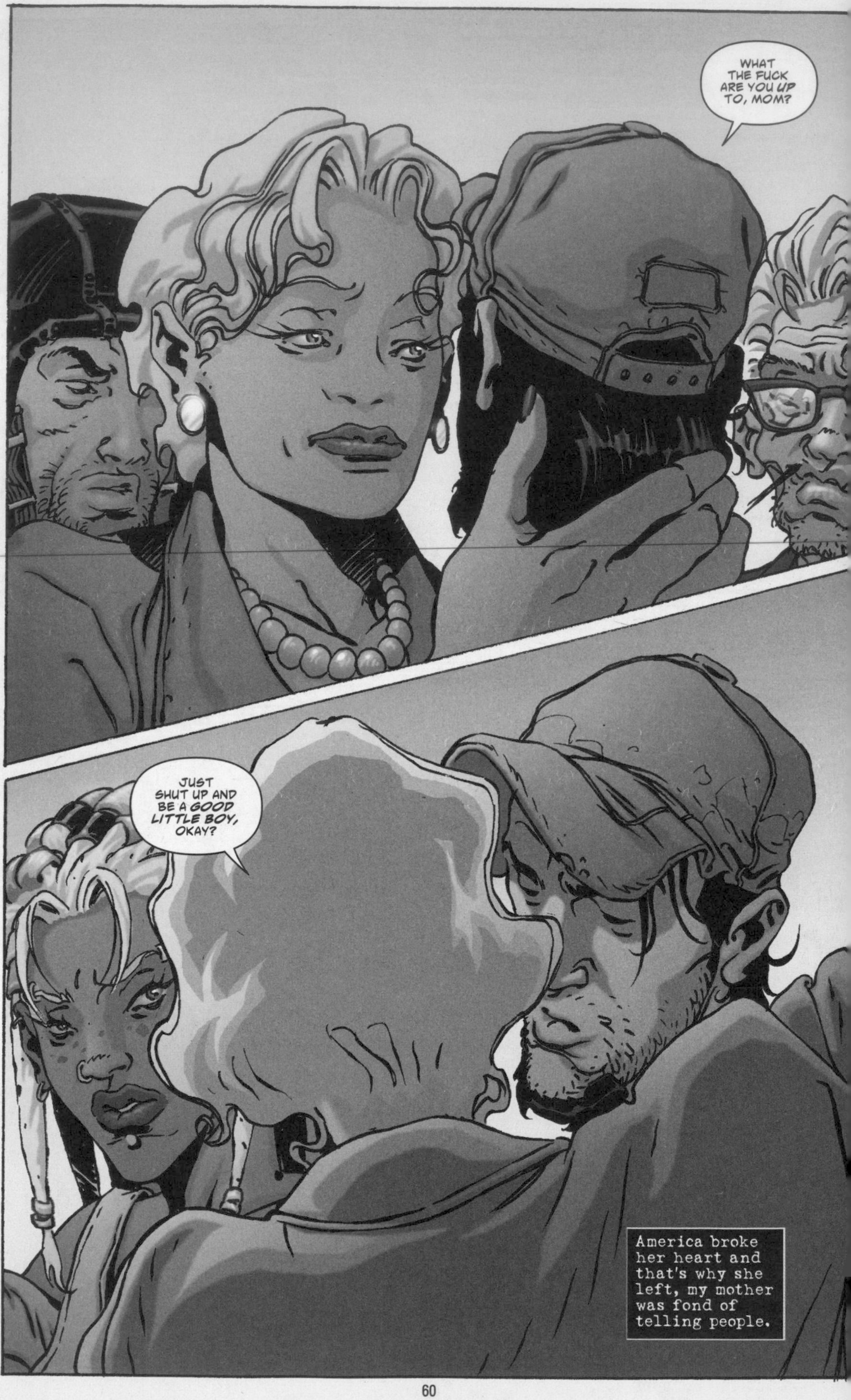
WHAT THE FUCK ARE YOU UP TO, MOM?
JUST SHUT UP AND BE A GOOD LITTLE BOY, OKAY?
America broke her heart and that's why she left, my mother was fond of telling people.

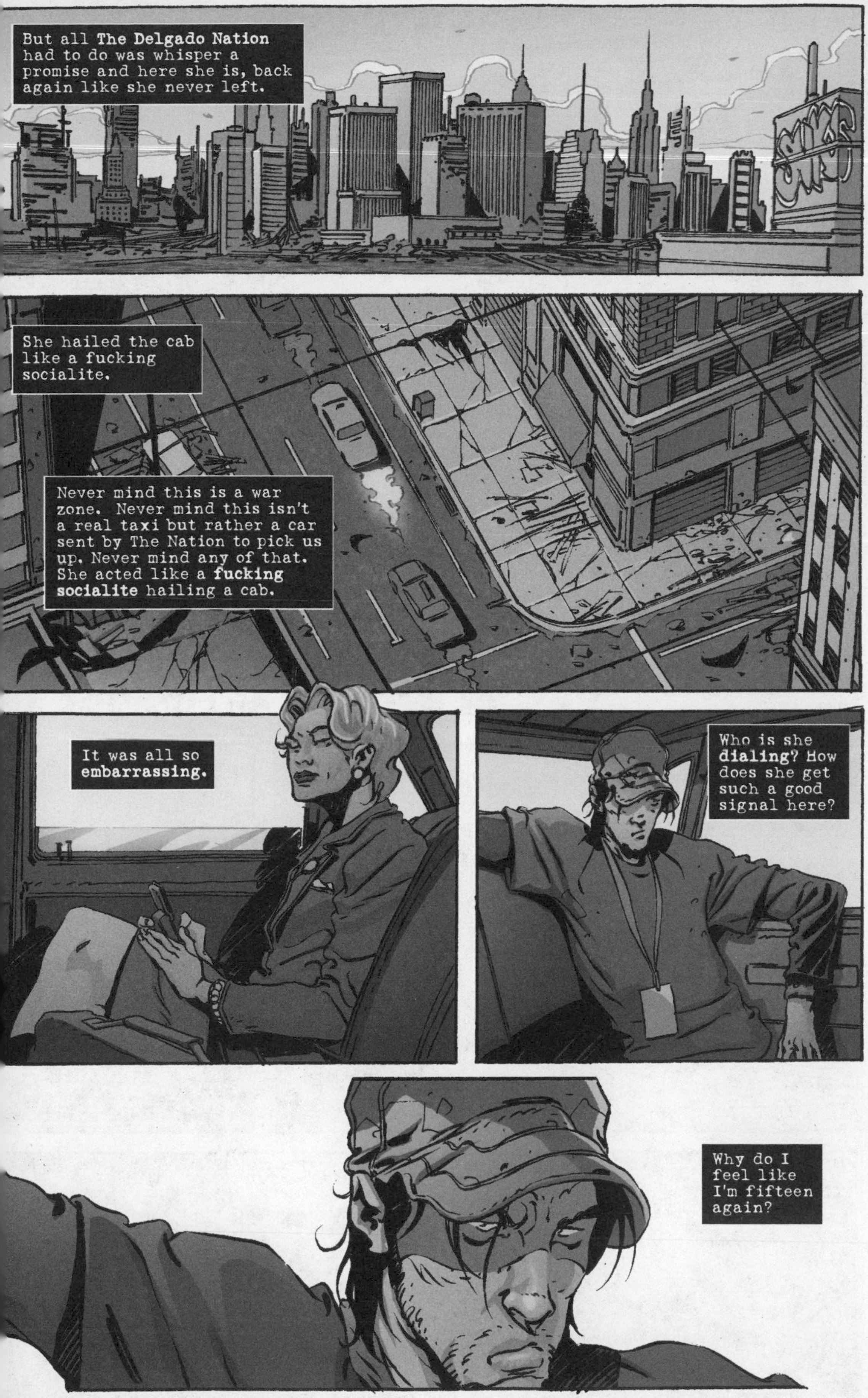
But all The Delgado Nation had to do was whisper a promise and here she is, back again like she never left.
She hailed the cab like a fucking socialite.
Never mind this is a war zone. Never mind this isn't a real taxi but rather a car sent by The Nation to pick us up. Never mind any of that. She acted like a fucking socialite hailing a cab.
It was all so embarrassing.
Who is she dialing? How does she get such a good signal here?
Why do I feel like I'm fifteen again?

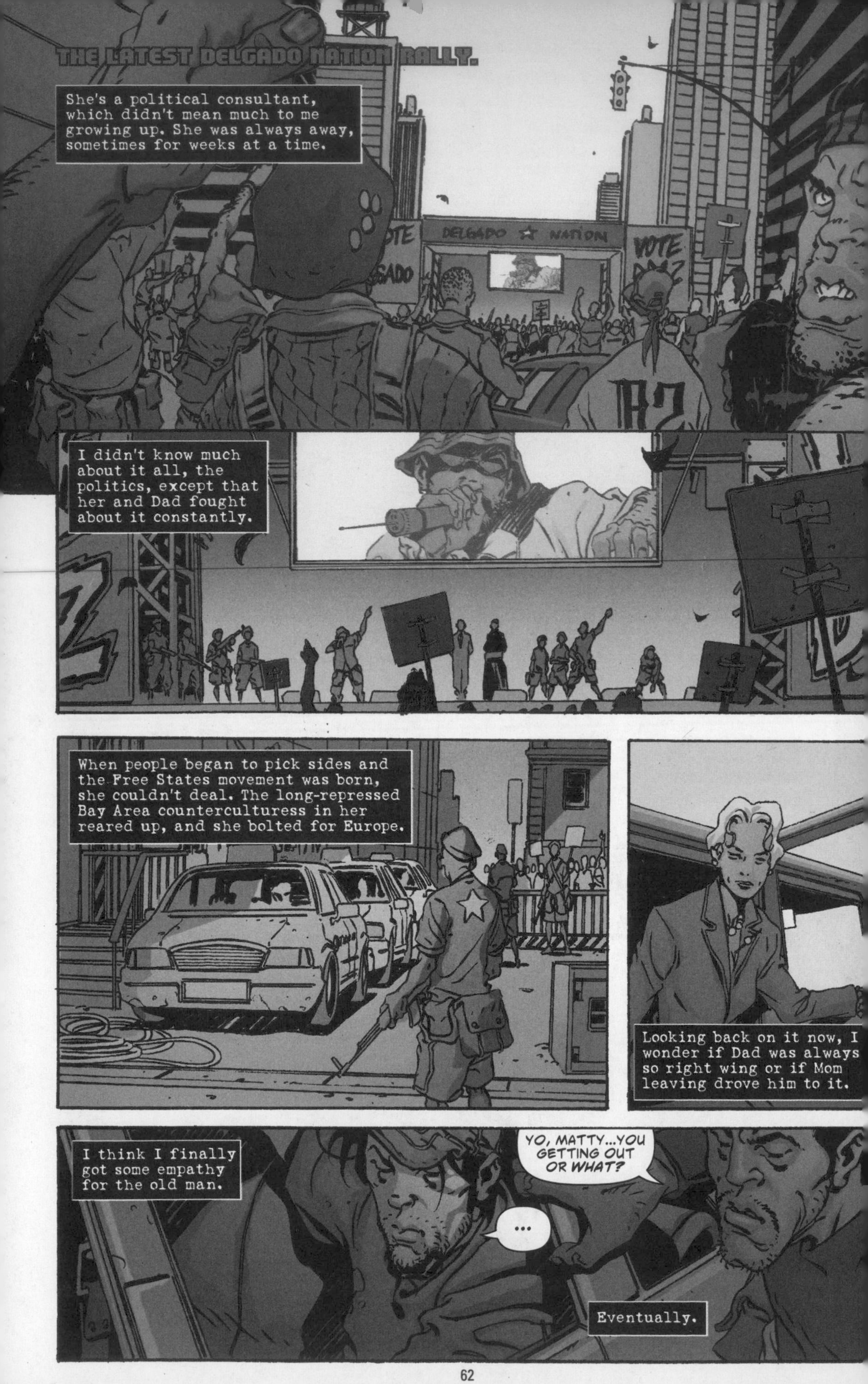
THE LATEST DELGADO NATION RALLY.
She's a political consultant, which didn't mean much to me growing up. She was always away, sometimes for weeks at a time.
DELGADO NATION
VOTE
I didn't know much about it all, the politics, except that her and Dad fought about it constantly.
When people began to pick sides and the Free States movement was born, she couldn't deal. The long-repressed Bay Area counterculturess in her reared up, and she bolted for Europe.
Looking back on it now, I wonder if Dad was always so right wing or if Mom leaving drove him to it.
I think I finally got some empathy for the old man.
YO, MATTY...YOU GETTING OUT OR WHAT?
...
Eventually.

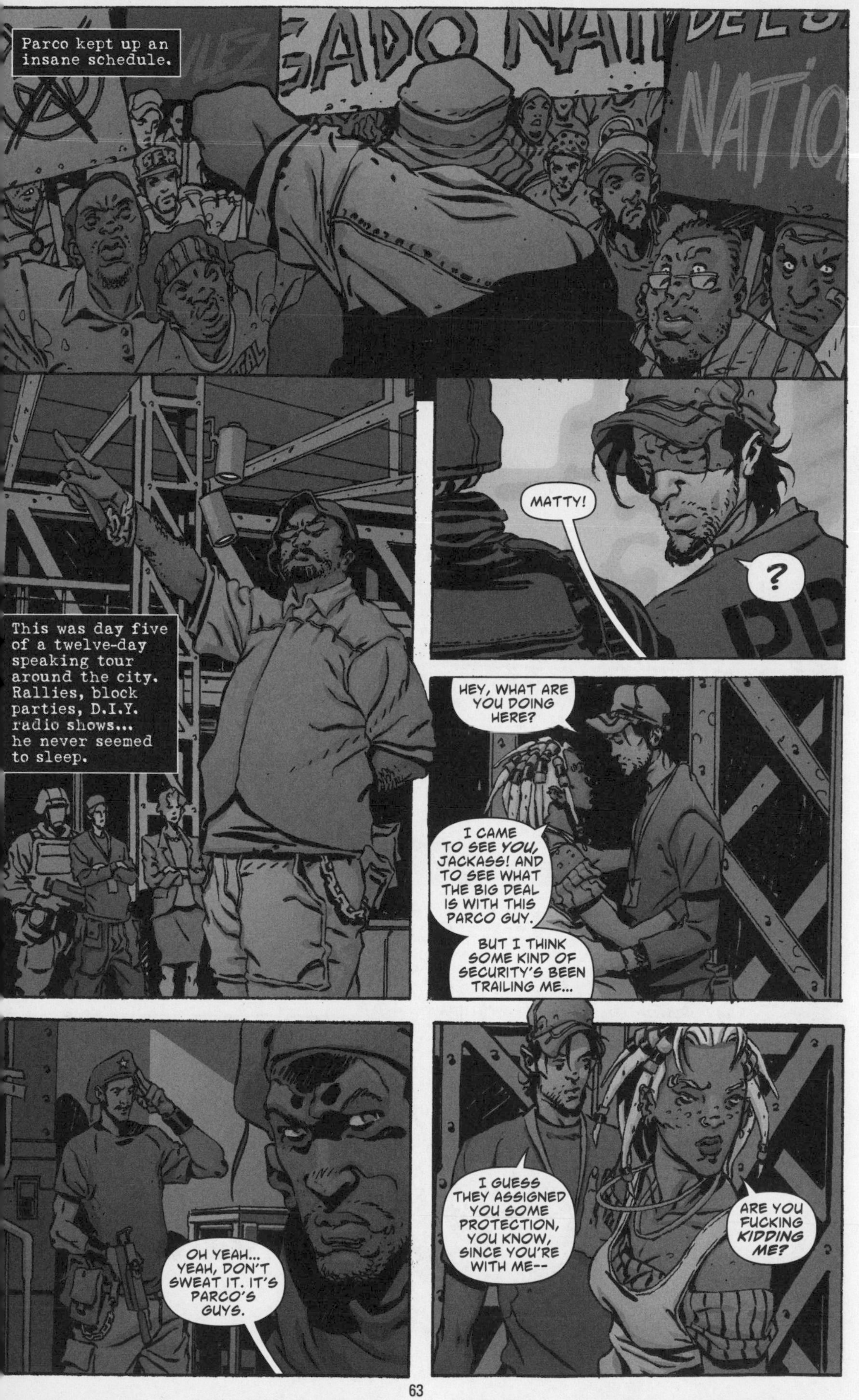
Parco kept up an insane schedule.
This was day five of a twelve-day speaking tour around the city. Rallies, block parties, D.I.Y. radio shows... he never seemed to sleep.
MATTY!
?
HEY, WHAT ARE YOU DOING HERE?
I CAME TO SEE YOU, JACKASS! AND TO SEE WHAT THE BIG DEAL IS WITH THIS PARCO GUY.
BUT I THINK SOME KIND OF SECURITY'S BEEN TRAILING ME...
OH YEAH... YEAH, DON'T SWEAT IT. IT'S PARCO'S GUYS.
I GUESS THEY ASSIGNED YOU SOME PROTECTION, YOU KNOW, SINCE YOU'RE WITH ME--
ARE YOU FUCKING KIDDING ME?

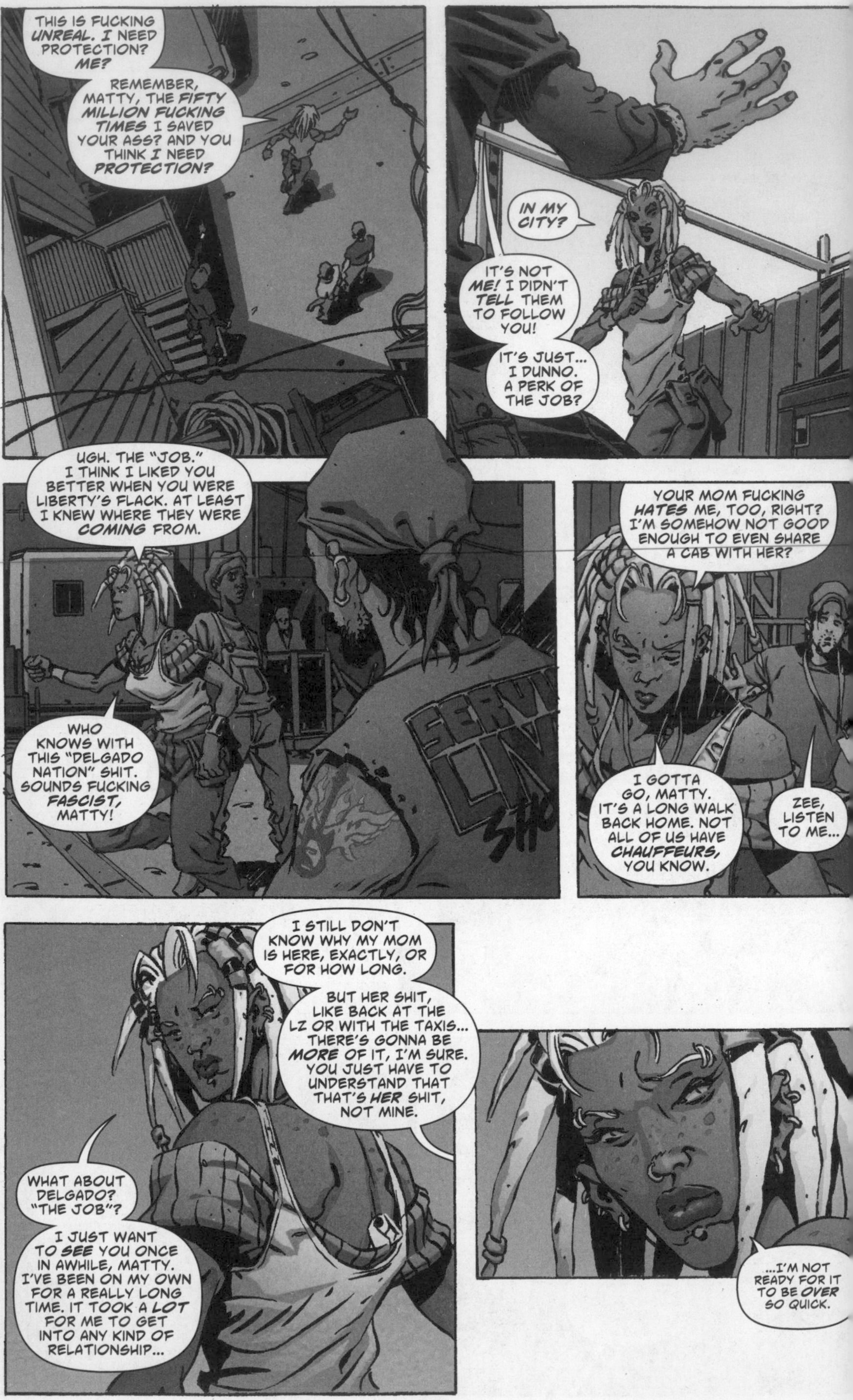
THIS IS FUCKING UNREAL. I NEED PROTECTION? ME?
REMEMBER, MATTY, THE FIFTY MILLION FUCKING TIMES I SAVED YOUR ASS? AND YOU THINK I NEED PROTECTION?
IN MY CITY?
IT'S NOT ME! I DIDN'T TELL THEM TO FOLLOW YOU!
IT'S JUST... I DUNNO. A PERK OF THE JOB?
UGH. THE "JOB." I THINK I LIKED YOU BETTER WHEN YOU WERE LIBERTY'S FLACK. AT LEAST I KNEW WHERE THEY WERE COMING FROM.
WHO KNOWS WITH THIS "DELGADO NATION" SHIT. SOUNDS FUCKING FASCIST, MATTY!
YOUR MOM FUCKING HATES ME, TOO, RIGHT? I'M SOMEHOW NOT GOOD ENOUGH TO EVEN SHARE A CAB WITH HER?
I GOTTA GO, MATTY. IT'S A LONG WALK BACK HOME. NOT ALL OF US HAVE CHAUFFEURS, YOU KNOW.
ZEE, LISTEN TO ME...
I STILL DON'T KNOW WHY MY MOM IS HERE, EXACTLY, OR FOR HOW LONG.
BUT HER SHIT, LIKE BACK AT THE LZ OR WITH THE TAXIS... THERE'S GONNA BE MORE OF IT, I'M SURE. YOU JUST HAVE TO UNDERSTAND THAT THAT'S HER SHIT, NOT MINE.
WHAT ABOUT DELGADO? "THE JOB"?
I JUST WANT TO SEE YOU ONCE IN AWHILE, MATTY. I'VE BEEN ON MY OWN FOR A REALLY LONG TIME. IT TOOK A LOT FOR ME TO GET INTO ANY KIND OF RELATIONSHIP...
...I'M NOT READY FOR IT TO BE OVER SO QUICK.

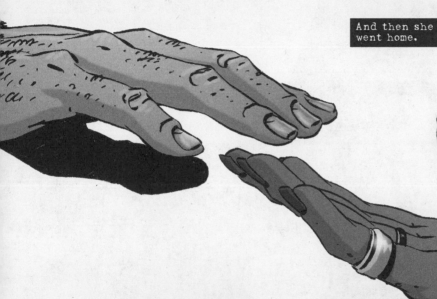

And then she went home.

And I went back to work.

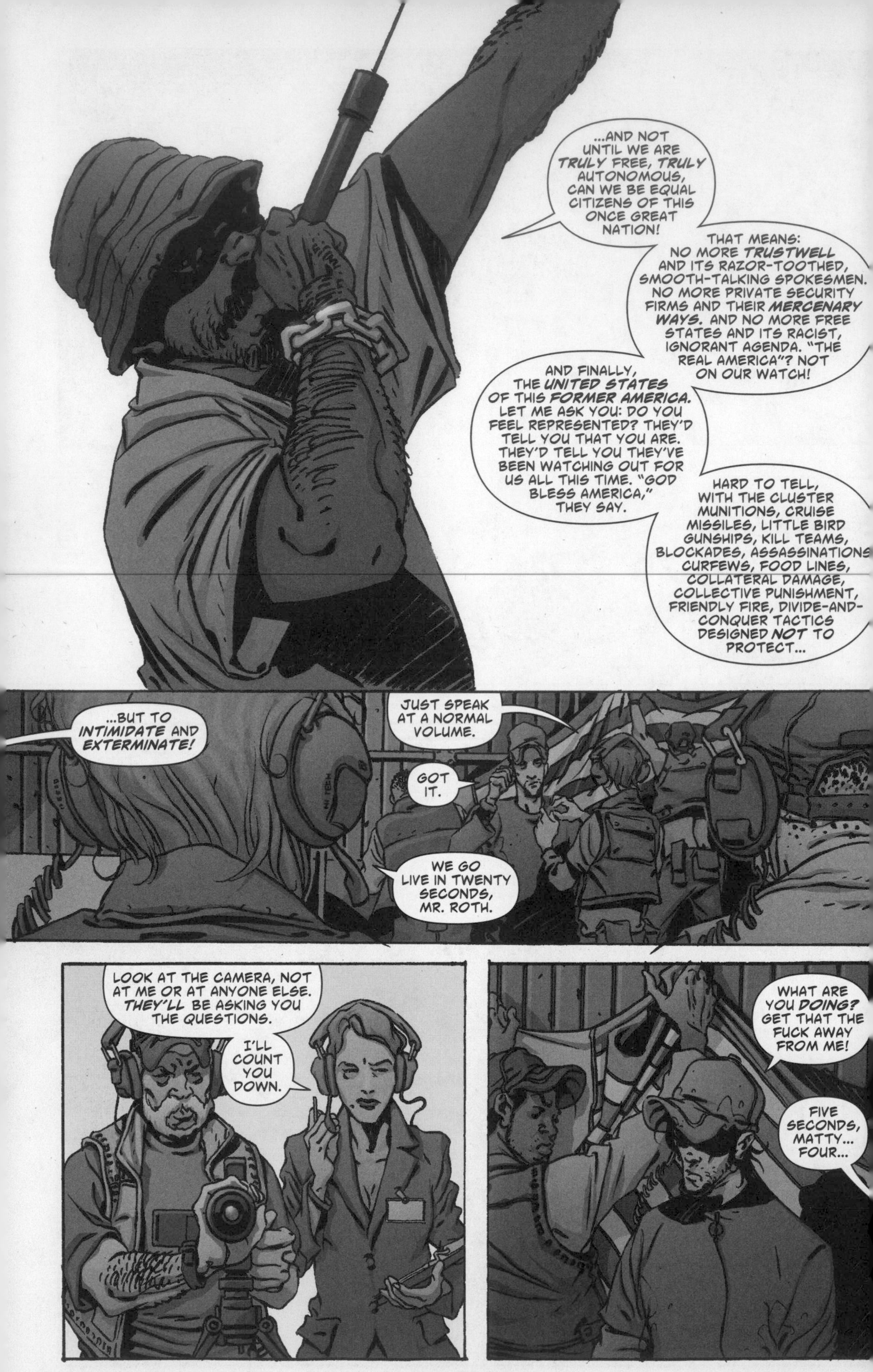
...AND NOT UNTIL WE ARE TRULY FREE, TRULY AUTONOMOUS, CAN WE BE EQUAL CITIZENS OF THIS ONCE GREAT NATION!
THAT MEANS: NO MORE TRUSTWELL AND ITS RAZOR-TOOTHED, SMOOTH-TALKING SPOKESMEN. NO MORE PRIVATE SECURITY FIRMS AND THEIR MERCENARY WAYS. AND NO MORE FREE STATES AND ITS RACIST, IGNORANT AGENDA. "THE REAL AMERICA"? NOT ON OUR WATCH!
AND FINALLY, THE UNITED STATES OF THIS FORMER AMERICA. LET ME ASK YOU: DO YOU FEEL REPRESENTED? THEY'D TELL YOU THAT YOU ARE. THEY'D TELL YOU THEY'VE BEEN WATCHING OUT FOR US ALL THIS TIME. "GOD BLESS AMERICA," THEY SAY.
HARD TO TELL, WITH THE CLUSTER MUNITIONS, CRUISE MISSILES, LITTLE BIRD GUNSHIPS, KILL TEAMS, BLOCKADES, ASSASSINATIONS CURFEWS, FOOD LINES, COLLATERAL DAMAGE, COLLECTIVE PUNISHMENT, FRIENDLY FIRE, DIVIDE-AND-CONQUER TACTICS DESIGNED NOT TO PROTECT...
...BUT TO INTIMIDATE AND EXTERMINATE!
JUST SPEAK AT A NORMAL VOLUME.
GOT IT.
WE GO LIVE IN TWENTY SECONDS, MR. ROTH.
LOOK AT THE CAMERA, NOT AT ME OR AT ANYONE ELSE. THEY'LL BE ASKING YOU THE QUESTIONS.
I'LL COUNT YOU DOWN.
WHAT ARE YOU DOING? GET THAT THE FUCK AWAY FROM ME!
FIVE SECONDS, MATTY... FOUR...

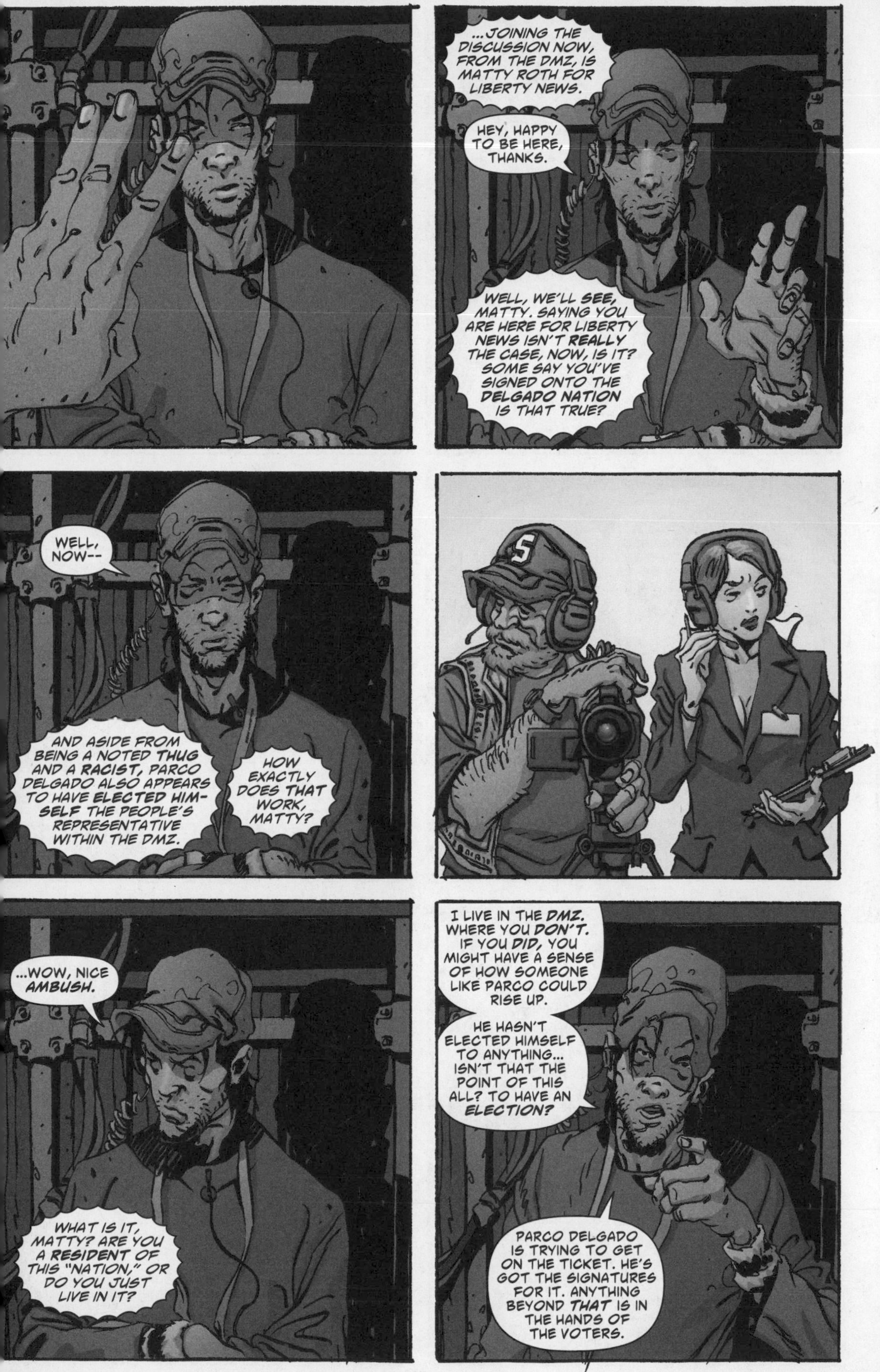
...JOINING THE DISCUSSION NOW, FROM THE DMZ, IS MATTY ROTH FOR LIBERTY NEWS.
HEY, HAPPY TO BE HERE, THANKS.
WELL, WE'LL SEE, MATTY. SAYING YOU ARE HERE FOR LIBERTY NEWS ISN'T REALLY THE CASE, NOW, IS IT? SOME SAY YOU'VE SIGNED ONTO THE DELGADO NATION IS THAT TRUE?
WELL, NOW--
AND ASIDE FROM BEING A NOTED THUG AND A RACIST, PARCO DELGADO ALSO APPEARS TO HAVE ELECTED HIM-SELF THE PEOPLE'S REPRESENTATIVE WITHIN THE DMZ.
HOW EXACTLY DOES THAT WORK, MATTY?
...WOW, NICE AMBUSH.
WHAT IS IT, MATTY? ARE YOU A RESIDENT OF THIS "NATION," OR DO YOU JUST LIVE IN IT?
I LIVE IN THE DMZ. WHERE YOU DON'T. IF YOU DID, YOU MIGHT HAVE A SENSE OF HOW SOMEONE LIKE PARCO COULD RISE UP.
HE HASN'T ELECTED HIMSELF TO ANYTHING... ISN'T THAT THE POINT OF THIS ALL? TO HAVE AN ELECTION?
PARCO DELGADO IS TRYING TO GET ON THE TICKET. HE'S GOT THE SIGNATURES FOR IT. ANYTHING BEYOND THAT IS IN THE HANDS OF THE VOTERS.

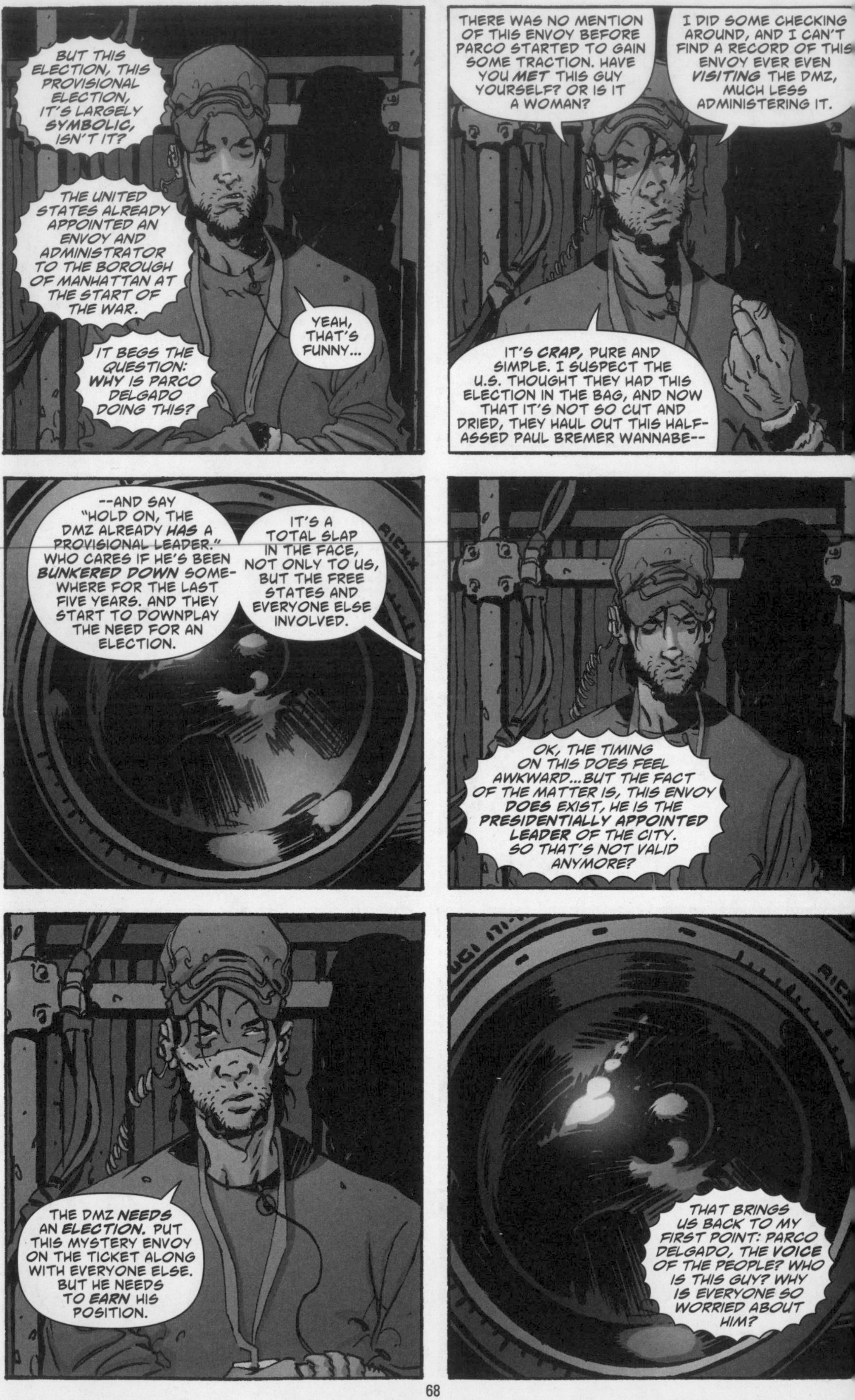
BUT THIS ELECTION, THIS PROVISIONAL ELECTION, IT'S LARGELY SYMBOLIC, ISN'T IT?
THE UNITED STATES ALREADY APPOINTED AN ENVOY AND ADMINISTRATOR TO THE BOROUGH OF MANHATTAN AT THE START OF THE WAR.
IT BEGS THE QUESTION: WHY IS PARCO DELGADO DOING THIS?
YEAH, THAT'S FUNNY...
THERE WAS NO MENTION OF THIS ENVOY BEFORE PARCO STARTED TO GAIN SOME TRACTION. HAVE YOU MET THIS GUY YOURSELF? OR IS IT A WOMAN?
I DID SOME CHECKING AROUND, AND I CAN'T FIND A RECORD OF THIS ENVOY EVER EVEN VISITING THE DMZ, MUCH LESS ADMINISTERING IT.
IT'S CRAP, PURE AND SIMPLE. I SUSPECT THE U.S. THOUGHT THEY HAD THIS ELECTION IN THE BAG, AND NOW THAT IT'S NOT SO CUT AND DRIED, THEY HAUL OUT THIS HALF-ASSED PAUL BREMER WANNABE--
--AND SAY "HOLD ON, THE DMZ ALREADY HAS A PROVISIONAL LEADER." WHO CARES IF HE'S BEEN BUNKERED DOWN SOMEWHERE FOR THE LAST FIVE YEARS. AND THEY START TO DOWNPLAY THE NEED FOR AN ELECTION.
IT'S A TOTAL SLAP IN THE FACE, NOT ONLY TO US, BUT THE FREE STATES AND EVERYONE ELSE INVOLVED.
OK, THE TIMING ON THIS DOES FEEL AWKWARD...BUT THE FACT OF THE MATTER IS, THIS ENVOY DOES EXIST, HE IS THE PRESIDENTIALLY APPOINTED LEADER OF THE CITY. SO THAT'S NOT VALID ANYMORE?
THE DMZ NEEDS AN ELECTION. PUT THIS MYSTERY ENVOY ON THE TICKET ALONG WITH EVERYONE ELSE. BUT HE NEEDS TO EARN HIS POSITION.
THAT BRINGS US BACK TO MY FIRST POINT: PARCO DELGADO, THE VOICE OF THE PEOPLE? WHO IS THIS GUY? WHY IS EVERYONE SO WORRIED ABOUT HIM?

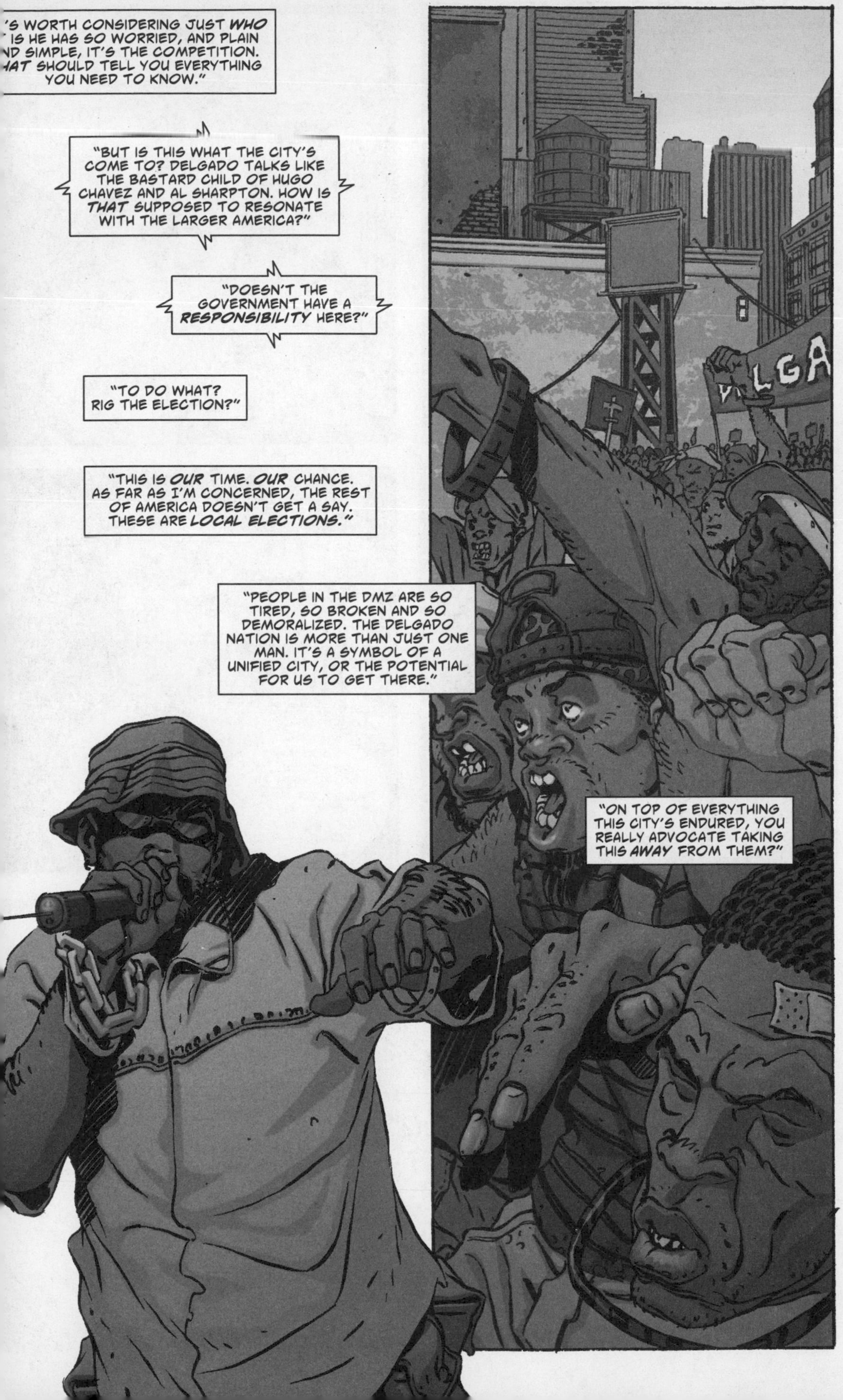
'S WORTH CONSIDERING JUST WHO IS HE HAS SO WORRIED, AND PLAIN ND SIMPLE, IT'S THE COMPETITION. HAT SHOULD TELL YOU EVERYTHING YOU NEED TO KNOW."
"BUT IS THIS WHAT THE CITY'S COME TO? DELGADO TALKS LIKE THE BASTARD CHILD OF HUGO CHAVEZ AND AL SHARPTON. HOW IS THAT SUPPOSED TO RESONATE WITH THE LARGER AMERICA?"
"DOESN'T THE GOVERNMENT HAVE A RESPONSIBILITY HERE?"
"TO DO WHAT? RIG THE ELECTION?"
"THIS IS OUR TIME. OUR CHANCE. AS FAR AS I'M CONCERNED, THE REST OF AMERICA DOESN'T GET A SAY. THESE ARE LOCAL ELECTIONS."
"PEOPLE IN THE DMZ ARE SO TIRED, SO BROKEN AND SO DEMORALIZED. THE DELGADO NATION IS MORE THAN JUST ONE MAN. IT'S A SYMBOL OF A UNIFIED CITY, OR THE POTENTIAL FOR US TO GET THERE."
"ON TOP OF EVERYTHING THIS CITY'S ENDURED, YOU REALLY ADVOCATE TAKING THIS AWAY FROM THEM?"

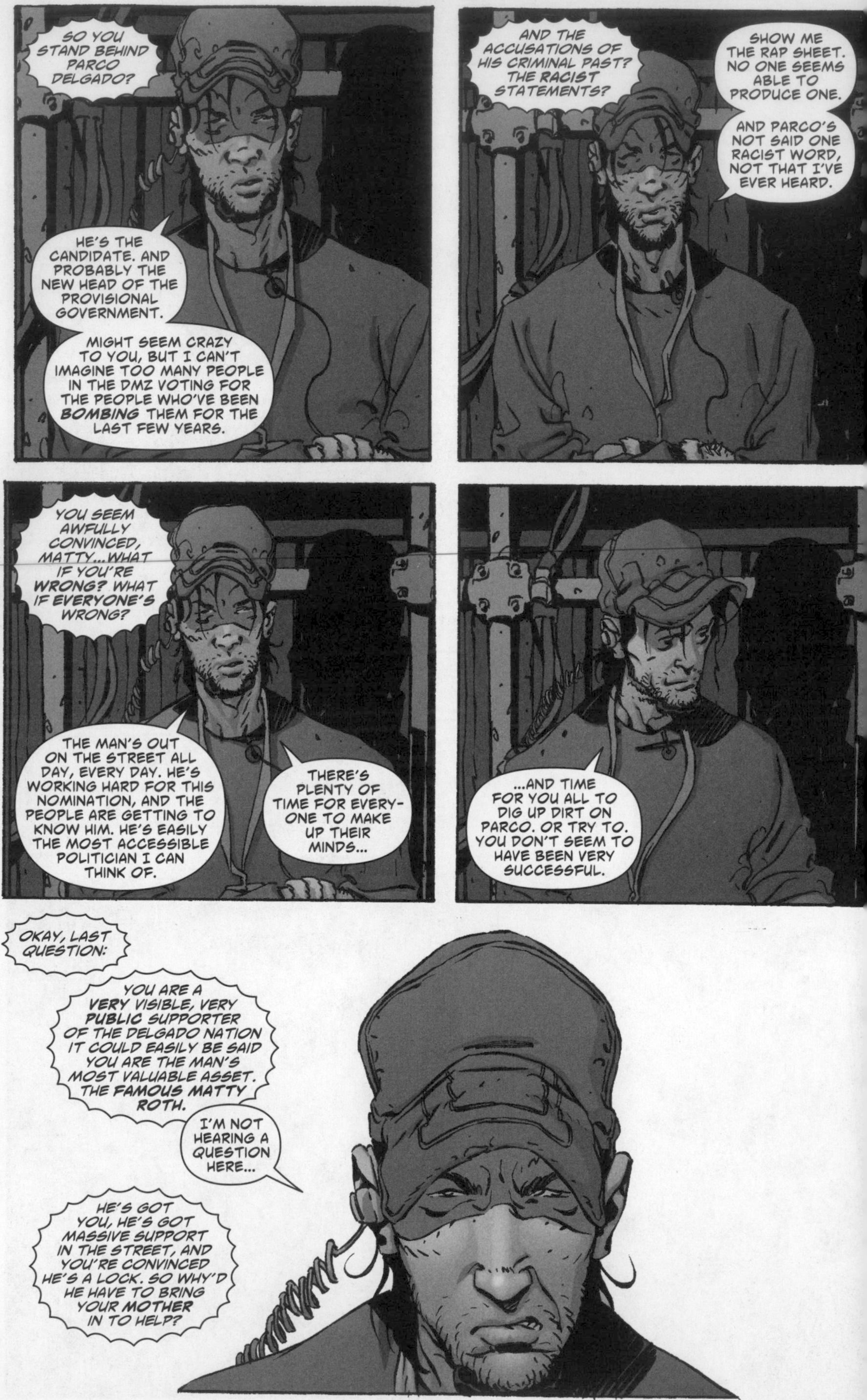
SO YOU STAND BEHIND PARCO DELGADO?
HE'S THE CANDIDATE. AND PROBABLY THE NEW HEAD OF THE PROVISIONAL GOVERNMENT.
MIGHT SEEM CRAZY TO YOU, BUT I CAN'T IMAGINE TOO MANY PEOPLE IN THE DMZ VOTING FOR THE PEOPLE WHO'VE BEEN BOMBING THEM FOR THE LAST FEW YEARS.
AND THE ACCUSATIONS OF HIS CRIMINAL PAST? THE RACIST STATEMENTS?
SHOW ME THE RAP SHEET. NO ONE SEEMS ABLE TO PRODUCE ONE.
AND PARCO'S NOT SAID ONE RACIST WORD, NOT THAT I'VE EVER HEARD.
YOU SEEM AWFULLY CONVINCED, MATTY... WHAT IF YOU'RE WRONG? WHAT IF EVERYONE'S WRONG?
THE MAN'S OUT ON THE STREET ALL DAY, EVERY DAY. HE'S WORKING HARD FOR THIS NOMINATION, AND THE PEOPLE ARE GETTING TO KNOW HIM. HE'S EASILY THE MOST ACCESSIBLE POLITICIAN I CAN THINK OF.
THERE'S PLENTY OF TIME FOR EVERY-ONE TO MAKE UP THEIR MINDS...
...AND TIME FOR YOU ALL TO DIG UP DIRT ON PARCO. OR TRY TO. YOU DON'T SEEM TO HAVE BEEN VERY SUCCESSFUL.
OKAY, LAST QUESTION:
YOU ARE A VERY VISIBLE, VERY PUBLIC SUPPORTER OF THE DELGADO NATION IT COULD EASILY BE SAID YOU ARE THE MAN'S MOST VALUABLE ASSET. THE FAMOUS MATTY ROTH.
I'M NOT HEARING A QUESTION HERE...
HE'S GOT YOU, HE'S GOT MASSIVE SUPPORT IN THE STREET, AND YOU'RE CONVINCED HE'S A LOCK. SO WHY'D HE HAVE TO BRING YOUR MOTHER IN TO HELP?

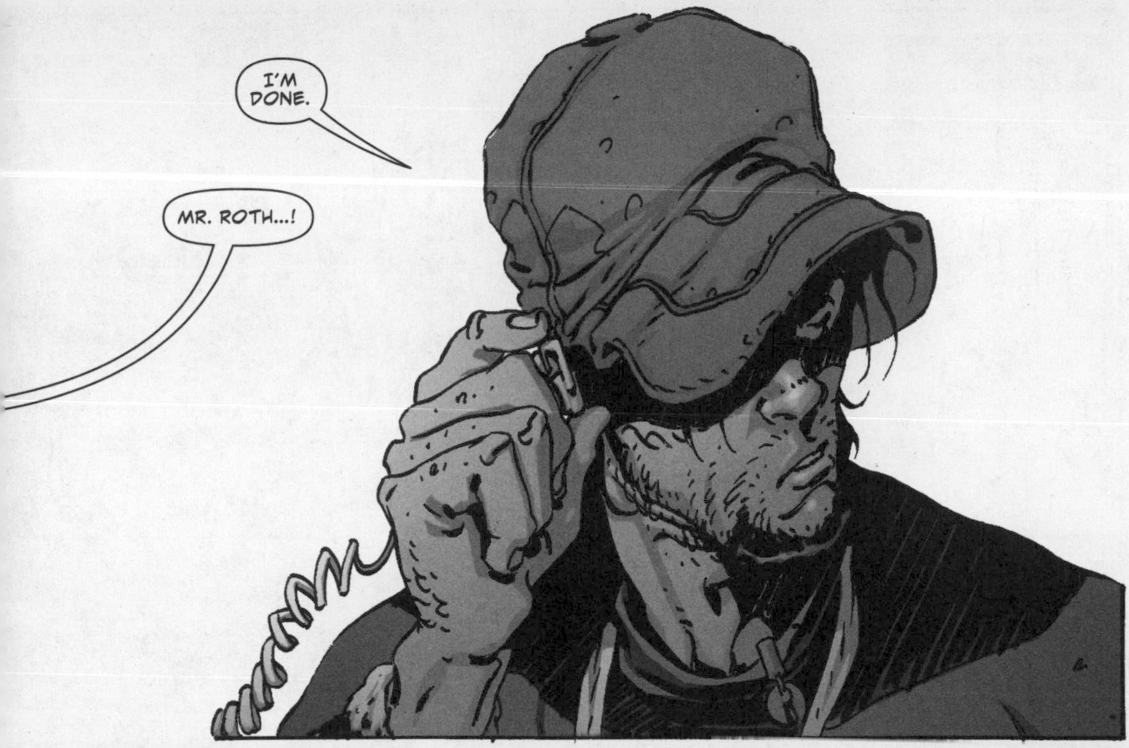
I'M DONE.
MR. ROTH...!

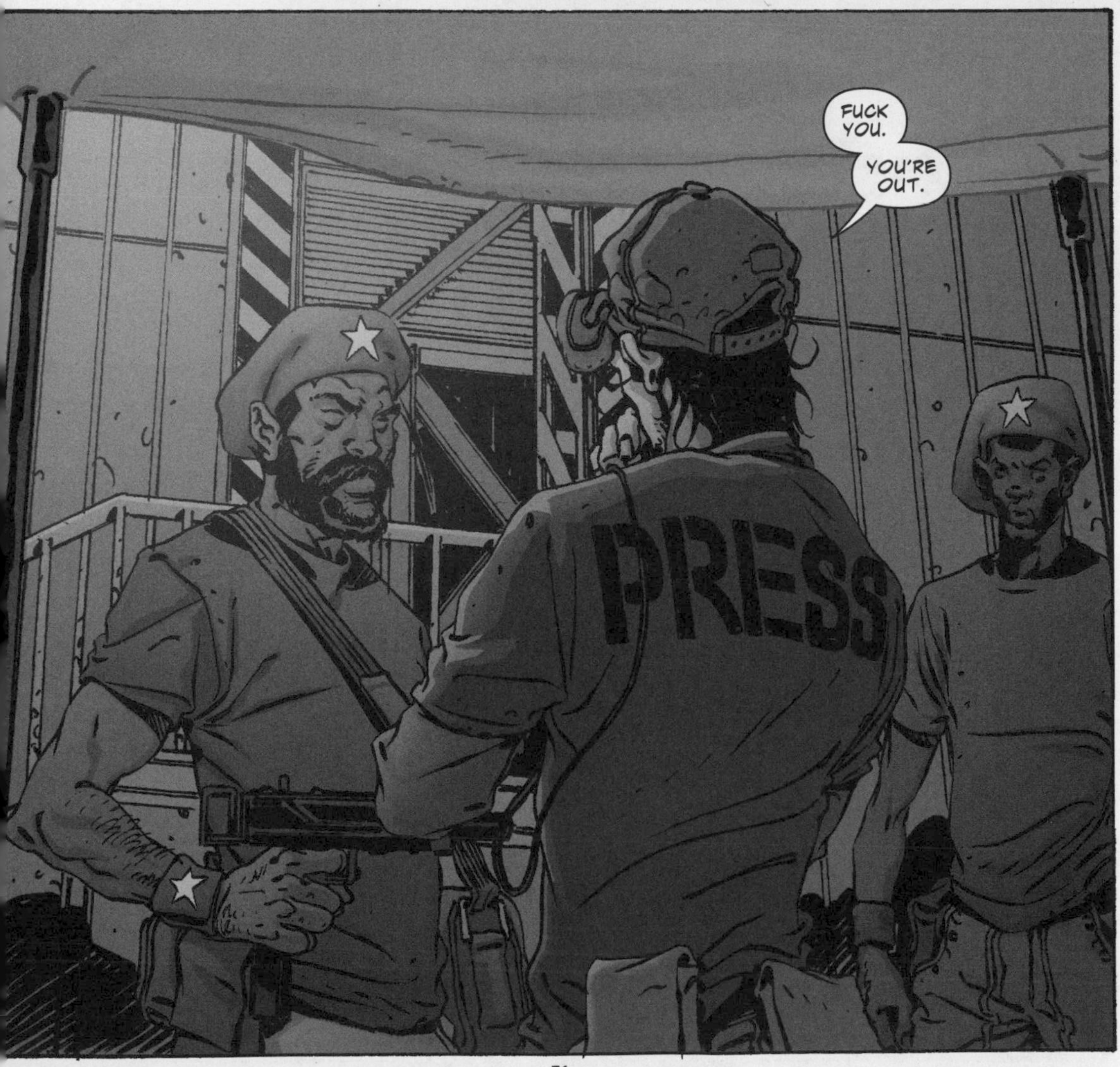
FUCK YOU.
YOU'RE OUT.
PRESS

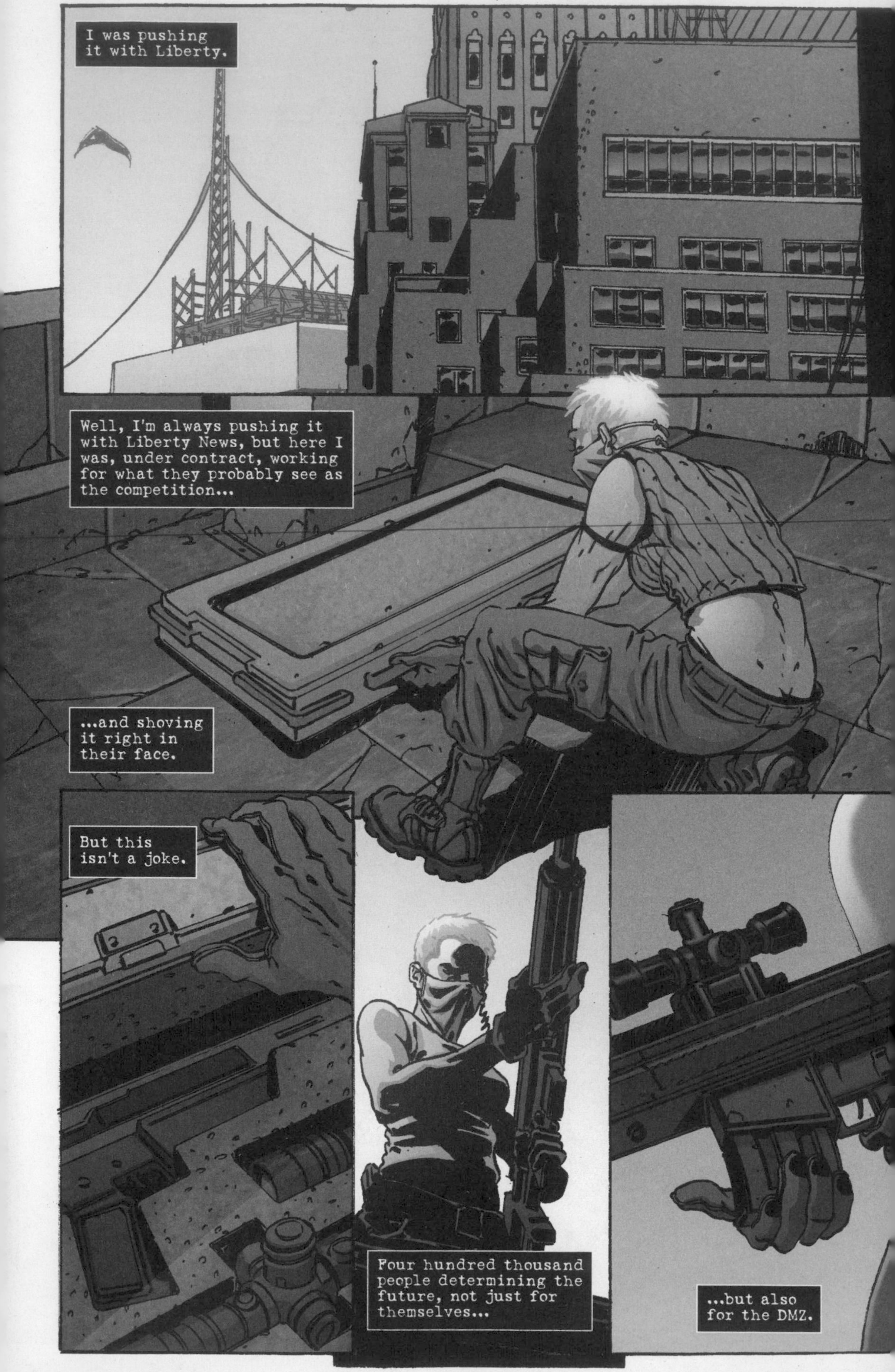
I was pushing it with Liberty.
Well, I'm always pushing it with Liberty News, but here I was, under contract, working for what they probably see as the competition...
...and shoving it right in their face.
But this isn't a joke.
Four hundred thousand people determining the future, not just for themselves...
...but also for the DMZ.

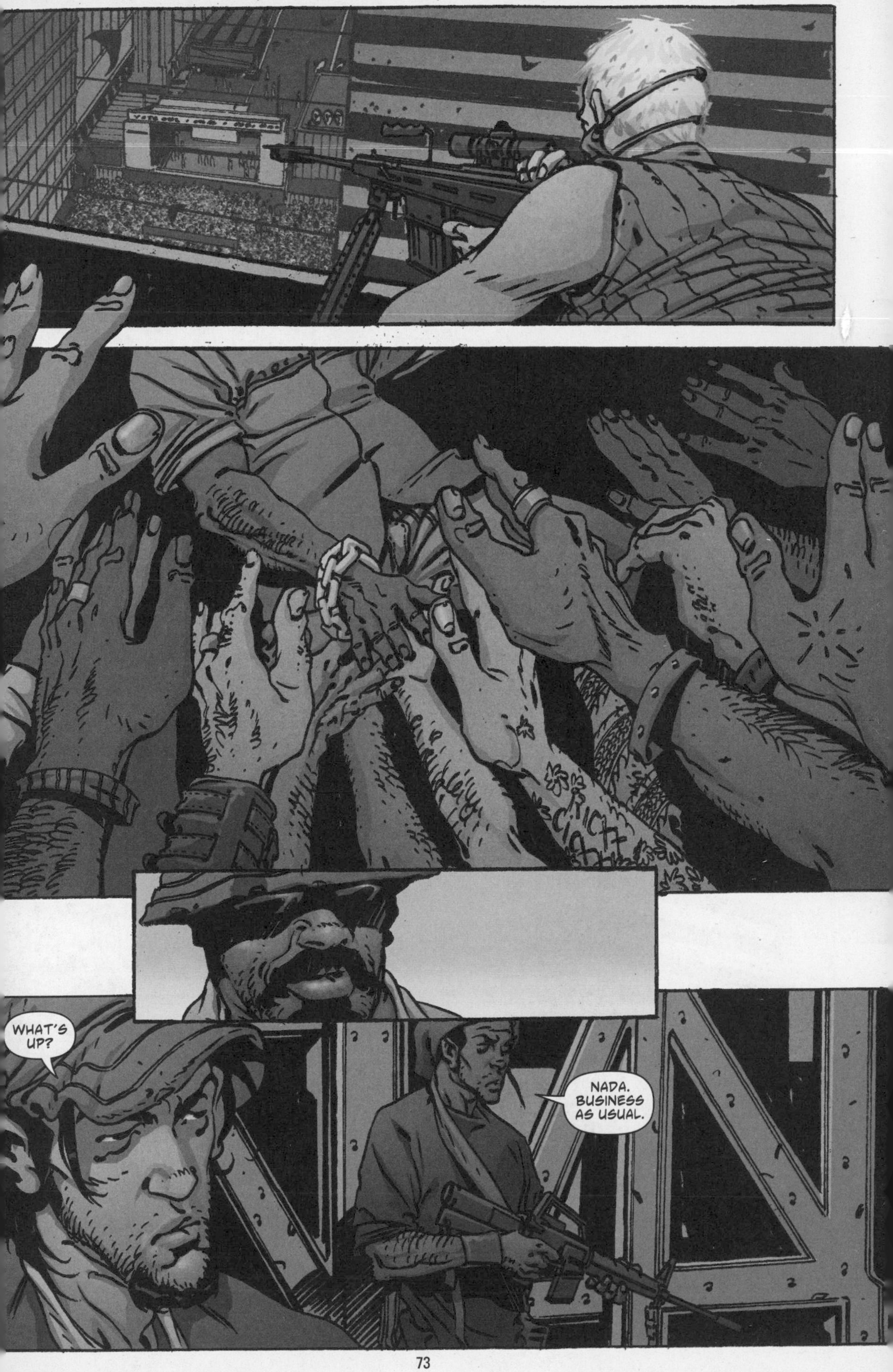
WHAT'S UP?
NADA. BUSINESS AS USUAL.

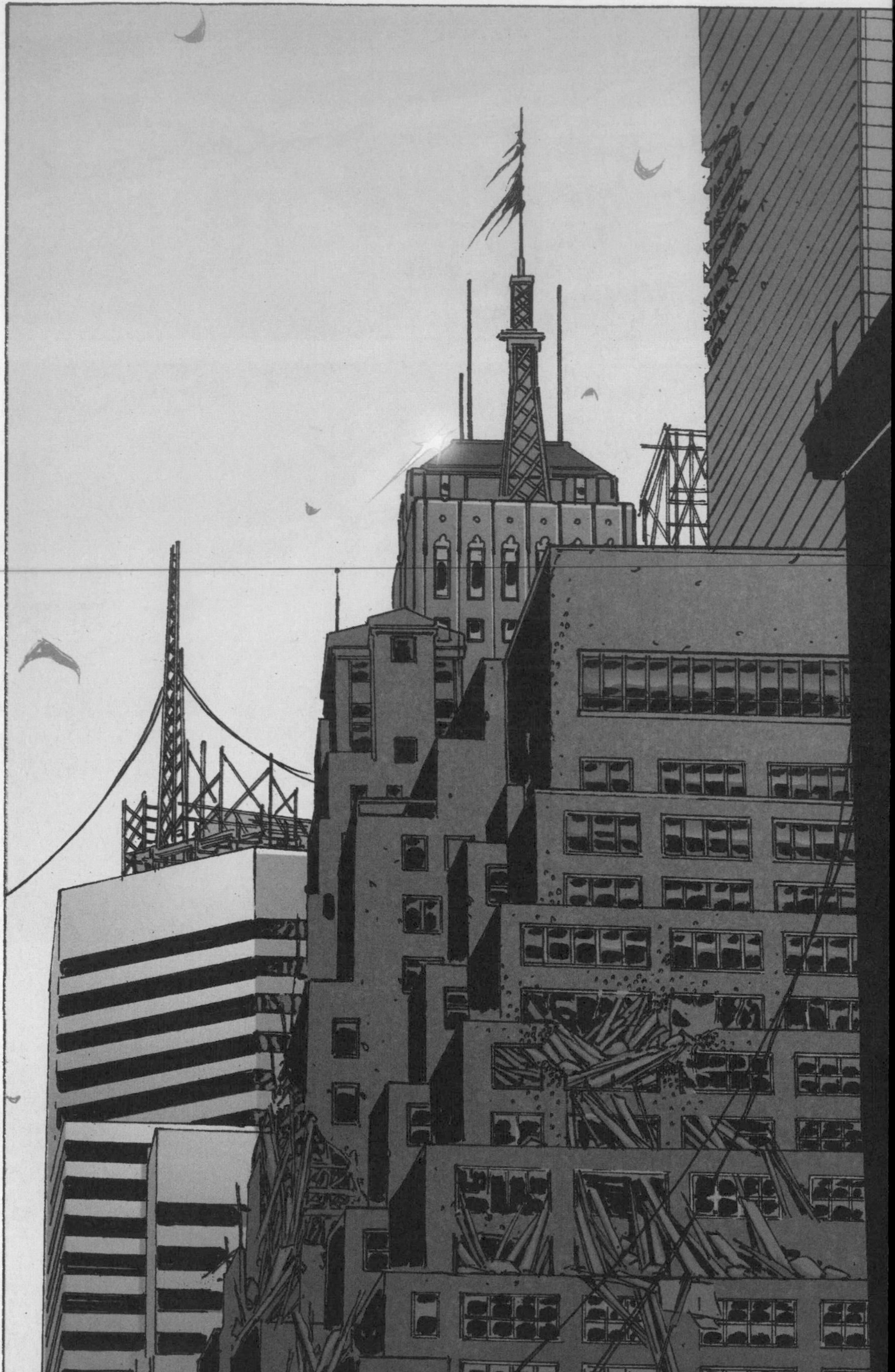

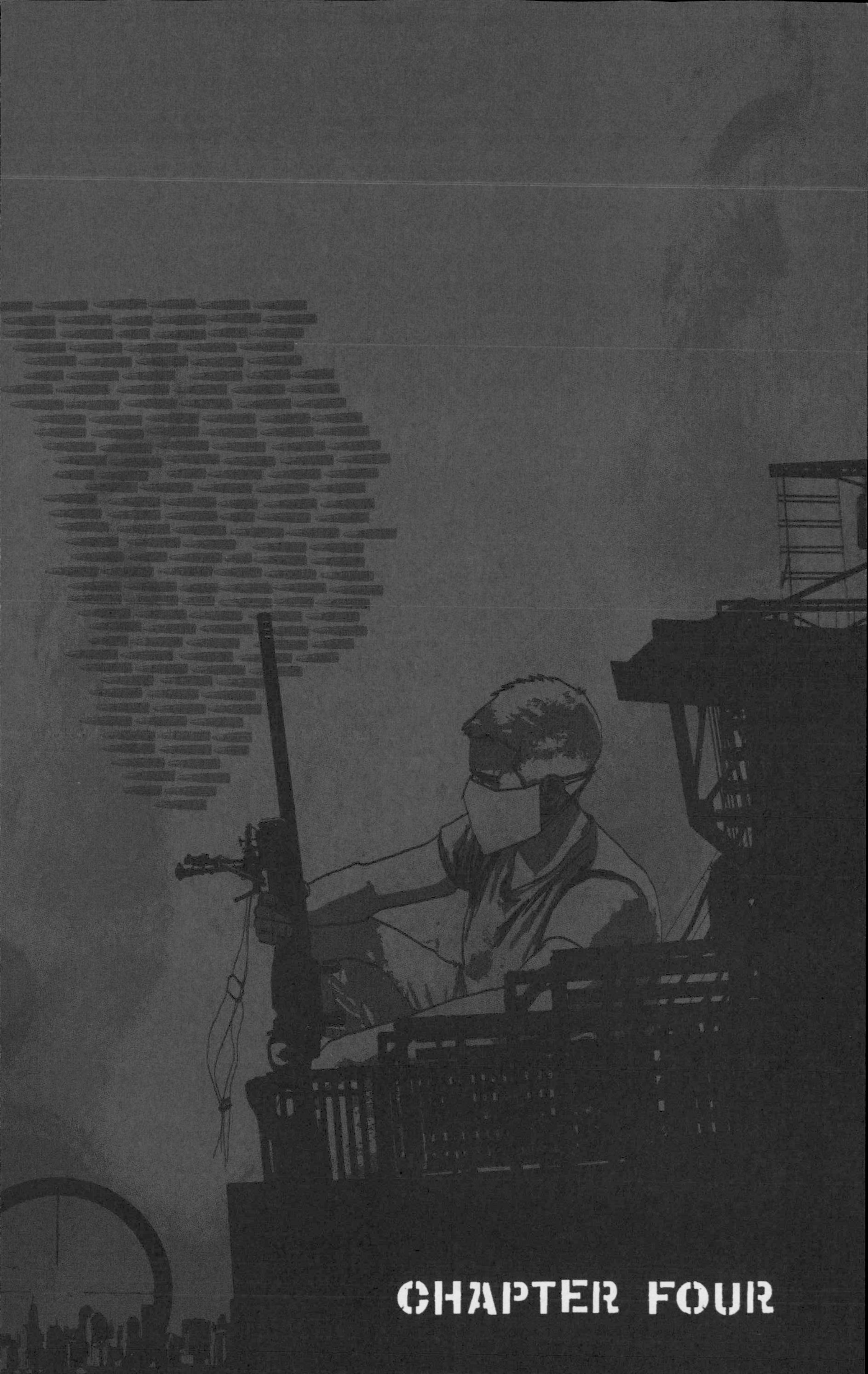

CHAPTER FOUR

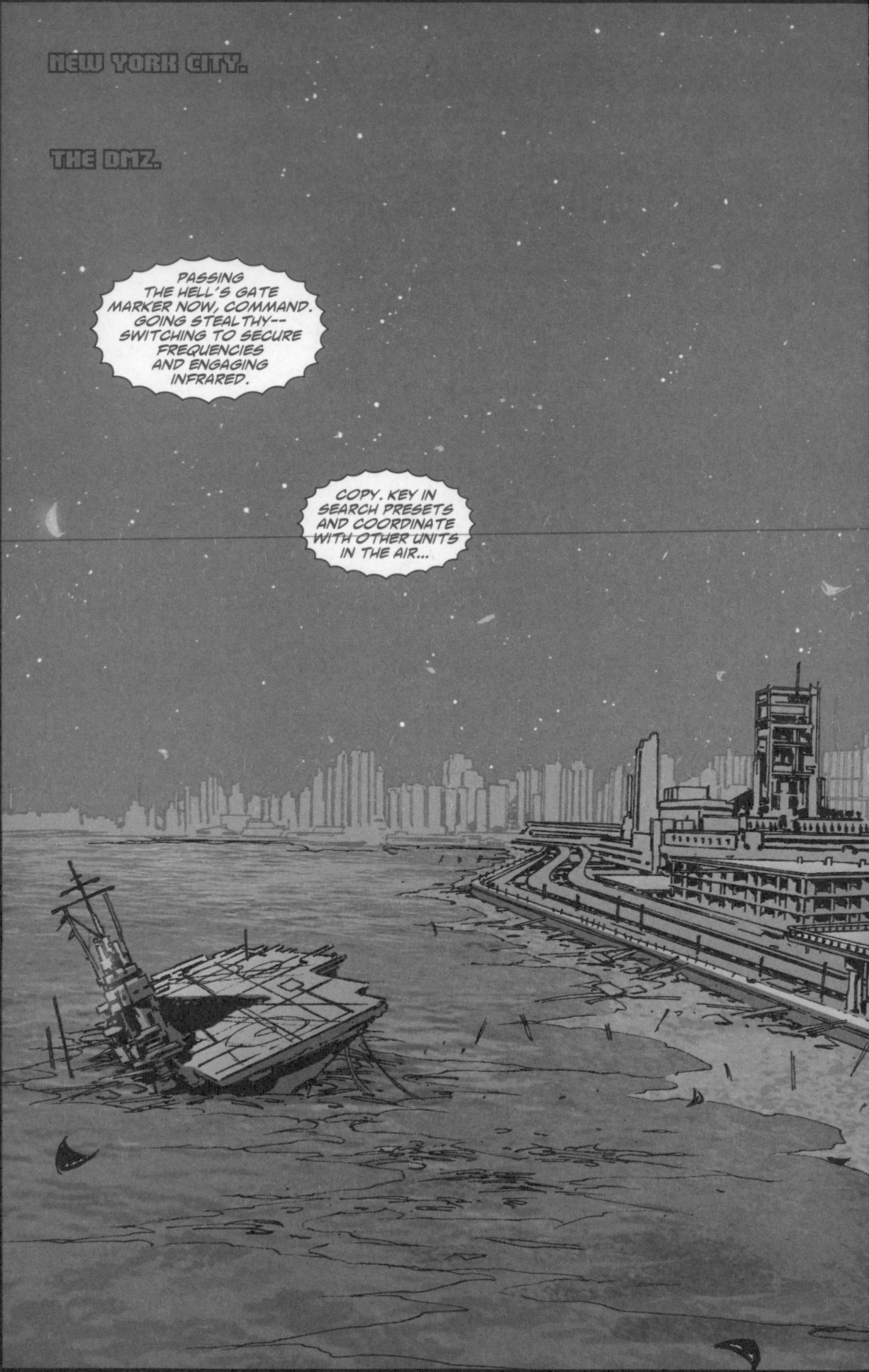
NEW YORK CITY.
THE DMZ.
PASSING THE HELL'S GATE MARKER NOW, COMMAND. GOING STEALTHY-- SWITCHING TO SECURE FREQUENCIES AND ENGAGING INFRARED.
COPY. KEY IN SEARCH PRESETS AND COORDINATE WITH OTHER UNITS IN THE AIR...

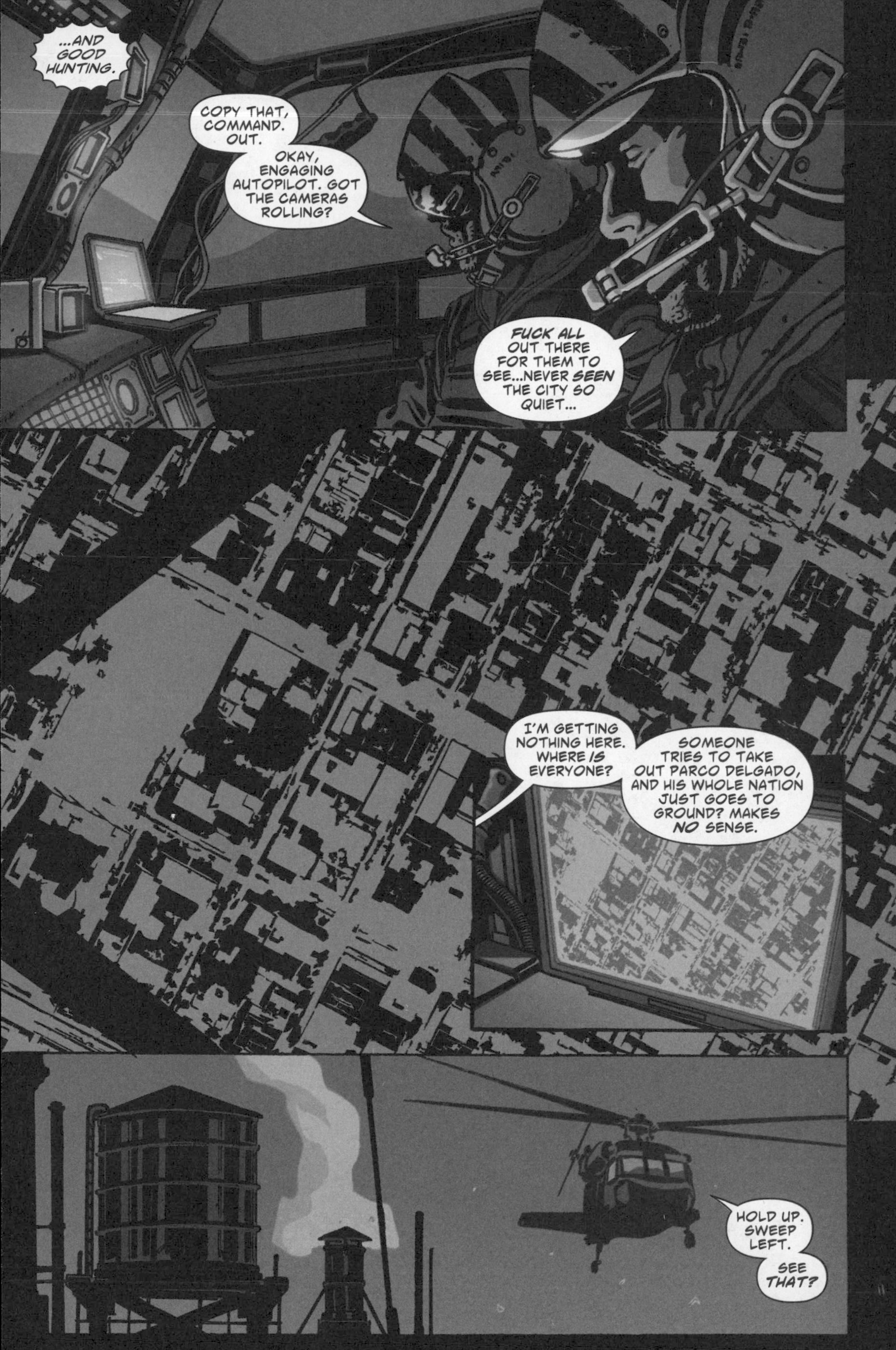
...AND GOOD HUNTING.
COPY THAT, COMMAND. OUT.
OKAY, ENGAGING AUTOPILOT. GOT THE CAMERAS ROLLING?
FUCK ALL OUT THERE FOR THEM TO SEE...NEVER SEEN THE CITY SO QUIET...
I'M GETTING NOTHING HERE. WHERE IS EVERYONE?
SOMEONE TRIES TO TAKE OUT PARCO DELGADO, AND HIS WHOLE NATION JUST GOES TO GROUND? MAKES NO SENSE.
HOLD UP. SWEEP LEFT.
SEE THAT?

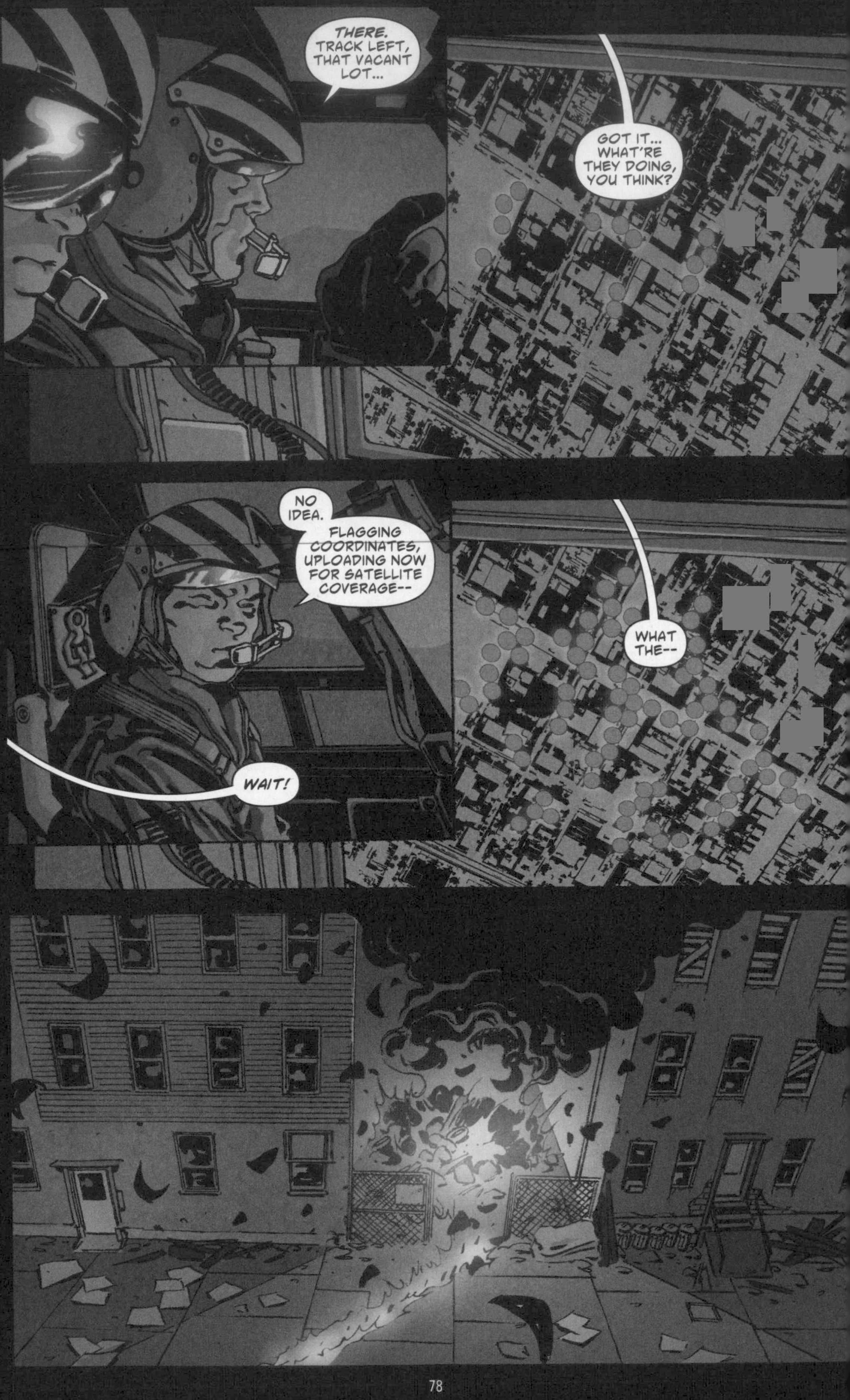
THERE. TRACK LEFT, THAT VACANT LOT...
GOT IT... WHAT'RE THEY DOING, YOU THINK?
NO IDEA.
FLAGGING COORDINATES, UPLOADING NOW FOR SATELLITE COVERAGE--
WHAT THE--
WAIT!

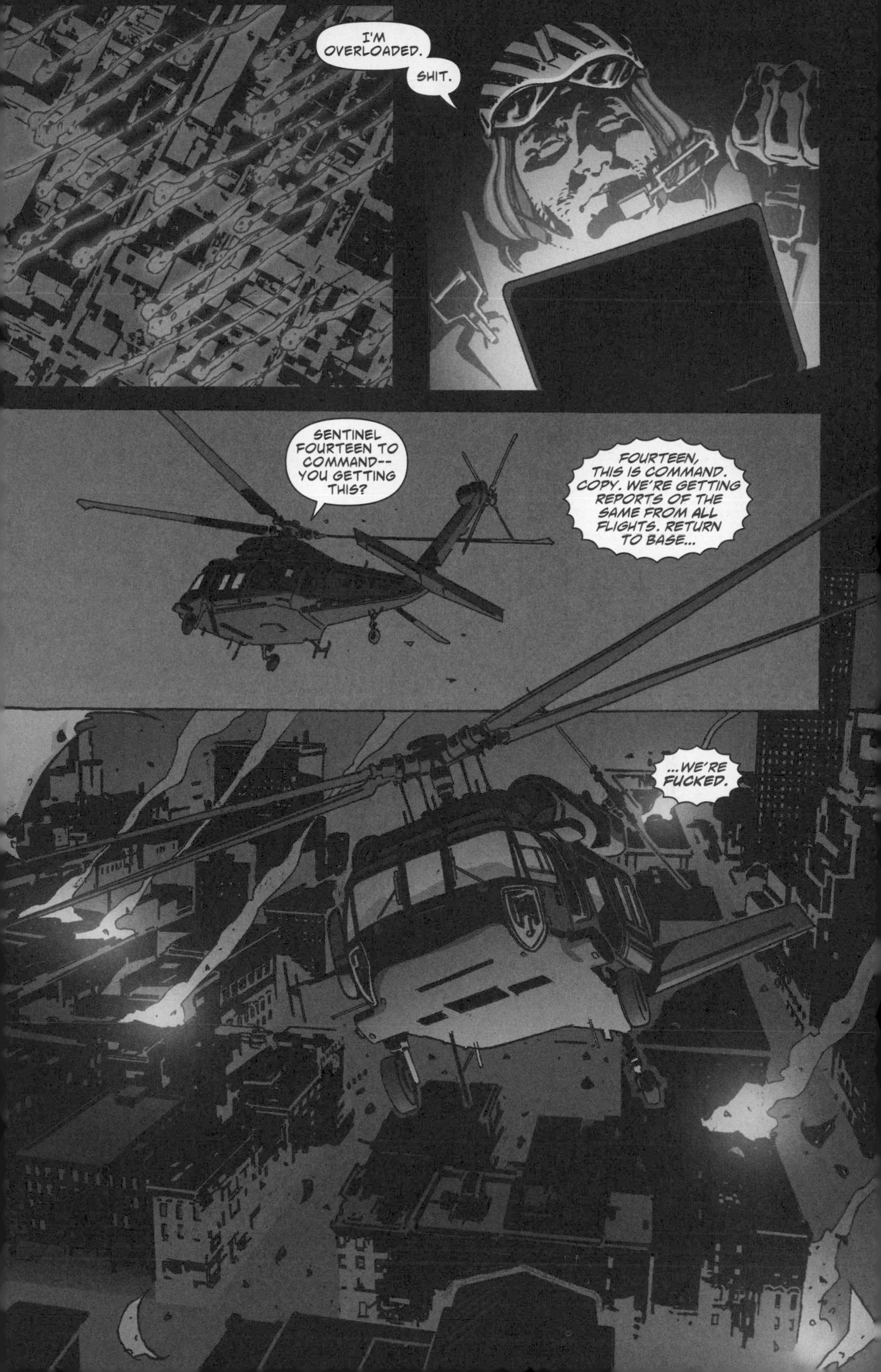
I'M OVERLOADED.
SHIT.
SENTINEL FOURTEEN TO COMMAND-- YOU GETTING THIS?
FOURTEEN, THIS IS COMMAND. COPY. WE'RE GETTING REPORTS OF THE SAME FROM ALL FLIGHTS. RETURN TO BASE...
...WE'RE FUCKED.

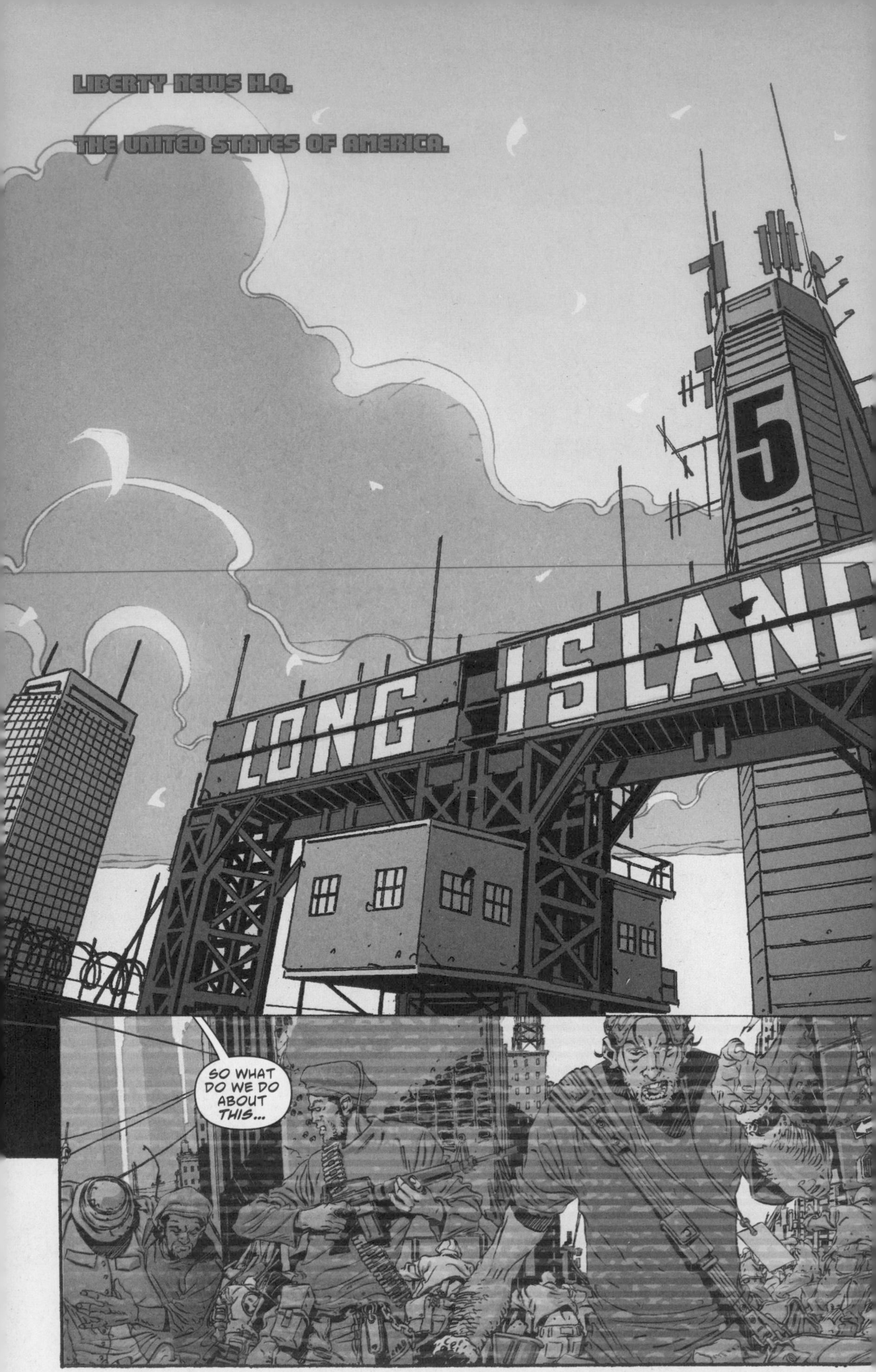
LIBERTY NEWS H.Q.
THE UNITED STATES OF AMERICA.
5
LONG ISLAND
SO WHAT DO WE DO ABOUT THIS...

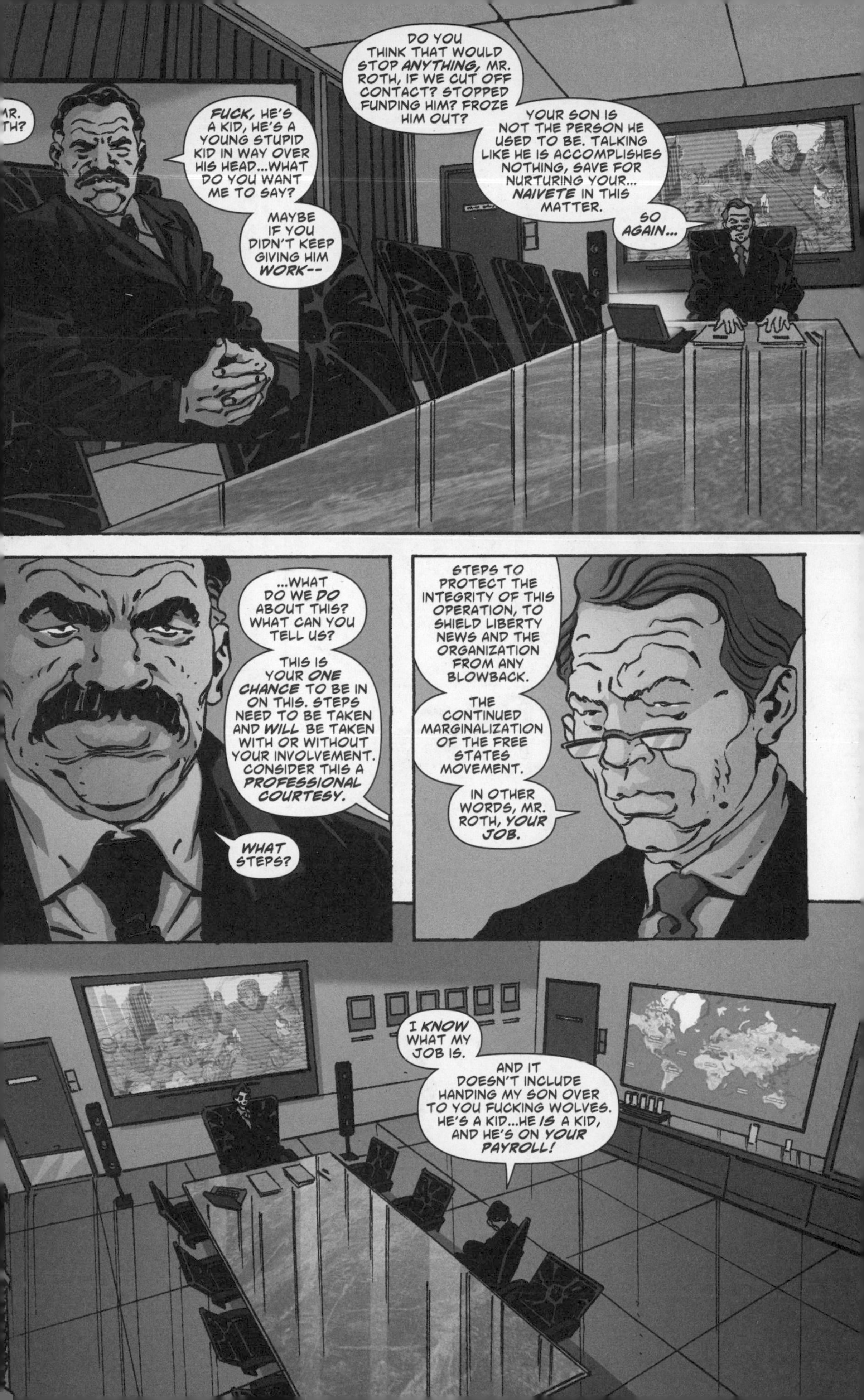
MR. ...TH?
FUCK, HE'S A KID, HE'S A YOUNG STUPID KID IN WAY OVER HIS HEAD...WHAT DO YOU WANT ME TO SAY?
MAYBE IF YOU DIDN'T KEEP GIVING HIM WORK--
DO YOU THINK THAT WOULD STOP ANYTHING, MR. ROTH, IF WE CUT OFF CONTACT? STOPPED FUNDING HIM? FROZE HIM OUT?
YOUR SON IS NOT THE PERSON HE USED TO BE. TALKING LIKE HE IS ACCOMPLISHES NOTHING, SAVE FOR NURTURING YOUR... NAIVETE IN THIS MATTER.
SO AGAIN...
...WHAT DO WE DO ABOUT THIS? WHAT CAN YOU TELL US?
THIS IS YOUR ONE CHANCE TO BE IN ON THIS. STEPS NEED TO BE TAKEN AND WILL BE TAKEN WITH OR WITHOUT YOUR INVOLVEMENT. CONSIDER THIS A PROFESSIONAL COURTESY.
WHAT STEPS?
STEPS TO PROTECT THE INTEGRITY OF THIS OPERATION, TO SHIELD LIBERTY NEWS AND THE ORGANIZATION FROM ANY BLOWBACK.
THE CONTINUED MARGINALIZATION OF THE FREE STATES MOVEMENT.
IN OTHER WORDS, MR. ROTH, YOUR JOB.
I KNOW WHAT MY JOB IS.
AND IT DOESN'T INCLUDE HANDING MY SON OVER TO YOU FUCKING WOLVES. HE'S A KID...HE IS A KID, AND HE'S ON YOUR PAYROLL!

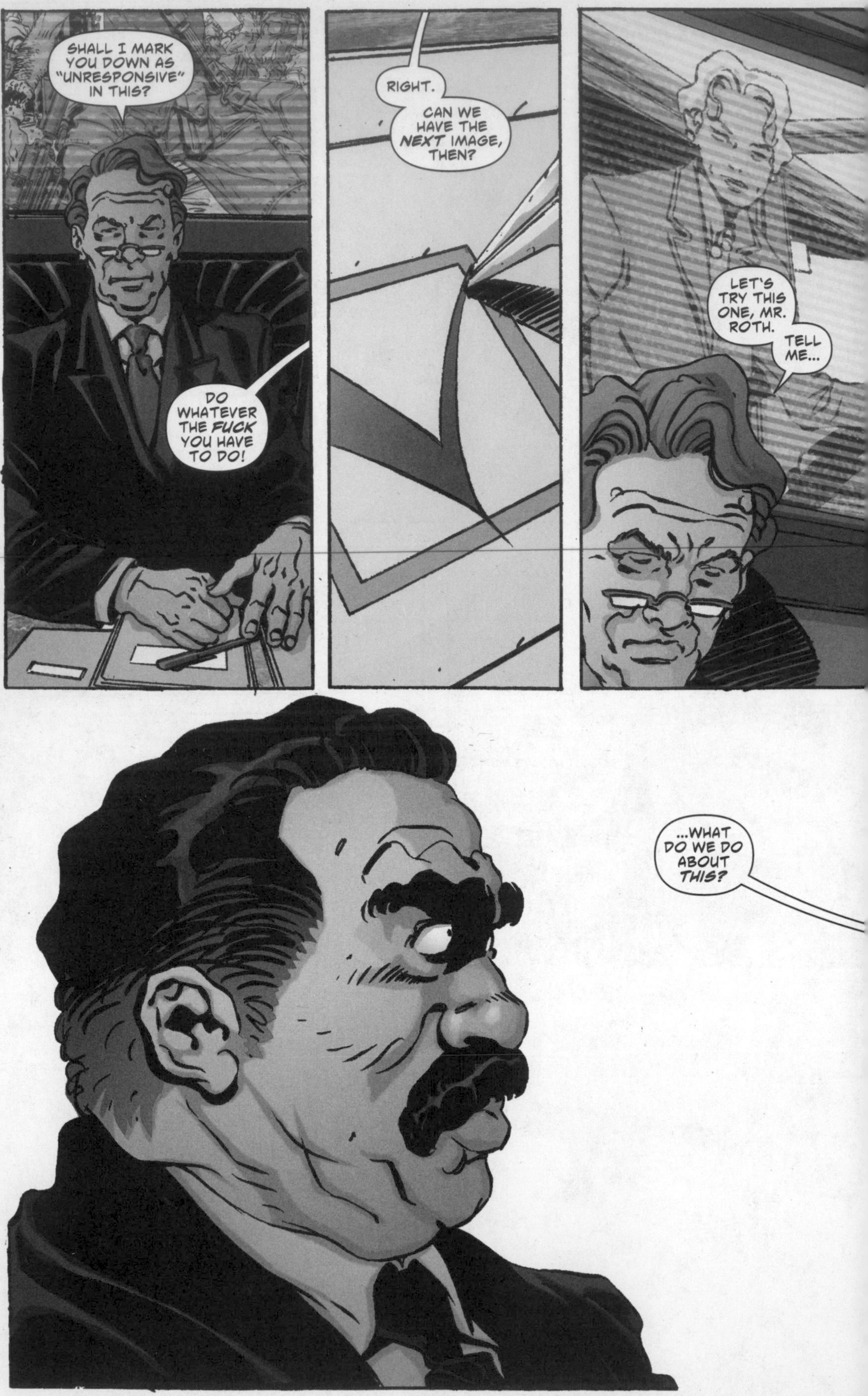
SHALL I MARK YOU DOWN AS "UNRESPONSIVE" IN THIS?
DO WHATEVER THE FUCK YOU HAVE TO DO!
RIGHT.
CAN WE HAVE THE NEXT IMAGE, THEN?
LET'S TRY THIS ONE, MR. ROTH.
TELL ME...
...WHAT DO WE DO ABOUT THIS?

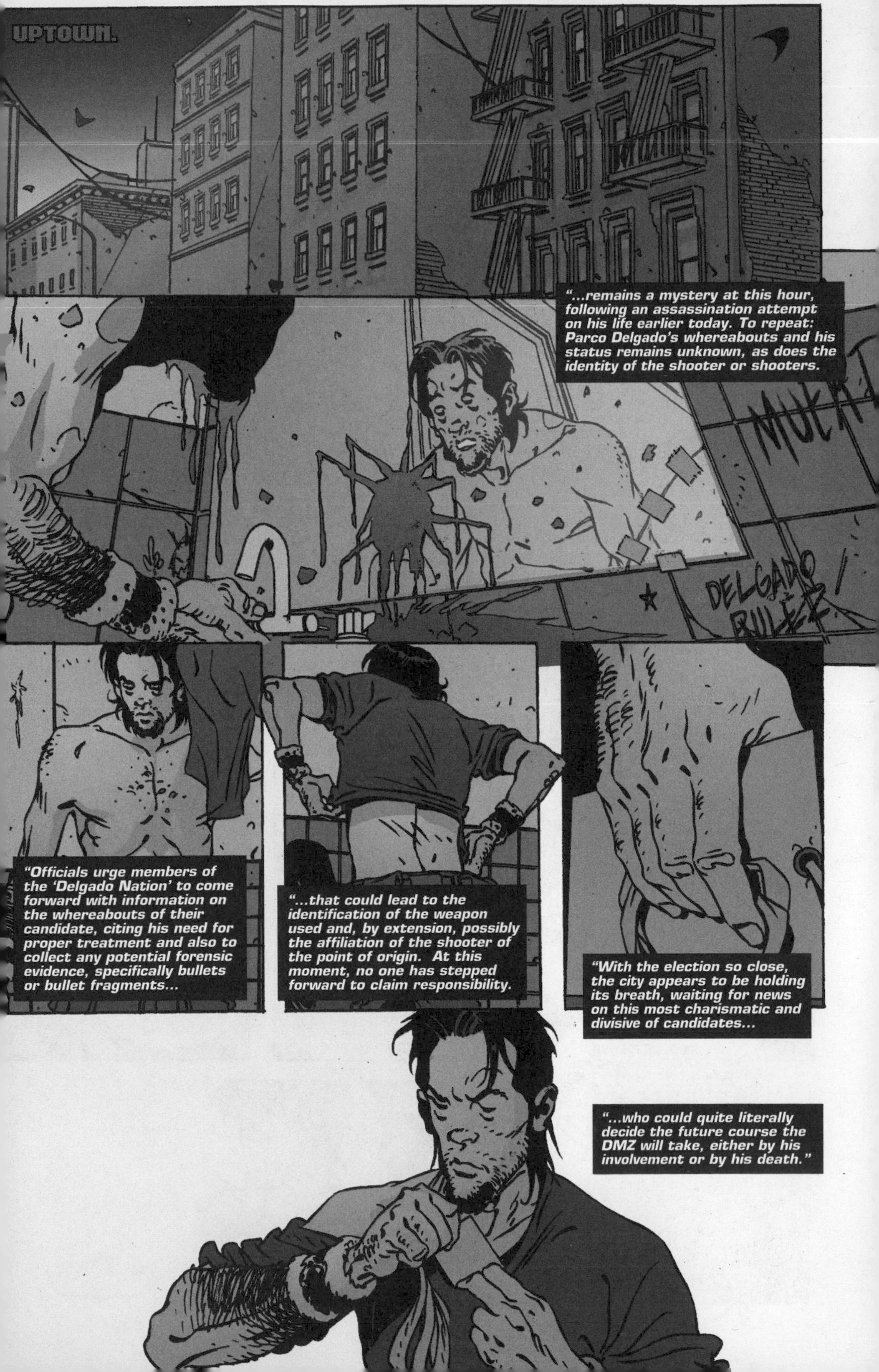
UPTOWN.
"...remains a mystery at this hour, following an assassination attempt on his life earlier today. To repeat: Parco Delgado's whereabouts and his status remains unknown, as does the identity of the shooter or shooters.
DELGADO RULEZ
"Officials urge members of the 'Delgado Nation' to come forward with information on the whereabouts of their candidate, citing his need for proper treatment and also to collect any potential forensic evidence, specifically bullets or bullet fragments...
"...that could lead to the identification of the weapon used and, by extension, possibly the affiliation of the shooter of the point of origin. At this moment, no one has stepped forward to claim responsibility.
"With the election so close, the city appears to be holding its breath, waiting for news on this most charismatic and divisive of candidates...
"...who could quite literally decide the future course the DMZ will take, either by his involvement or by his death."

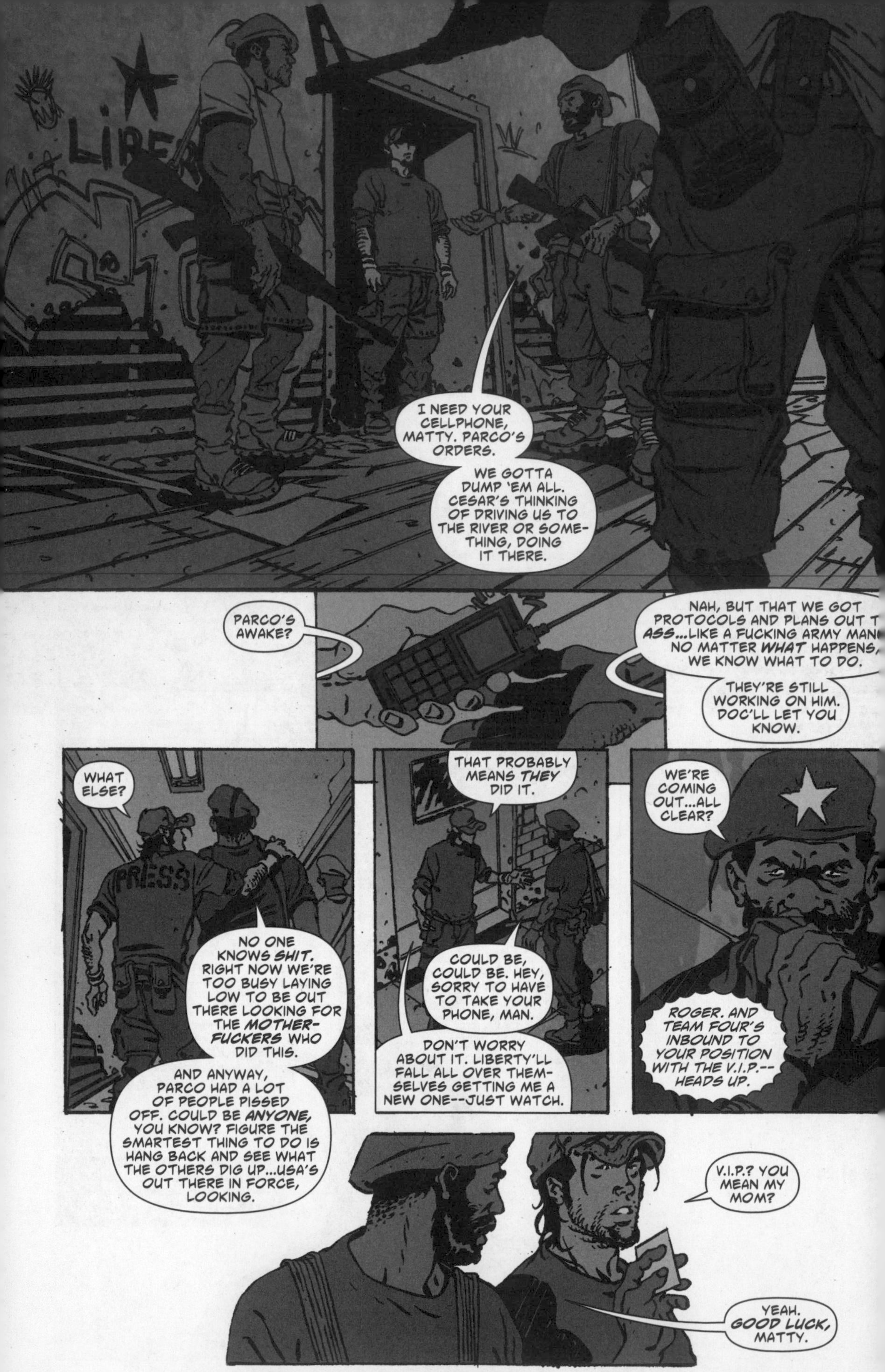
I NEED YOUR CELLPHONE, MATTY. PARCO'S ORDERS.
WE GOTTA DUMP 'EM ALL. CESAR'S THINKING OF DRIVING US TO THE RIVER OR SOME-THING, DOING IT THERE.
PARCO'S AWAKE?
NAH, BUT THAT WE GOT PROTOCOLS AND PLANS OUT T ASS...LIKE A FUCKING ARMY MAN NO MATTER *WHAT* HAPPENS, WE KNOW WHAT TO DO.
THEY'RE STILL WORKING ON HIM. DOC'LL LET YOU KNOW.
WHAT ELSE?
NO ONE KNOWS *SHIT*. RIGHT NOW WE'RE TOO BUSY LAYING LOW TO BE OUT THERE LOOKING FOR THE *MOTHER-FUCKERS* WHO DID THIS.
AND ANYWAY, PARCO HAD A LOT OF PEOPLE PISSED OFF. COULD BE *ANYONE*, YOU KNOW? FIGURE THE SMARTEST THING TO DO IS HANG BACK AND SEE WHAT THE OTHERS DIG UP...USA'S OUT THERE IN FORCE, LOOKING.
THAT PROBABLY MEANS *THEY* DID IT.
COULD BE, COULD BE. HEY, SORRY TO HAVE TO TAKE YOUR PHONE, MAN.
DON'T WORRY ABOUT IT. LIBERTY'LL FALL ALL OVER THEM-SELVES GETTING ME A NEW ONE--JUST WATCH.
WE'RE COMING OUT...ALL CLEAR?
ROGER. AND TEAM FOUR'S INBOUND TO YOUR POSITION WITH THE V.I.P.--HEADS UP.
V.I.P.? YOU MEAN MY MOM?
YEAH. *GOOD LUCK,* MATTY.

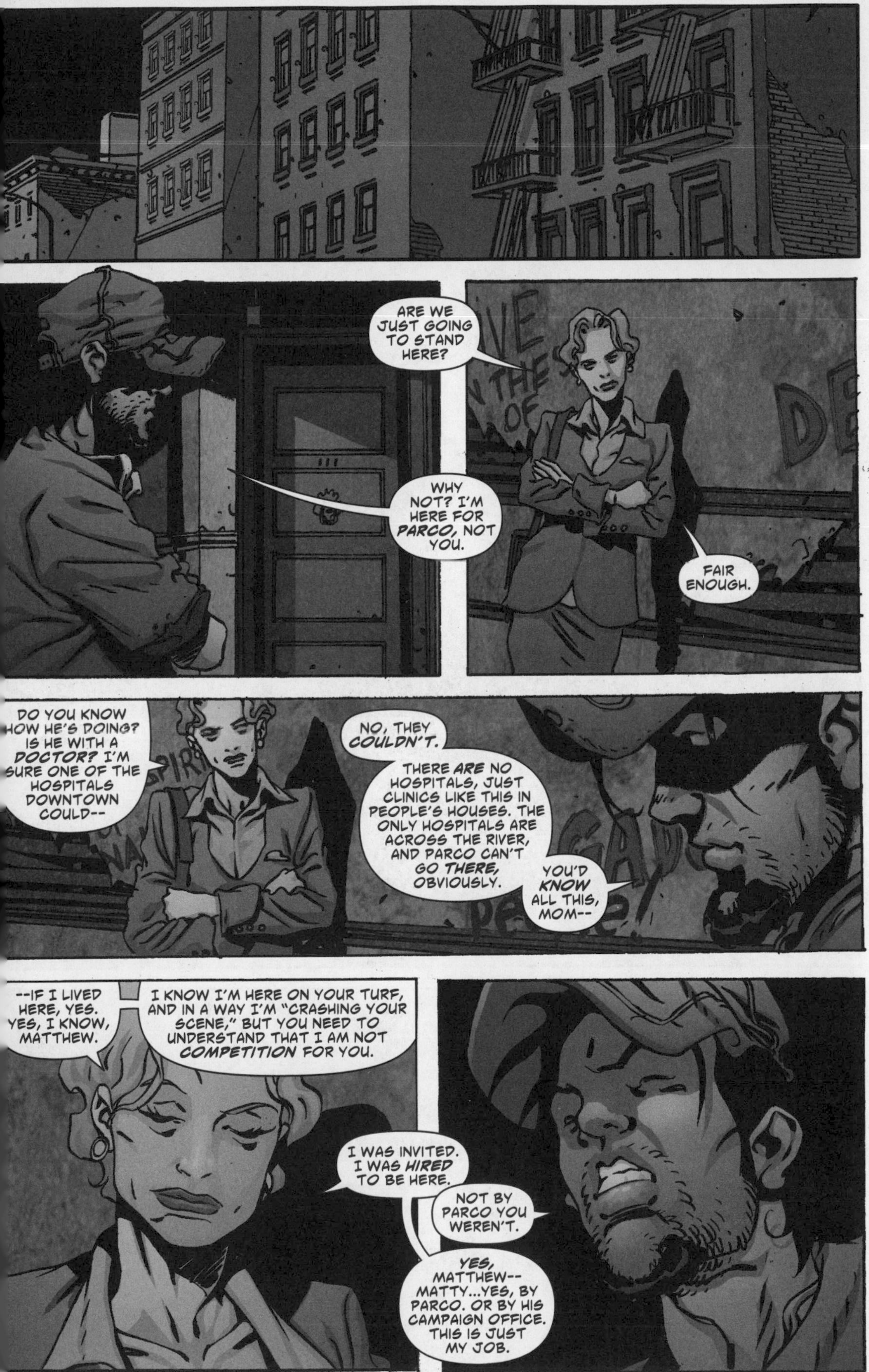
ARE WE JUST GOING TO STAND HERE?
WHY NOT? I'M HERE FOR PARCO, NOT YOU.
FAIR ENOUGH.
DO YOU KNOW HOW HE'S DOING? IS HE WITH A DOCTOR? I'M SURE ONE OF THE HOSPITALS DOWNTOWN COULD--
NO, THEY COULDN'T.
THERE ARE NO HOSPITALS, JUST CLINICS LIKE THIS IN PEOPLE'S HOUSES. THE ONLY HOSPITALS ARE ACROSS THE RIVER, AND PARCO CAN'T GO THERE, OBVIOUSLY.
YOU'D KNOW ALL THIS, MOM--
--IF I LIVED HERE, YES. YES, I KNOW, MATTHEW.
I KNOW I'M HERE ON YOUR TURF, AND IN A WAY I'M "CRASHING YOUR SCENE," BUT YOU NEED TO UNDERSTAND THAT I AM NOT COMPETITION FOR YOU.
I WAS INVITED. I WAS HIRED TO BE HERE.
NOT BY PARCO YOU WEREN'T.
YES, MATTHEW-- MATTY...YES, BY PARCO. OR BY HIS CAMPAIGN OFFICE. THIS IS JUST MY JOB.

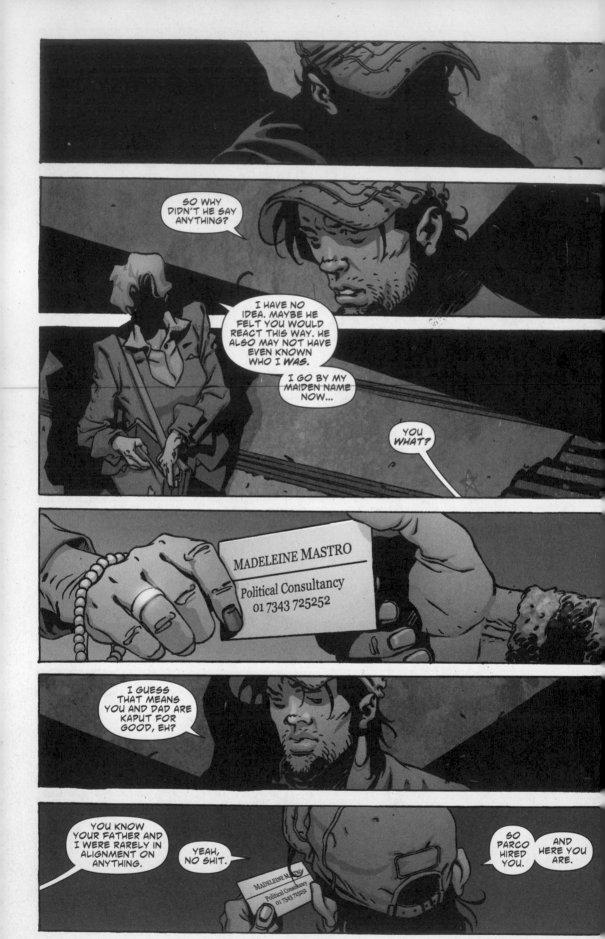

SO WHY DIDN'T HE SAY ANYTHING?

I HAVE NO IDEA. MAYBE HE FELT YOU WOULD REACT THIS WAY. HE ALSO MAY NOT HAVE EVEN KNOWN WHO I *WAS*.

I GO BY MY MAIDEN NAME NOW...

YOU WHAT?

MADELEINE MASTRO

Political Consultancy

01 7343 725252

I GUESS THAT MEANS YOU AND DAD ARE KAPUT FOR GOOD, EH?

YOU KNOW YOUR FATHER AND I WERE RARELY IN ALIGNMENT ON ANYTHING.

YEAH, NO SHIT.

MADELEINE MASTRO

Political Consultancy

01 7343 725252

SO PARCO HIRED YOU.

AND HERE YOU ARE.

 THIS THING WITH PARCO...THIS IS *BIG,* AND IT CAN GO BOTH WAYS. AND I DON'T MEAN IN A WILL-HE-MAKE-IT-OR-NOT WAY...

BUT IN A HOW-DO-WE-SPIN-IT WAY.

 THAT'S PRETTY *COLD,* MOM...

 IT'S HOW PEOPLE GET ELECTED, MATTY.

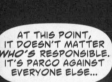 AT THIS POINT, IT DOESN'T MATTER *WHO'S* RESPONSIBLE. IT'S PARCO AGAINST EVERYONE ELSE...

 ...BY NOT NAMING A SHOOTER, BY NOT SAYING IT WAS THESE GUYS OVER HERE, WE WON'T RUN THE RISK OF BEING ALIGNED WITH THE OTHER GUYS OVER THERE BY DEFAULT.

PARCO IN A PUBLIC APPEARANCE LIMBO LIKE THIS CAN HELP US TREMENDOUSLY.

 HE'S GOTTA SHOW HIS FACE AT *SOME* POINT, THOUGH.

HIS ONE STRENGTH IS HIS CHARISMA, HIS APPEAL TO THE CROWDS. BUT THAT ONLY WORKS SO WELL WHEN HE'S ABOVE THE FRAY. WHEN HE'S UNTOUCHABLE.

 PARCO MAY GET BETTER... GOD KNOWS I PERSONALLY HOPE HE MAKES A FULL RECOVERY.

BUT FOR THE REASONS I WAS HIRED, FOR GETTING HIM ELECTED AND INTO OFFICE...FOR THE *POLITICS* OF IT ALL...

 IF HE NEVER LEFT THAT ROOM THIS ELECTION WOULD BE A *SLAM DUNK.*

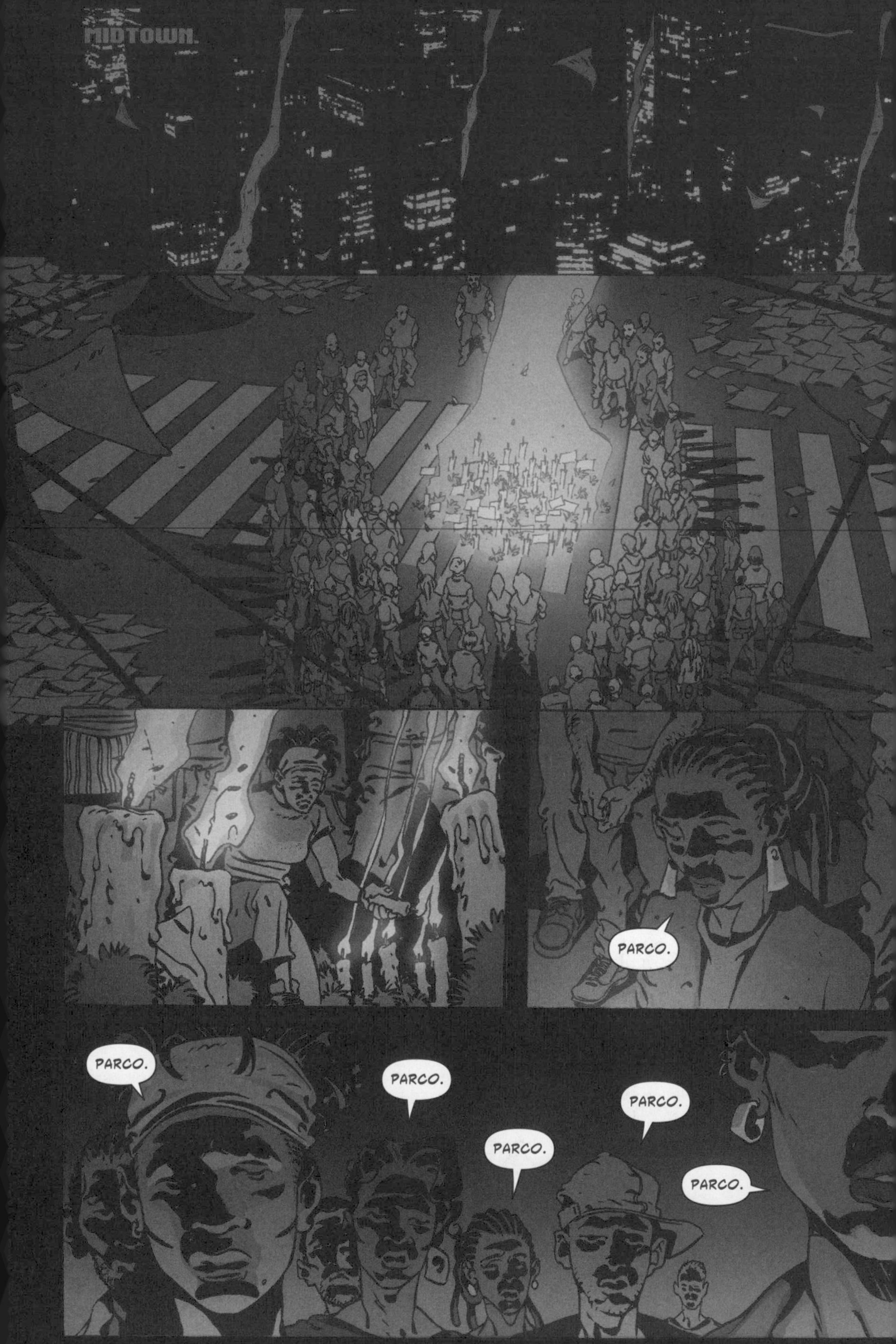
MIDTOWN.
PARCO.
PARCO.
PARCO.
PARCO.
PARCO.
PARCO.

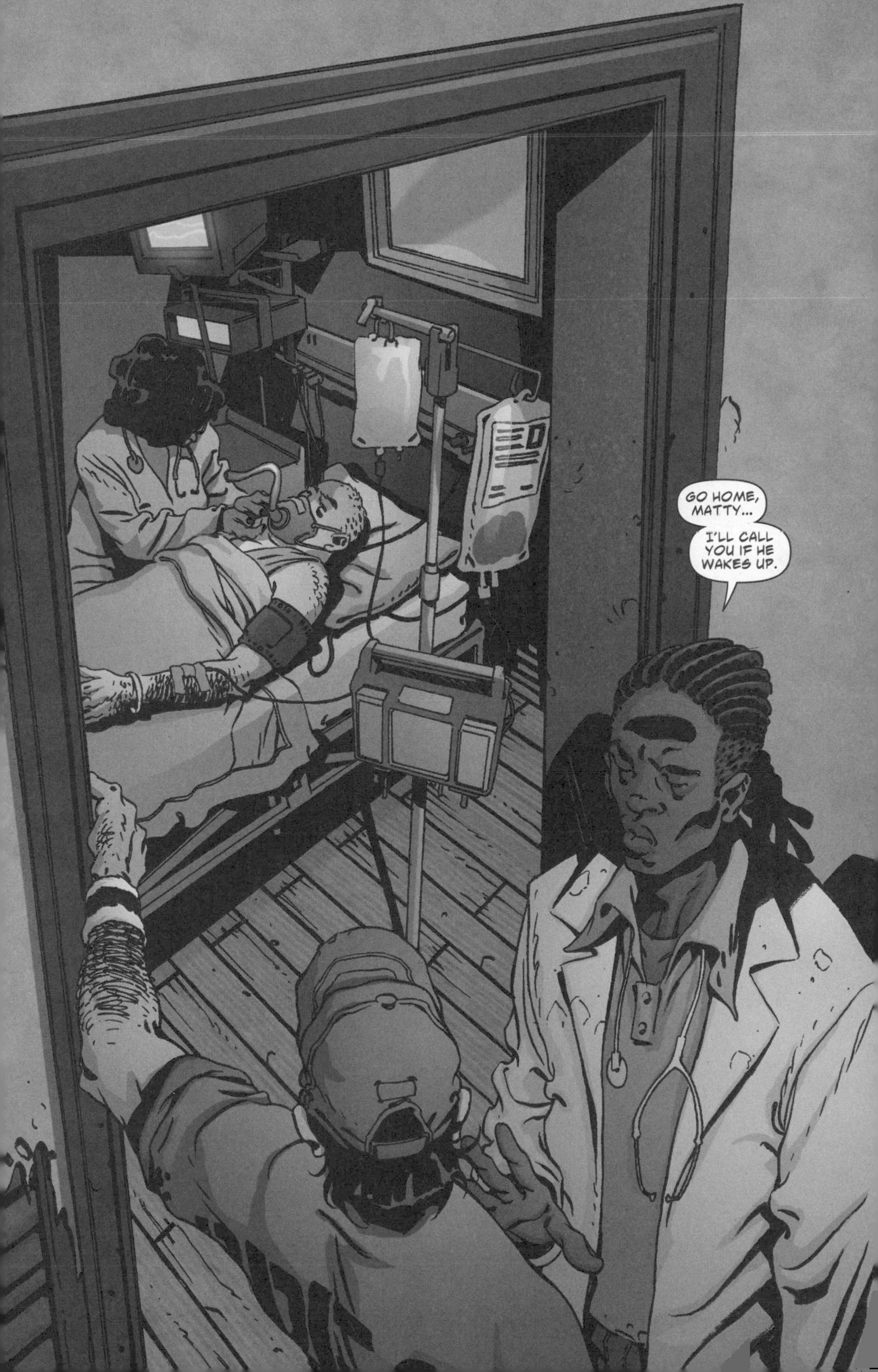
GO HOME, MATTY...
I'LL CALL YOU IF HE WAKES UP.

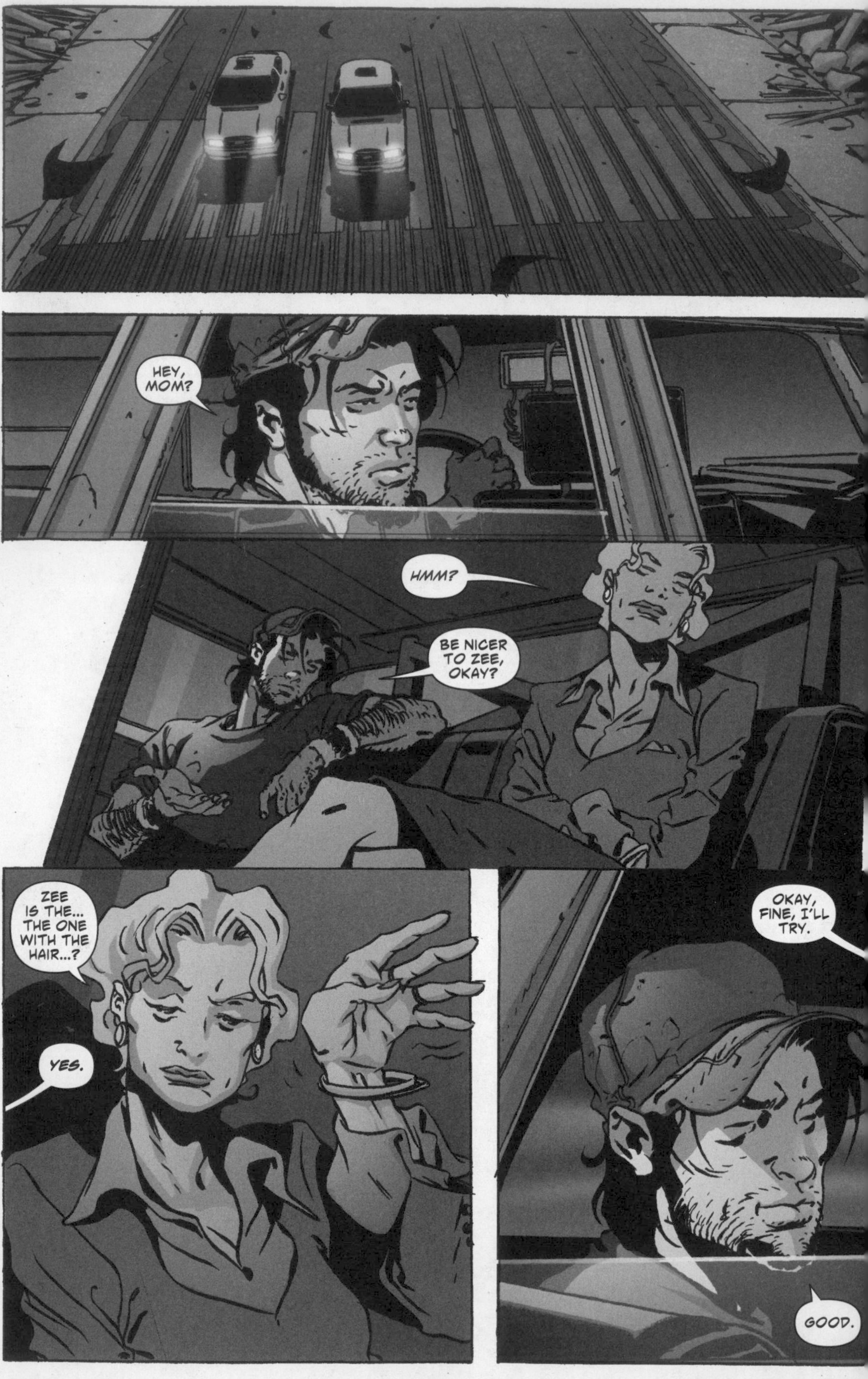
HEY, MOM?
HMM?
BE NICER TO ZEE, OKAY?
ZEE IS THE... THE ONE WITH THE HAIR...?
YES.
OKAY, FINE, I'LL TRY.
GOOD.

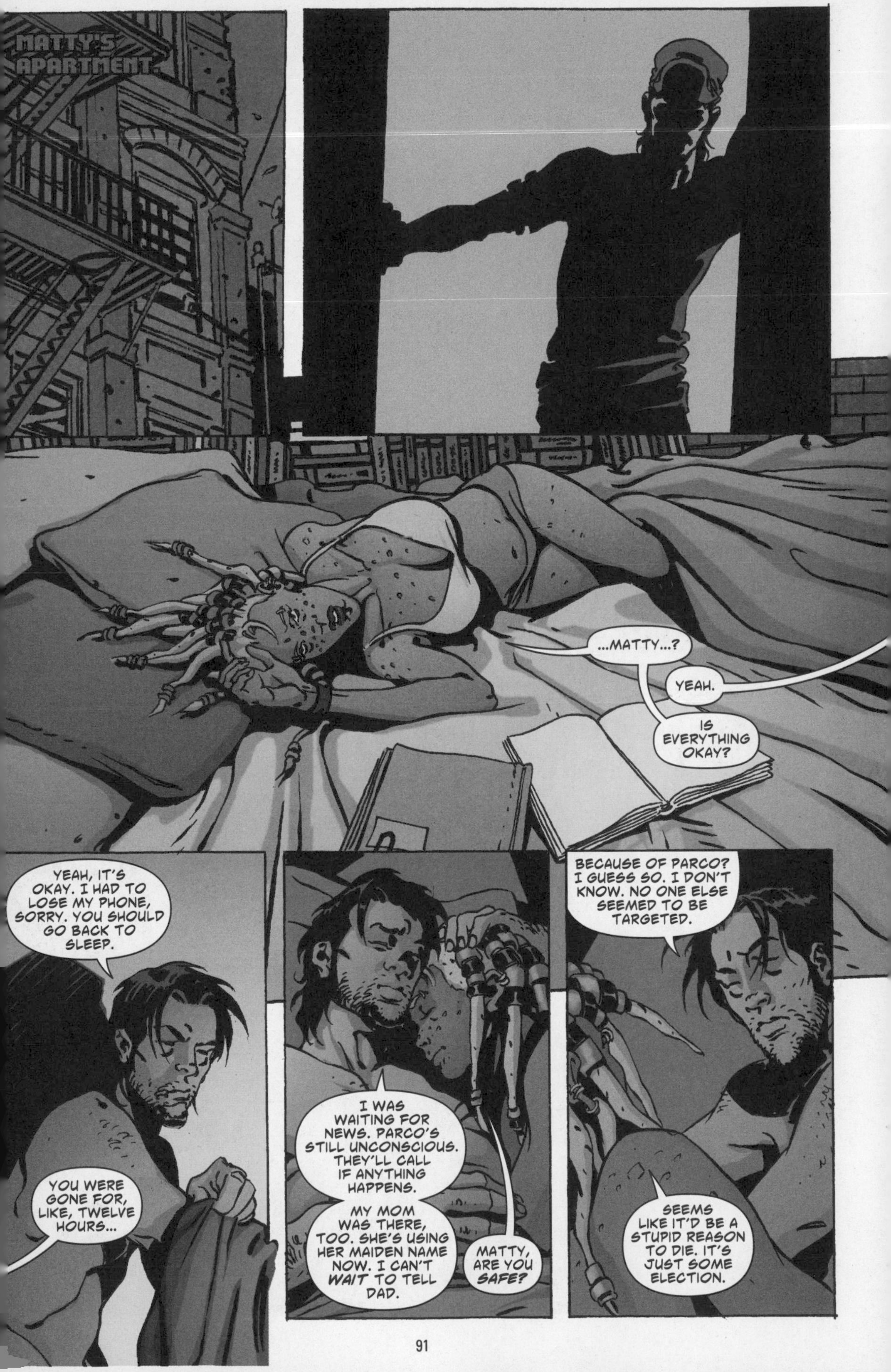
MATTY'S APARTMENT.
...MATTY...?
YEAH.
IS EVERYTHING OKAY?
YEAH, IT'S OKAY. I HAD TO LOSE MY PHONE, SORRY. YOU SHOULD GO BACK TO SLEEP.
YOU WERE GONE FOR, LIKE, TWELVE HOURS...
I WAS WAITING FOR NEWS. PARCO'S STILL UNCONSCIOUS. THEY'LL CALL IF ANYTHING HAPPENS.
MY MOM WAS THERE, TOO. SHE'S USING HER MAIDEN NAME NOW. I CAN'T WAIT TO TELL DAD.
MATTY, ARE YOU SAFE?
BECAUSE OF PARCO? I GUESS SO. I DON'T KNOW. NO ONE ELSE SEEMED TO BE TARGETED.
SEEMS LIKE IT'D BE A STUPID REASON TO DIE. IT'S JUST SOME ELECTION.

"It's not going to change anything" was on her lips when she drifted back to sleep.

And that's the thing, that's what keeps me up some nights. Will it change anything? If Parco wins, will they give him the office?

We have a long, ugly history of unseating democratically elected leaders...

...when the people voted "wrong."

Can they handle a Delgado government in the middle of this war? Is this just pissing in the wind?

Fuck.

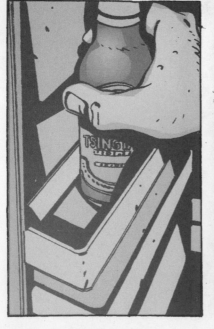

Long night.

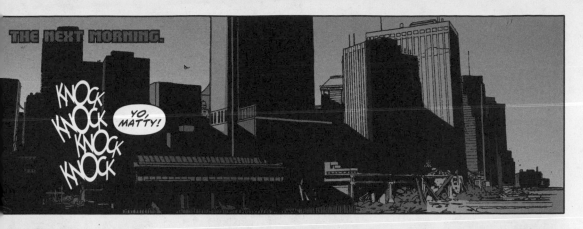

KNOCK
KNOCK
KNOCK
KNOCK

YO, MATTY!

IS IT PARCO...?

NO, WE HAVE A MEETING. GET UP, GET DRESSED, C'MON...

WHAT IS IT?

YOU WILL *NOT* BELIEVE THIS SHIT.

UNITED STATES WANTS A MEETING. A FUCKING *SIT-DOWN*, LIKE IN A MAFIA FILM. JESUS.

WITH YOU?

WITH THE *DELGADO NATION*.

BE CAREFUL, MATTY.

DON'T WORRY...

LIBERTY STILL HAS ME UNDER CONTRACT, REMEMBER?

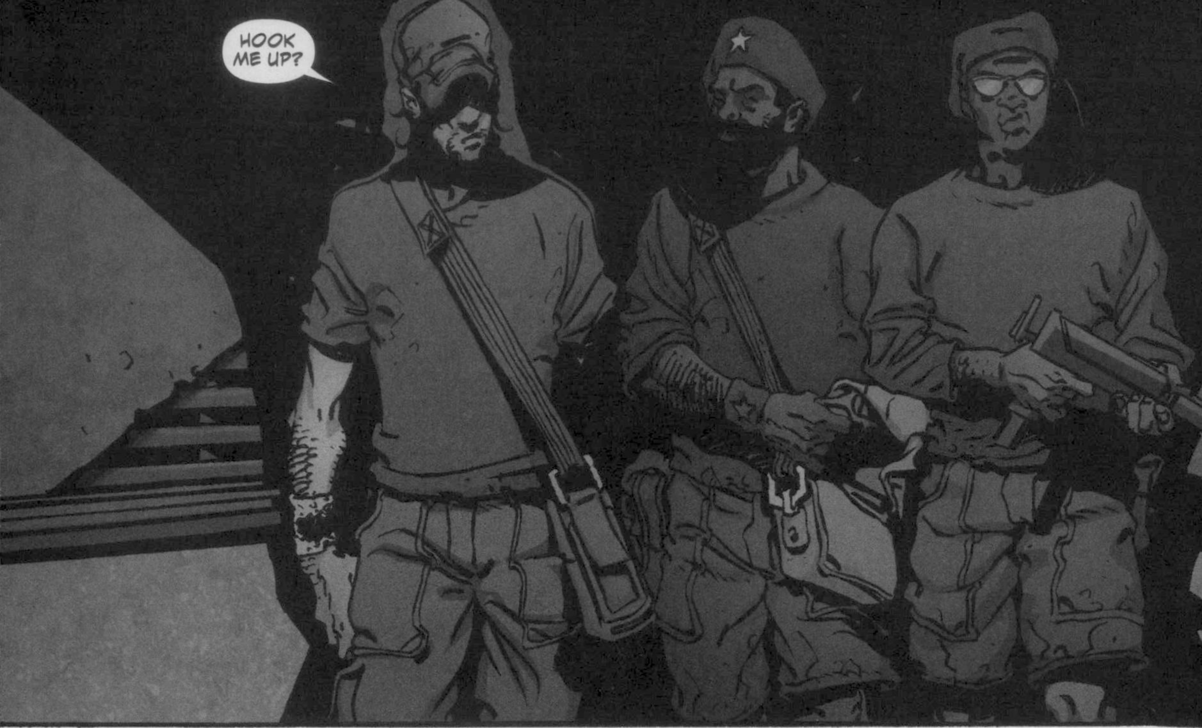
HOOK ME UP?

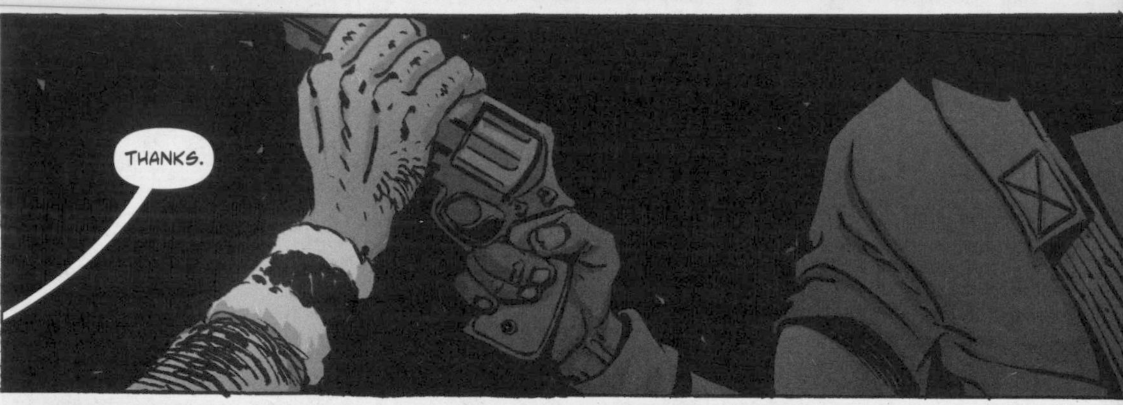
THANKS.

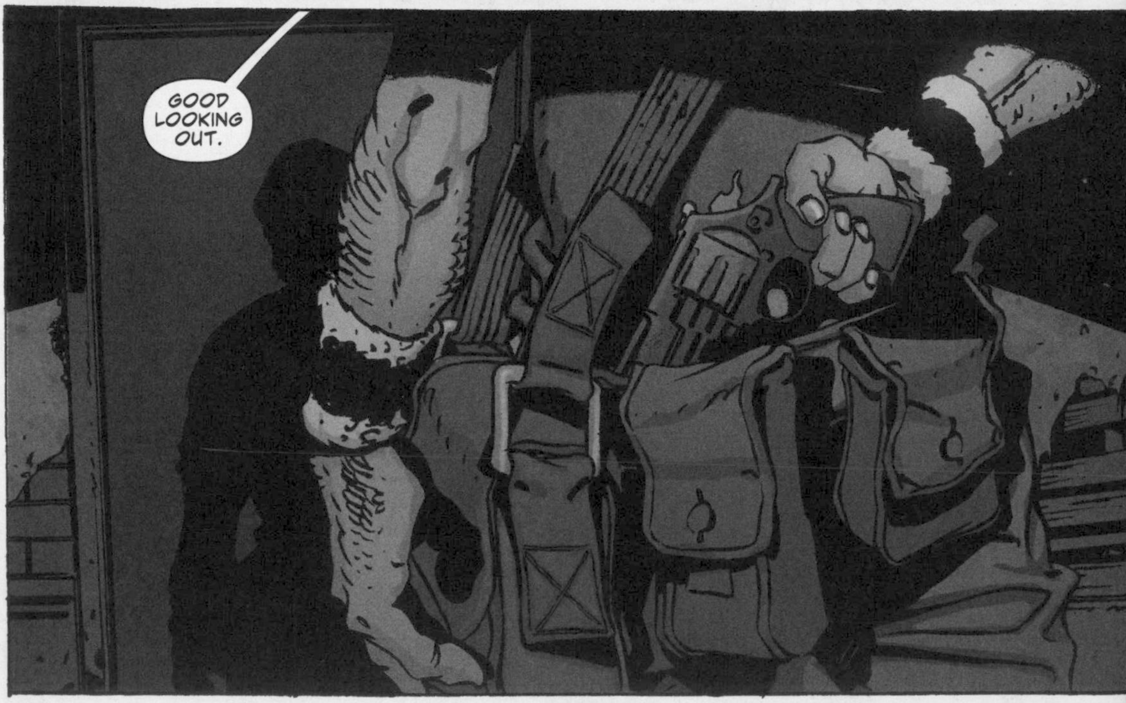
GOOD LOOKING OUT.

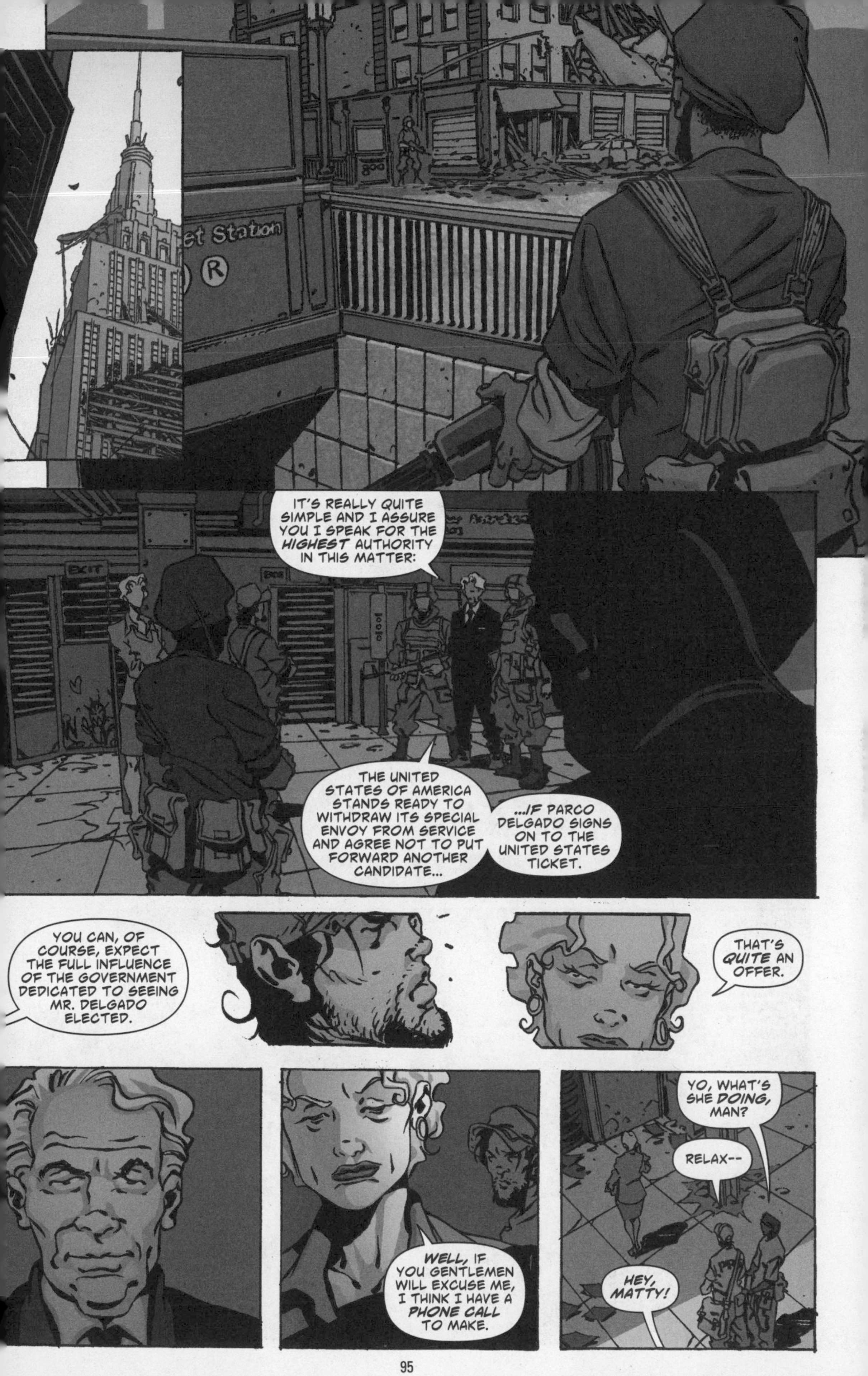

...et Station
R
IT'S REALLY QUITE SIMPLE AND I ASSURE YOU I SPEAK FOR THE HIGHEST AUTHORITY IN THIS MATTER:
EXIT
THE UNITED STATES OF AMERICA STANDS READY TO WITHDRAW ITS SPECIAL ENVOY FROM SERVICE AND AGREE NOT TO PUT FORWARD ANOTHER CANDIDATE...
...IF PARCO DELGADO SIGNS ON TO THE UNITED STATES TICKET.
YOU CAN, OF COURSE, EXPECT THE FULL INFLUENCE OF THE GOVERNMENT DEDICATED TO SEEING MR. DELGADO ELECTED.
THAT'S QUITE AN OFFER.
WELL, IF YOU GENTLEMEN WILL EXCUSE ME, I THINK I HAVE A PHONE CALL TO MAKE.
YO, WHAT'S SHE DOING, MAN?
RELAX--
HEY, MATTY!

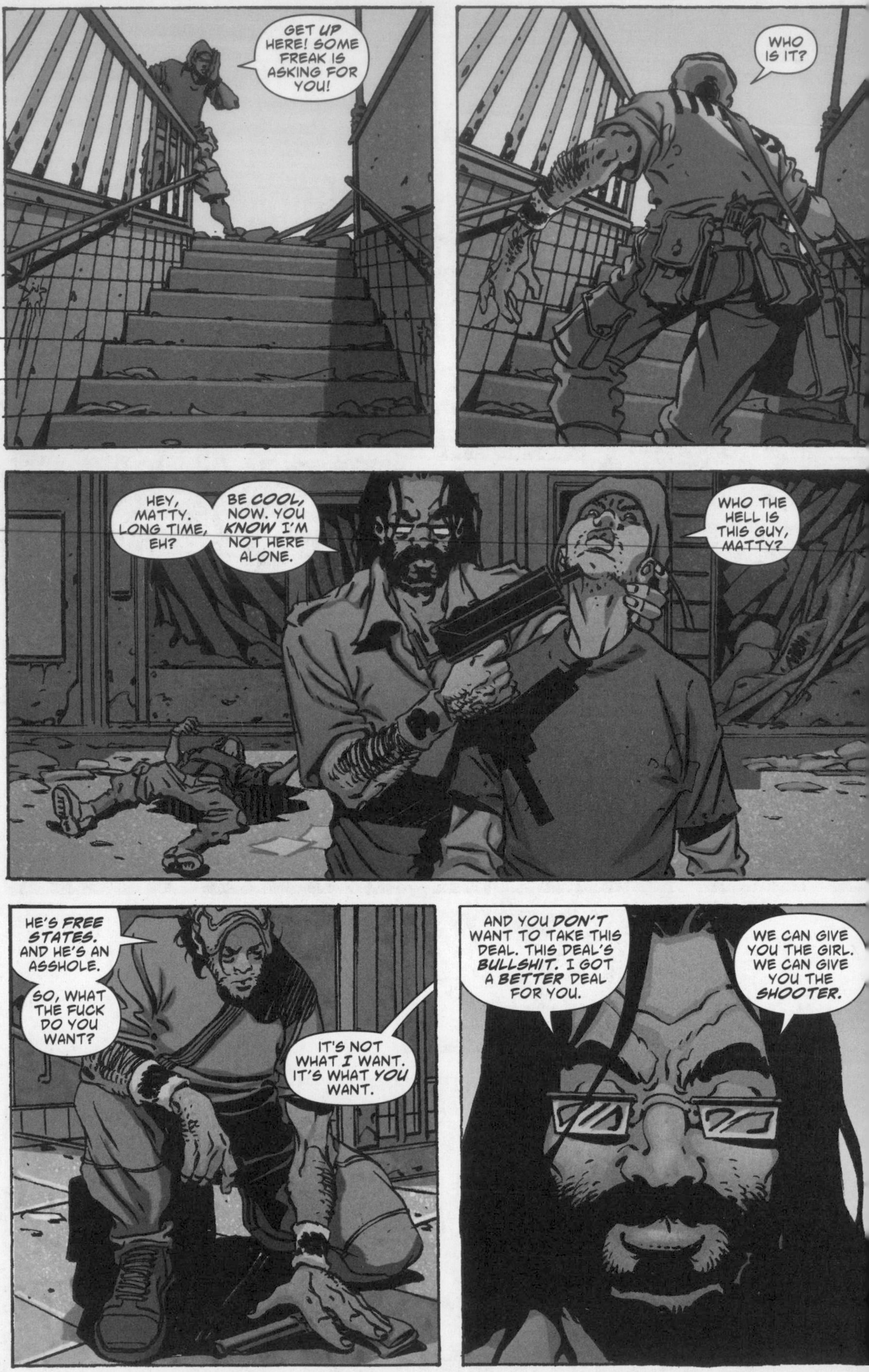
GET UP HERE! SOME FREAK IS ASKING FOR YOU!
WHO IS IT?
HEY, MATTY. LONG TIME, EH?
BE COOL, NOW. YOU KNOW I'M NOT HERE ALONE.
WHO THE HELL IS THIS GUY, MATTY?
HE'S FREE STATES. AND HE'S AN ASSHOLE.
SO, WHAT THE FUCK DO YOU WANT?
IT'S NOT WHAT I WANT. IT'S WHAT YOU WANT.
AND YOU DON'T WANT TO TAKE THIS DEAL. THIS DEAL'S BULLSHIT. I GOT A BETTER DEAL FOR YOU.
WE CAN GIVE YOU THE GIRL. WE CAN GIVE YOU THE SHOOTER.

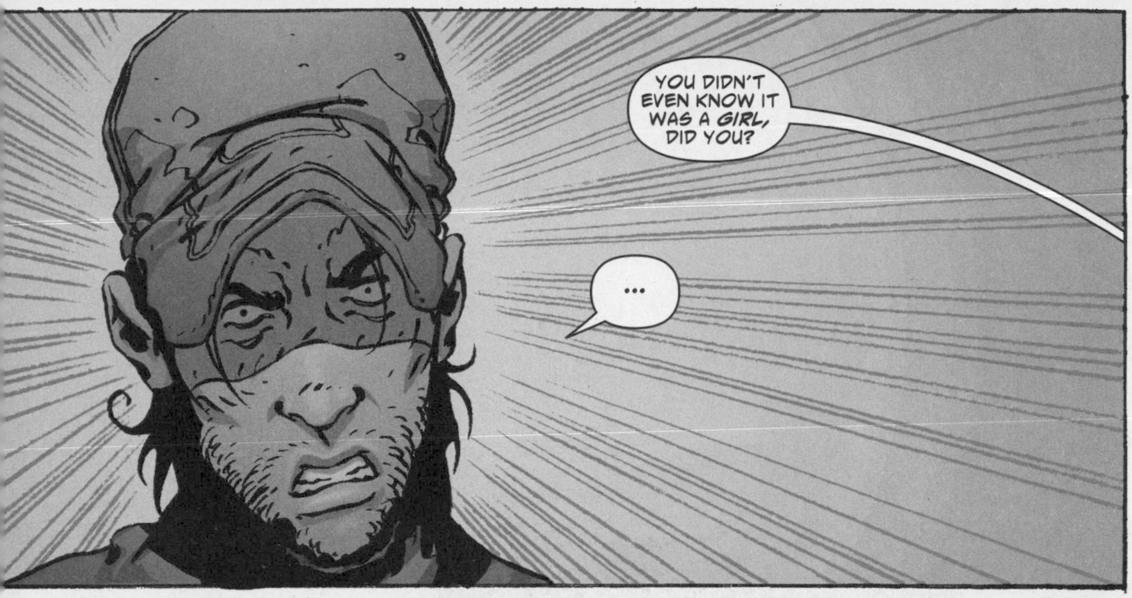
YOU DIDN'T EVEN KNOW IT WAS A GIRL, DID YOU?
...

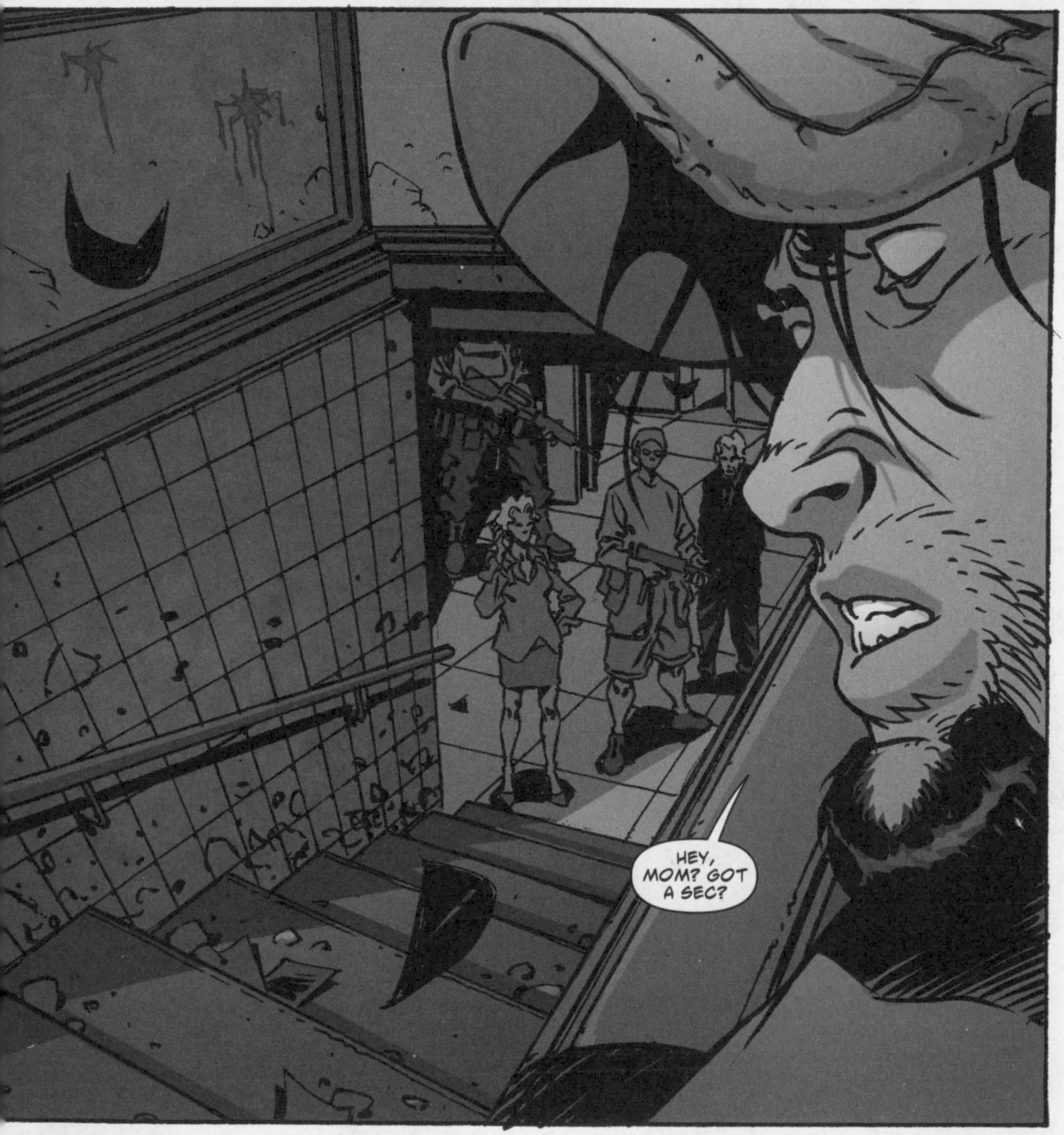
HEY, MOM? GOT A SEC?

CHAPTER FIVE

MAKE YOUR VOTE COUNT
(Asegure que cuente su voto.)

TO VOTE FOR A STATEMENT, CANDI
OR FOR A WRITE-IN, BLACK IN
BESIDE YOUR CHOICE.

(Para votar a favor de una declaración

OFFICIAL BALLOT
(BOLETA OFICIAL)

SAMPLE ELECTION
(ELECCION DE MUESTRA)

SAMPLE CUSTOMER

INSTRUCTION NOTE:

If you voted in this column you may
not vote in another column. Here is
column found on this page.

County Commissioner,
Precinct No. 1
(Comisionado del Condado,
Precinto Núm. 1)

Black Jack Pershing

Davie Crockett (State)

Joan Laride (May)

School Board Trustee,

IF YOU HAVE ANY QUESTIONS,
PLEASE ASK YOUR ELECTION OFFICIAL
(Si usted tiene alguna pregunta, favor de dirigirla a los oficiales electorales

3rd DIST
REPUBLIC

DO NOT FOLD YOUR BALLOT!
(Favor de no doblar su boleta.)

07 01920

⑦

e(s) by FILLING IN OVAL
BLACK or DARK PEN ONLY.
LLENANDO EL ÓVALO
on una PLUMA NEGRA o
CURO SOLAMENTE.

END OF BALLOT
FIN DE BOLETA

DELGADO
NATION

I HAVE VOTED – HAVE YOU?   OTO UD?   DETACH THIS STUB   80   90   95

BD   40

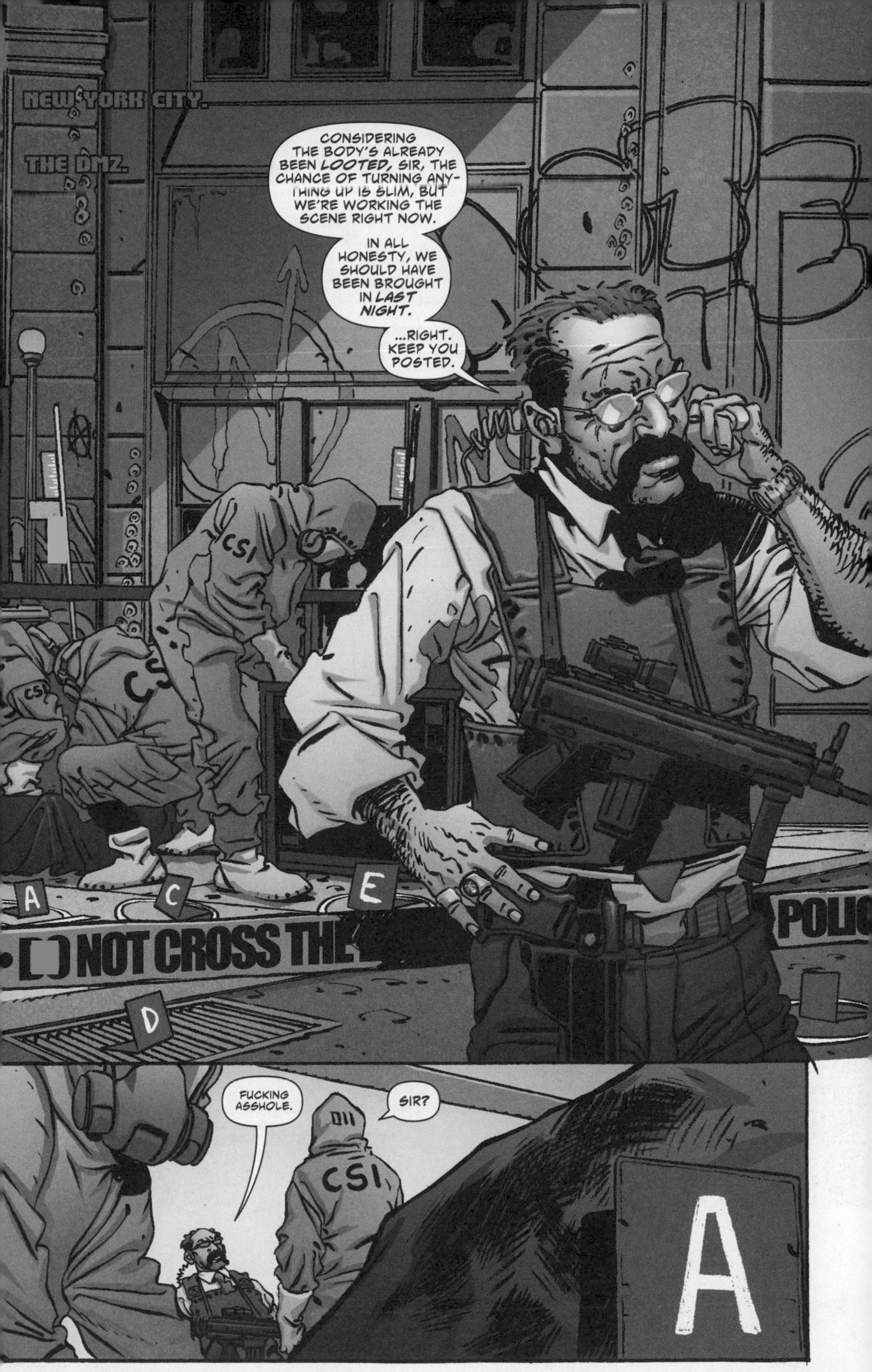
NEW YORK CITY.
THE DMZ.
CONSIDERING THE BODY'S ALREADY BEEN LOOTED, SIR, THE CHANCE OF TURNING ANY-THING UP IS SLIM, BUT WE'RE WORKING THE SCENE RIGHT NOW.
IN ALL HONESTY, WE SHOULD HAVE BEEN BROUGHT IN LAST NIGHT.
...RIGHT. KEEP YOU POSTED.
FUCKING ASSHOLE.
SIR?

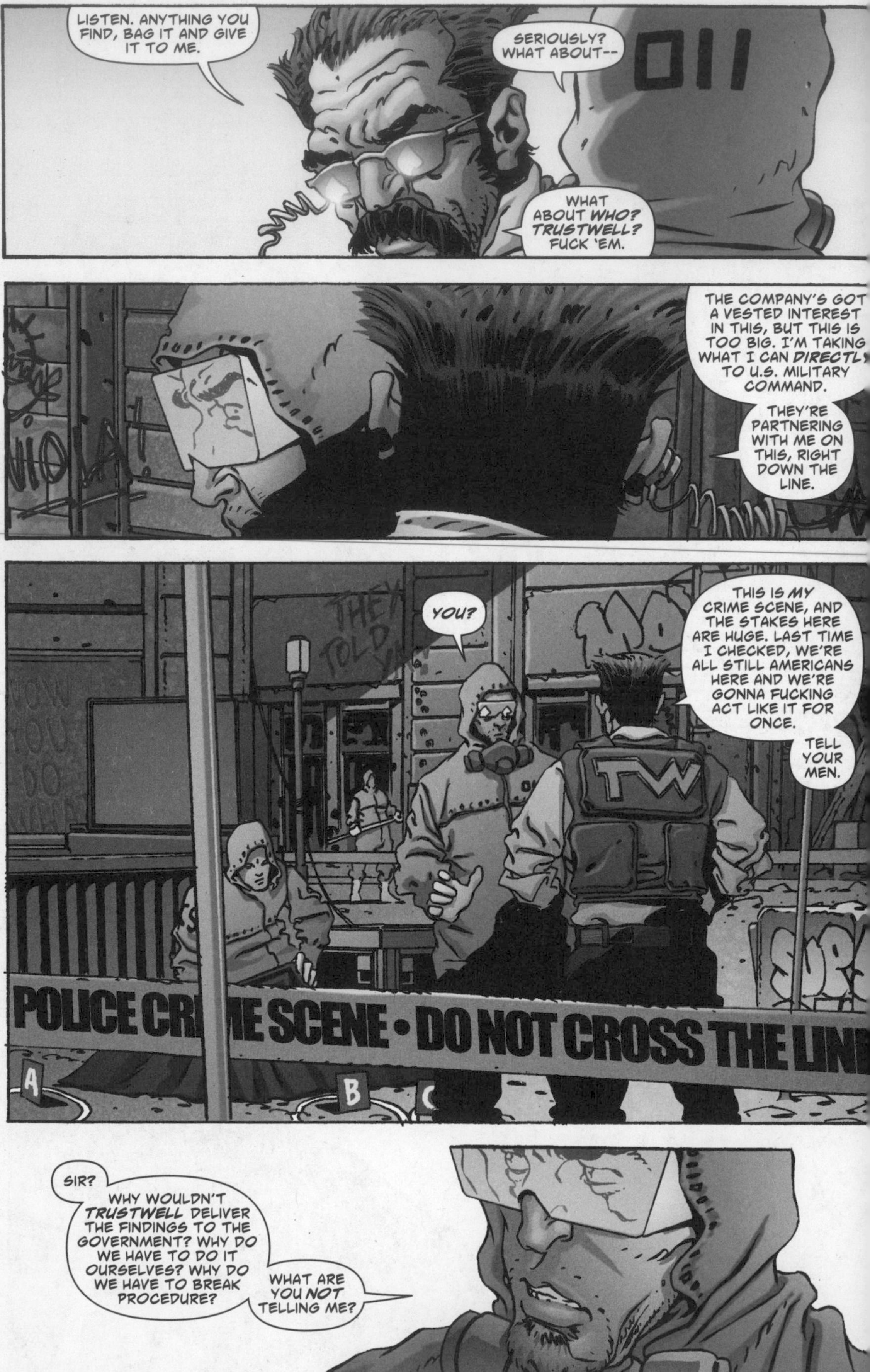
LISTEN. ANYTHING YOU FIND, BAG IT AND GIVE IT TO ME.
SERIOUSLY? WHAT ABOUT--
011
WHAT ABOUT WHO? TRUSTWELL? FUCK 'EM.
THE COMPANY'S GOT A VESTED INTEREST IN THIS, BUT THIS IS TOO BIG. I'M TAKING WHAT I CAN DIRECTL TO U.S. MILITARY COMMAND.
THEY'RE PARTNERING WITH ME ON THIS, RIGHT DOWN THE LINE.
YOU?
THIS IS MY CRIME SCENE, AND THE STAKES HERE ARE HUGE. LAST TIME I CHECKED, WE'RE ALL STILL AMERICANS HERE AND WE'RE GONNA FUCKING ACT LIKE IT FOR ONCE.
TELL YOUR MEN.
TW
POLICE CR ME SCENE • DO NOT CROSS THE LI
A
B
SIR?
WHY WOULDN'T TRUSTWELL DELIVER THE FINDINGS TO THE GOVERNMENT? WHY DO WE HAVE TO DO IT OURSELVES? WHY DO WE HAVE TO BREAK PROCEDURE?
WHAT ARE YOU NOT TELLING ME?

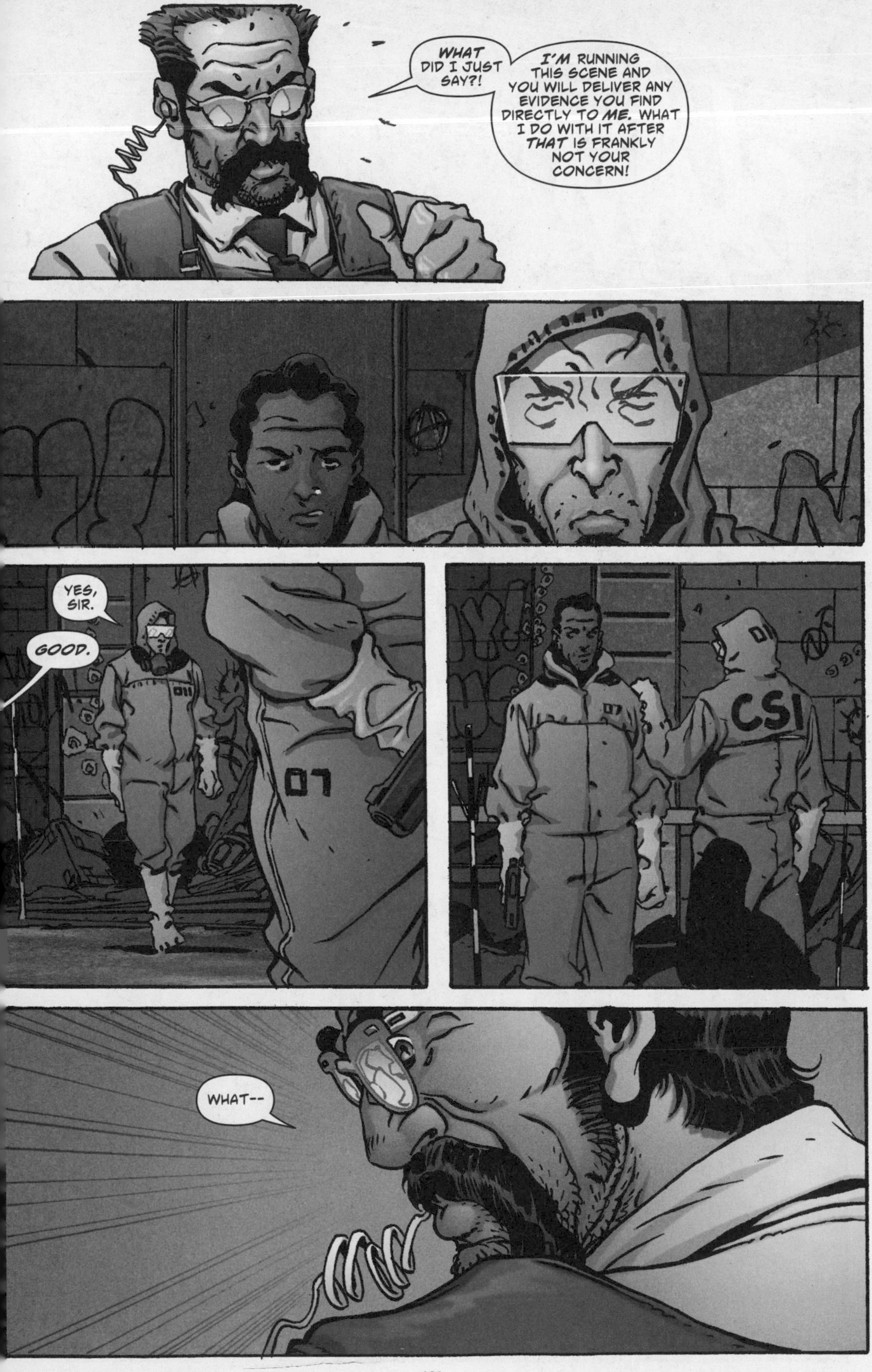

WHAT DID I JUST SAY?!
I'M RUNNING THIS SCENE AND YOU WILL DELIVER ANY EVIDENCE YOU FIND DIRECTLY TO ME. WHAT I DO WITH IT AFTER THAT IS FRANKLY NOT YOUR CONCERN!
YES, SIR.
GOOD.
07
07
CSI
WHAT--

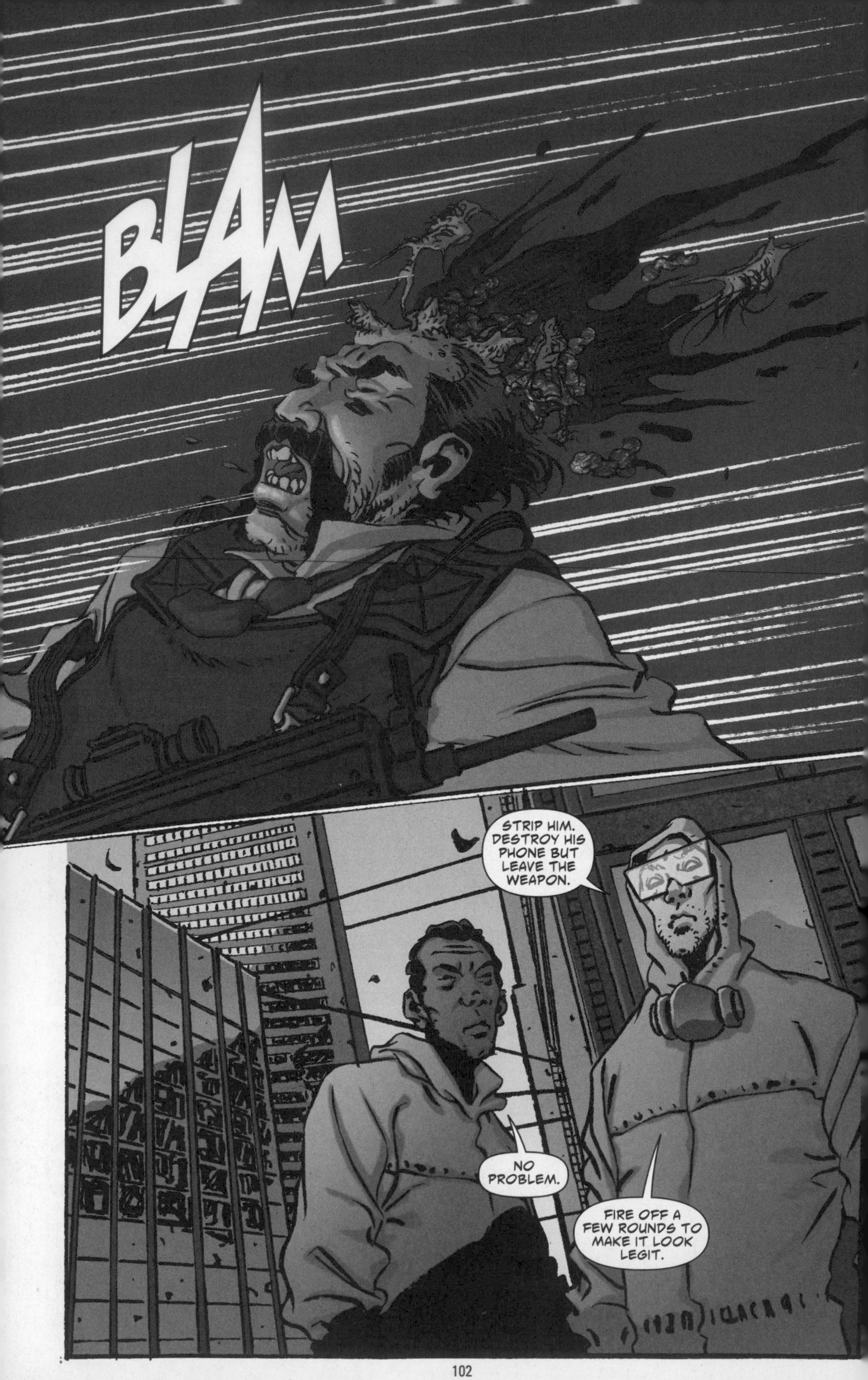
BLAM
STRIP HIM. DESTROY HIS PHONE BUT LEAVE THE WEAPON.
NO PROBLEM.
FIRE OFF A FEW ROUNDS TO MAKE IT LOOK LEGIT.

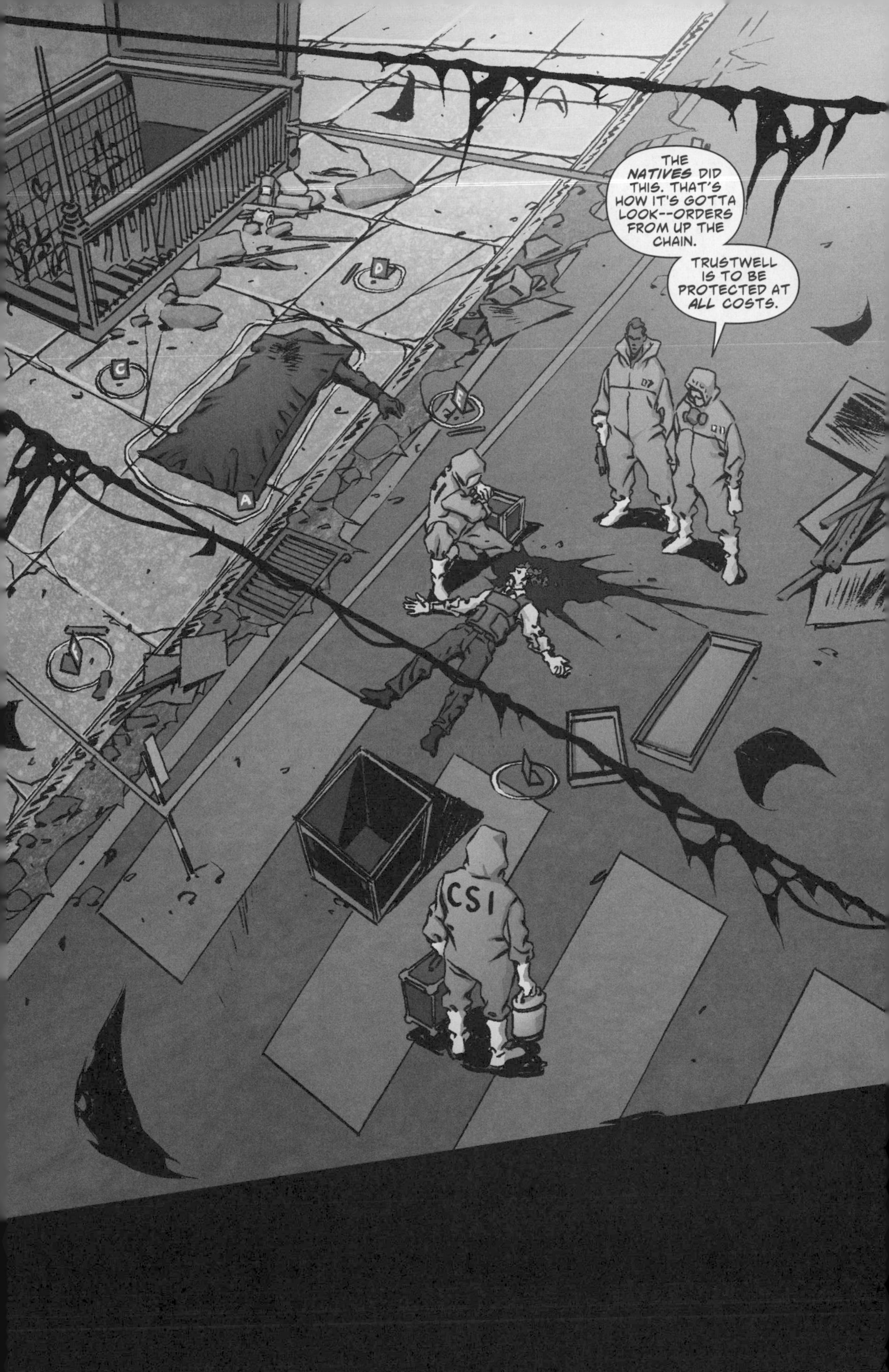
THE NATIVES DID THIS. THAT'S HOW IT'S GOTTA LOOK--ORDERS FROM UP THE CHAIN.
TRUSTWELL IS TO BE PROTECTED AT ALL COSTS.
CSI

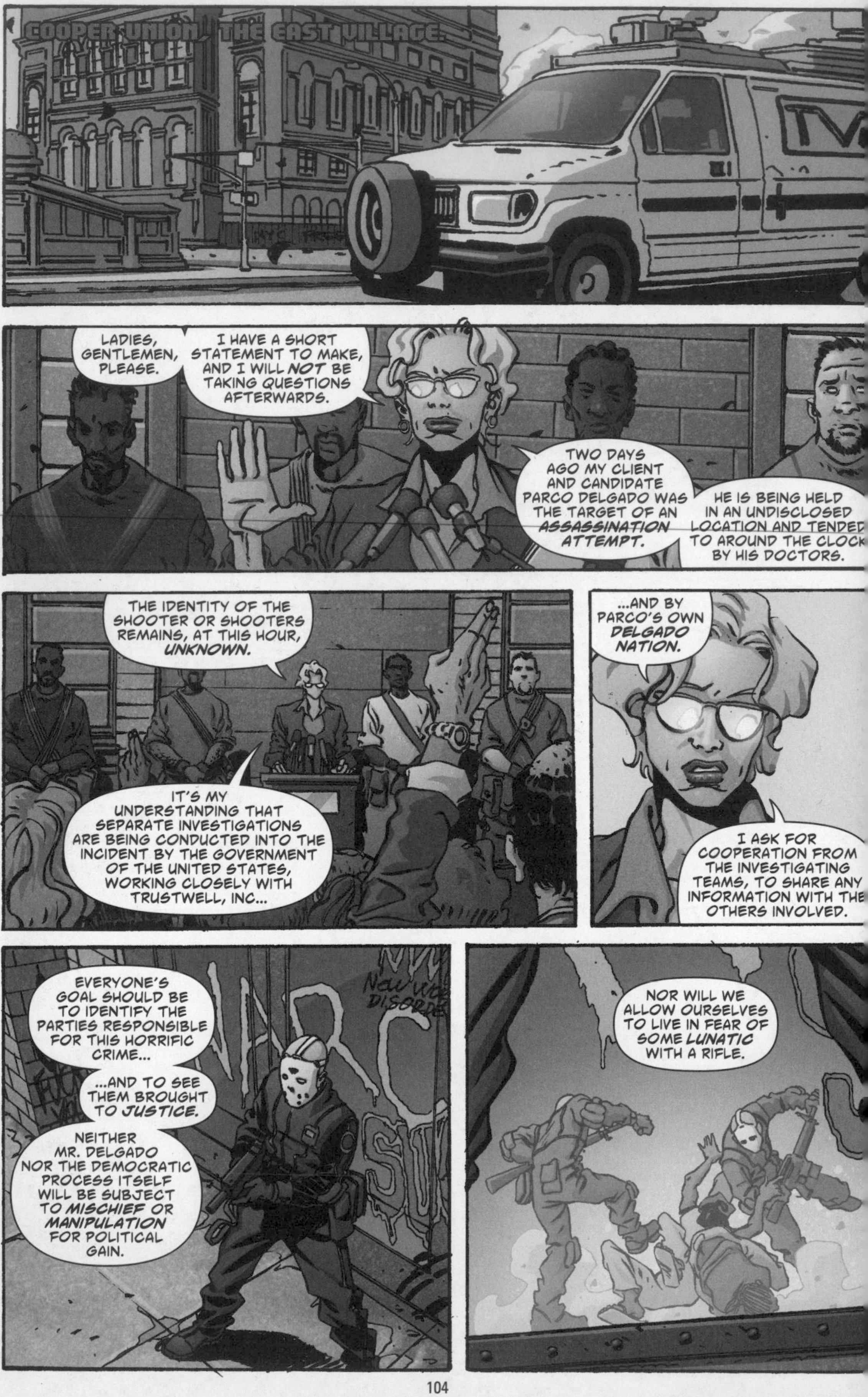
COOPER UNION. THE EAST VILLAGE.
TV
LADIES, GENTLEMEN, PLEASE.
I HAVE A SHORT STATEMENT TO MAKE, AND I WILL NOT BE TAKING QUESTIONS AFTERWARDS.
TWO DAYS AGO MY CLIENT AND CANDIDATE PARCO DELGADO WAS THE TARGET OF AN ASSASSINATION ATTEMPT.
HE IS BEING HELD IN AN UNDISCLOSED LOCATION AND TENDED TO AROUND THE CLOCK BY HIS DOCTORS.
...AND BY PARCO'S OWN DELGADO NATION.
THE IDENTITY OF THE SHOOTER OR SHOOTERS REMAINS, AT THIS HOUR, UNKNOWN.
IT'S MY UNDERSTANDING THAT SEPARATE INVESTIGATIONS ARE BEING CONDUCTED INTO THE INCIDENT BY THE GOVERNMENT OF THE UNITED STATES, WORKING CLOSELY WITH TRUSTWELL, INC...
I ASK FOR COOPERATION FROM THE INVESTIGATING TEAMS, TO SHARE ANY INFORMATION WITH THE OTHERS INVOLVED.
EVERYONE'S GOAL SHOULD BE TO IDENTIFY THE PARTIES RESPONSIBLE FOR THIS HORRIFIC CRIME...
...AND TO SEE THEM BROUGHT TO JUSTICE.
NEITHER MR. DELGADO NOR THE DEMOCRATIC PROCESS ITSELF WILL BE SUBJECT TO MISCHIEF OR MANIPULATION FOR POLITICAL GAIN.
NOR WILL WE ALLOW OURSELVES TO LIVE IN FEAR OF SOME LUNATIC WITH A RIFLE.

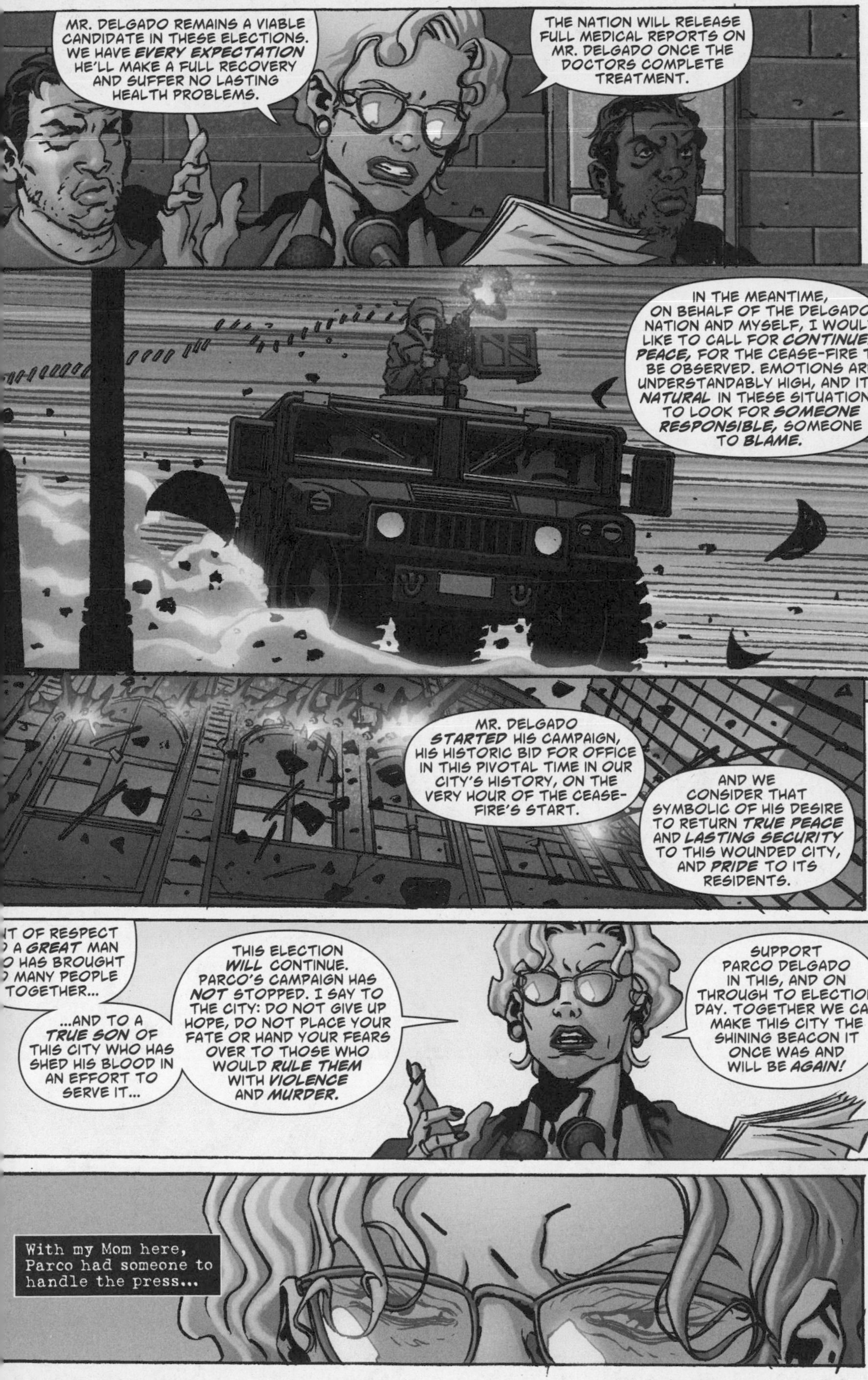
MR. DELGADO REMAINS A VIABLE CANDIDATE IN THESE ELECTIONS. WE HAVE EVERY EXPECTATION HE'LL MAKE A FULL RECOVERY AND SUFFER NO LASTING HEALTH PROBLEMS.
THE NATION WILL RELEASE FULL MEDICAL REPORTS ON MR. DELGADO ONCE THE DOCTORS COMPLETE TREATMENT.
IN THE MEANTIME, ON BEHALF OF THE DELGADO NATION AND MYSELF, I WOULD LIKE TO CALL FOR CONTINUED PEACE, FOR THE CEASE-FIRE TO BE OBSERVED. EMOTIONS ARE UNDERSTANDABLY HIGH, AND IT'S NATURAL IN THESE SITUATIONS TO LOOK FOR SOMEONE RESPONSIBLE, SOMEONE TO BLAME.
MR. DELGADO STARTED HIS CAMPAIGN, HIS HISTORIC BID FOR OFFICE IN THIS PIVOTAL TIME IN OUR CITY'S HISTORY, ON THE VERY HOUR OF THE CEASE-FIRE'S START.
AND WE CONSIDER THAT SYMBOLIC OF HIS DESIRE TO RETURN TRUE PEACE AND LASTING SECURITY TO THIS WOUNDED CITY, AND PRIDE TO ITS RESIDENTS.
NT OF RESPECT A GREAT MAN O HAS BROUGHT MANY PEOPLE TOGETHER...
...AND TO A TRUE SON OF THIS CITY WHO HAS SHED HIS BLOOD IN AN EFFORT TO SERVE IT...
THIS ELECTION WILL CONTINUE. PARCO'S CAMPAIGN HAS NOT STOPPED. I SAY TO THE CITY: DO NOT GIVE UP HOPE, DO NOT PLACE YOUR FATE OR HAND YOUR FEARS OVER TO THOSE WHO WOULD RULE THEM WITH VIOLENCE AND MURDER.
SUPPORT PARCO DELGADO IN THIS, AND ON THROUGH TO ELECTION DAY. TOGETHER WE CAN MAKE THIS CITY THE SHINING BEACON IT ONCE WAS AND WILL BE AGAIN!
With my Mom here, Parco had someone to handle the press...

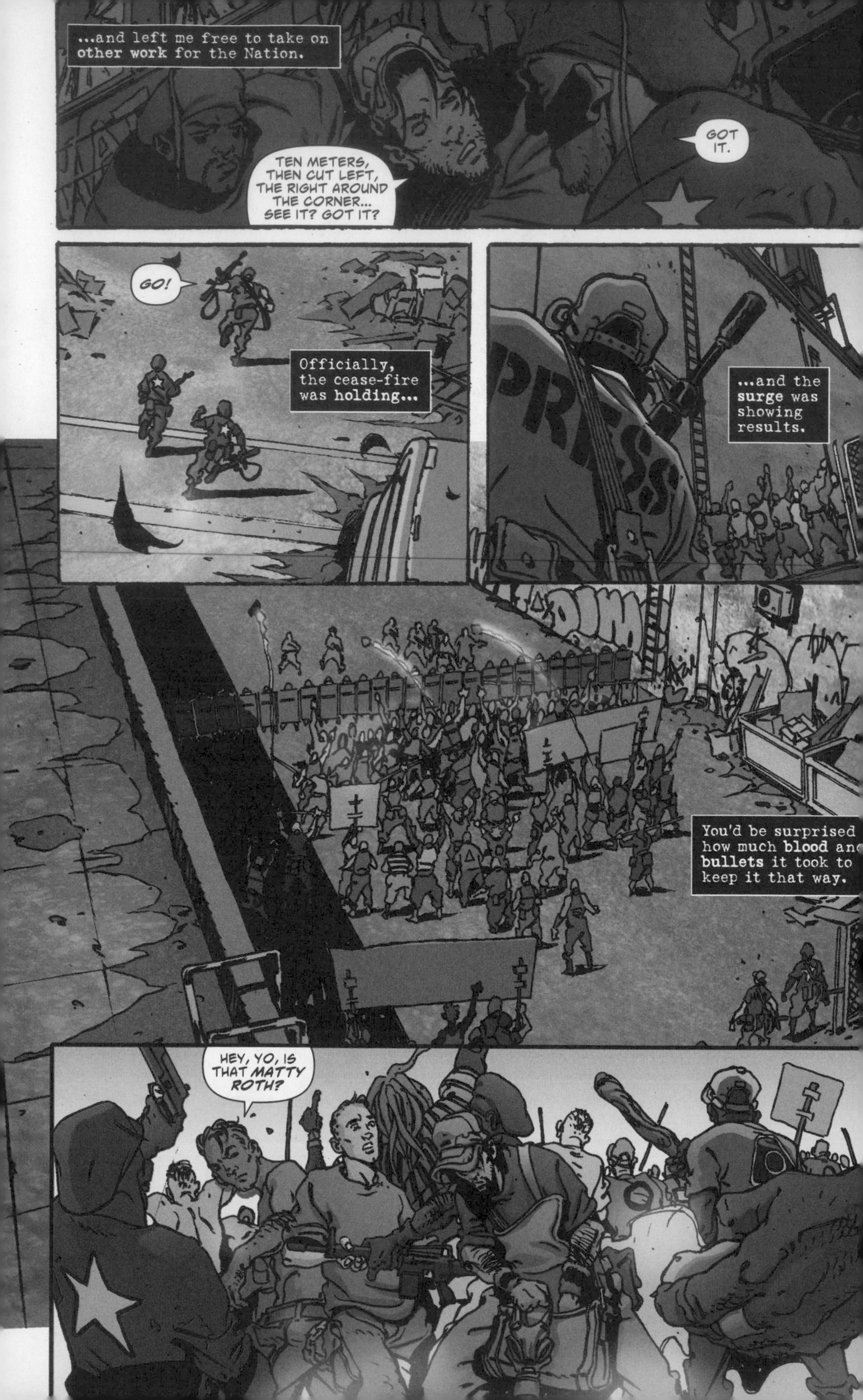
...and left me free to take on other work for the Nation.
TEN METERS, THEN CUT LEFT, THE RIGHT AROUND THE CORNER... SEE IT? GOT IT?
GOT IT.
GO!
Officially, the cease-fire was holding...
PRESS
...and the surge was showing results.
You'd be surprised how much blood and bullets it took to keep it that way.
HEY, YO, IS THAT MATTY ROTH?

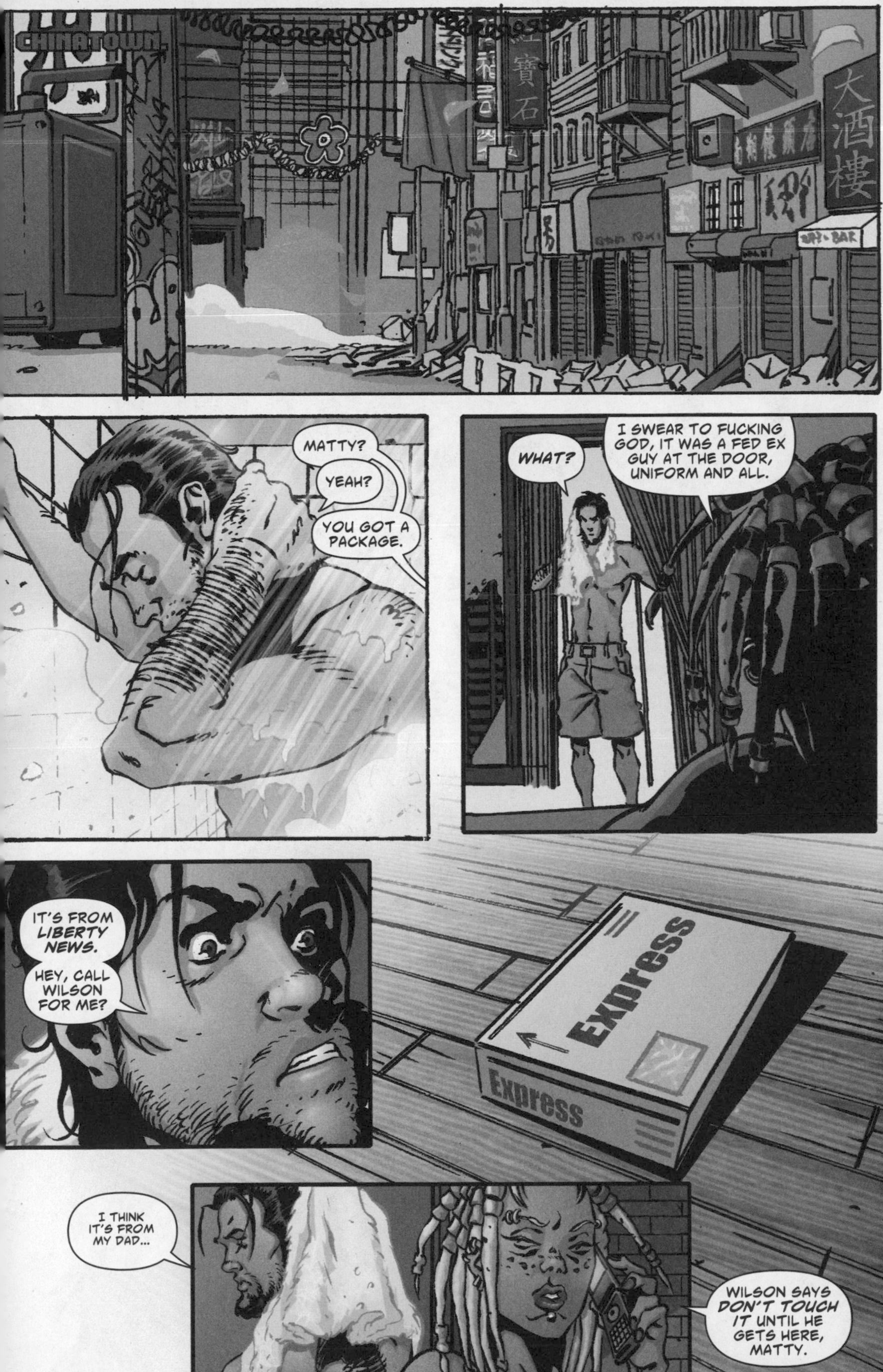
CHINATOWN
MATTY?
YEAH?
YOU GOT A PACKAGE.
WHAT?
I SWEAR TO FUCKING GOD, IT WAS A FED EX GUY AT THE DOOR, UNIFORM AND ALL.
IT'S FROM LIBERTY NEWS.
HEY, CALL WILSON FOR ME?
Express
Express
I THINK IT'S FROM MY DAD...
WILSON SAYS DON'T TOUCH IT UNTIL HE GETS HERE, MATTY.

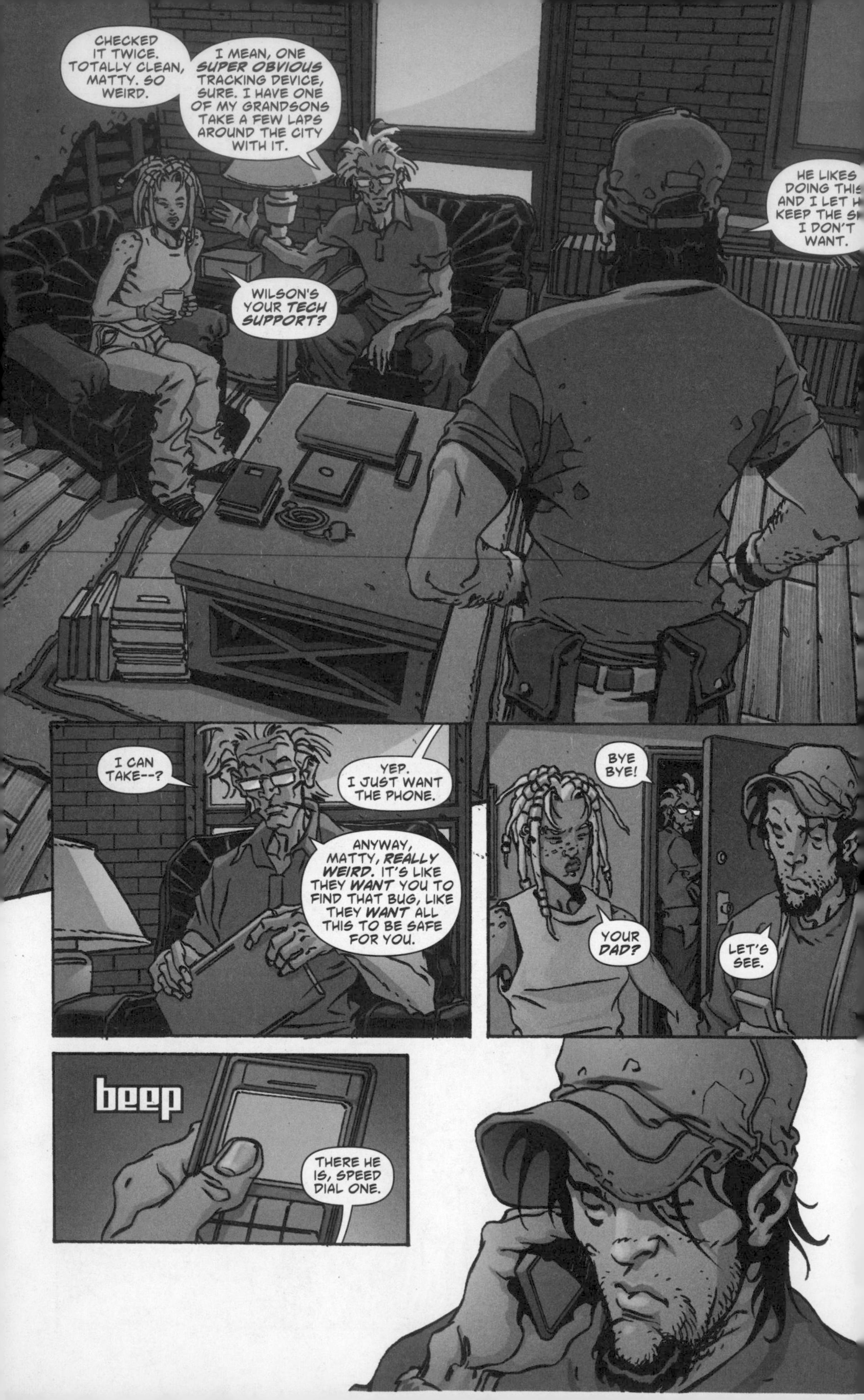
CHECKED IT TWICE. TOTALLY CLEAN, MATTY. SO WEIRD.
I MEAN, ONE SUPER OBVIOUS TRACKING DEVICE, SURE. I HAVE ONE OF MY GRANDSONS TAKE A FEW LAPS AROUND THE CITY WITH IT.
WILSON'S YOUR TECH SUPPORT?
HE LIKES DOING THIS AND I LET H KEEP THE S I DON'T WANT.
I CAN TAKE--?
YEP. I JUST WANT THE PHONE.
ANYWAY, MATTY, REALLY WEIRD. IT'S LIKE THEY WANT YOU TO FIND THAT BUG, LIKE THEY WANT ALL THIS TO BE SAFE FOR YOU.
BYE BYE!
YOUR DAD?
LET'S SEE.
beep
THERE HE IS, SPEED DIAL ONE.

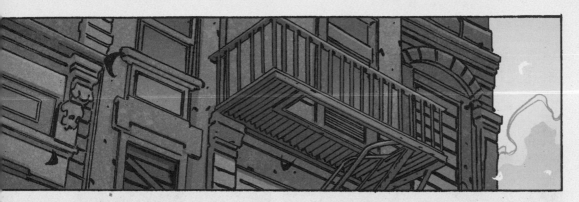

...DAD...DAD, LISTEN.

THEY AREN'T ON THE LEVEL, MATTY. THE DEAL-- THE DEAL IS GARBAGE.

I KNOW, DAD.

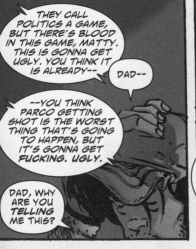

THEY CALL POLITICS A GAME, BUT THERE'S BLOOD IN THIS GAME, MATTY. THIS IS GONNA GET UGLY. YOU THINK IT IS ALREADY--

DAD--

--YOU THINK PARCO GETTING SHOT IS THE WORST THING THAT'S GOING TO HAPPEN, BUT IT'S GONNA GET FUCKING. UGLY.

DAD, WHY ARE YOU TELLING ME THIS?

THEY CAME ROUND TO SEE ME, ASKING ABOUT YOU. AND YOUR MOTHER.

I'M ON FORCED LEAVE. I'M AT HOME, MATTY, AND TO BE HONEST I DON'T THINK I'M MEANT TO LEAVE THE APARTMENT.

SHIT.

LISTEN. DON'T WORRY. JUST DON'T DO ANY- THING.

JUST FIND A DARK HOLE AND CRAWL INTO IT, AND STAY THERE UNTIL AFTER ELECTION DAY.

MAYBE THERE WILL STILL BE A CITY LEFT WHEN YOU DO.

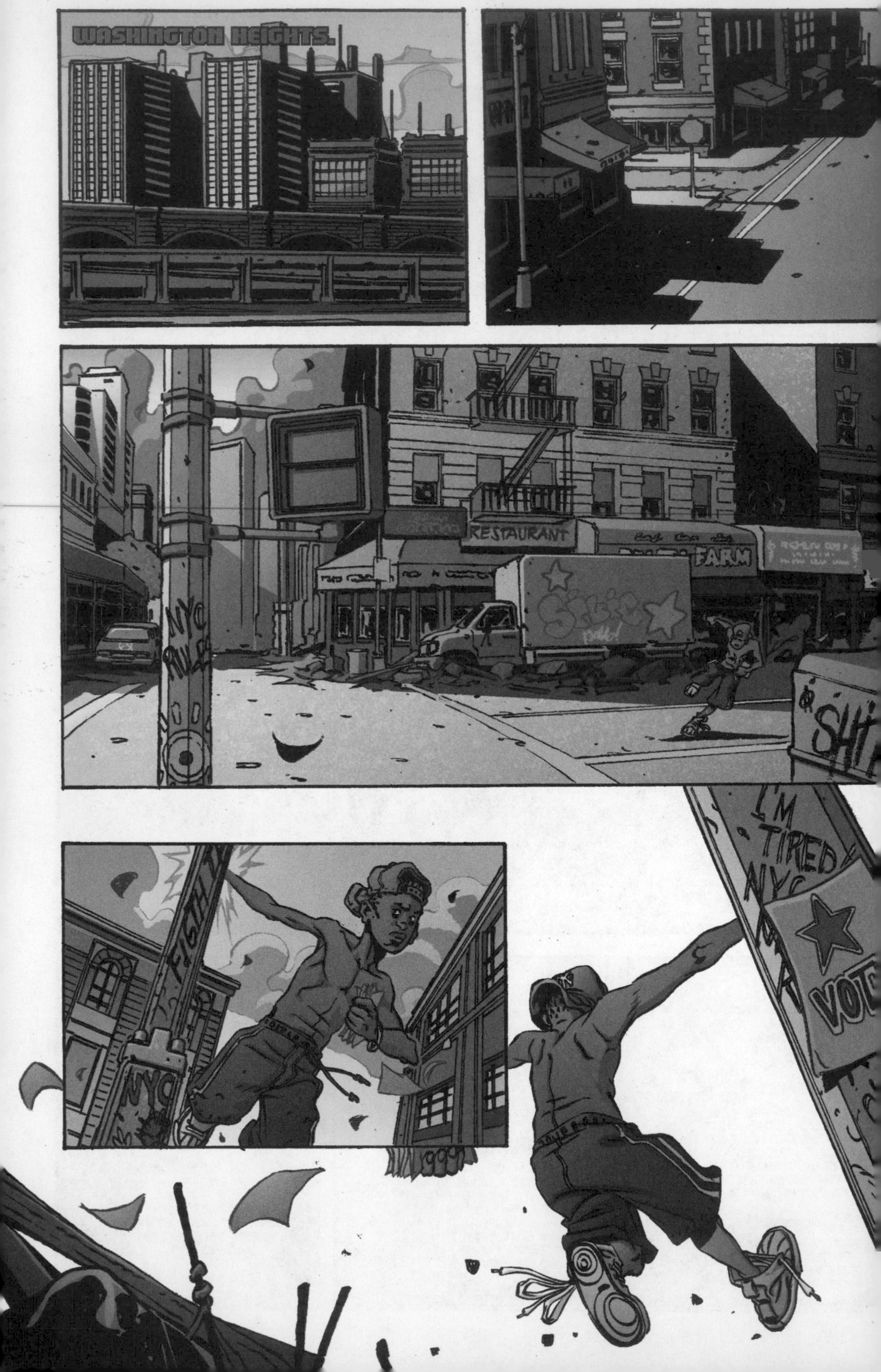
WASHINGTON HEIGHTS.
RESTAURANT
FARM
I'M TIRED

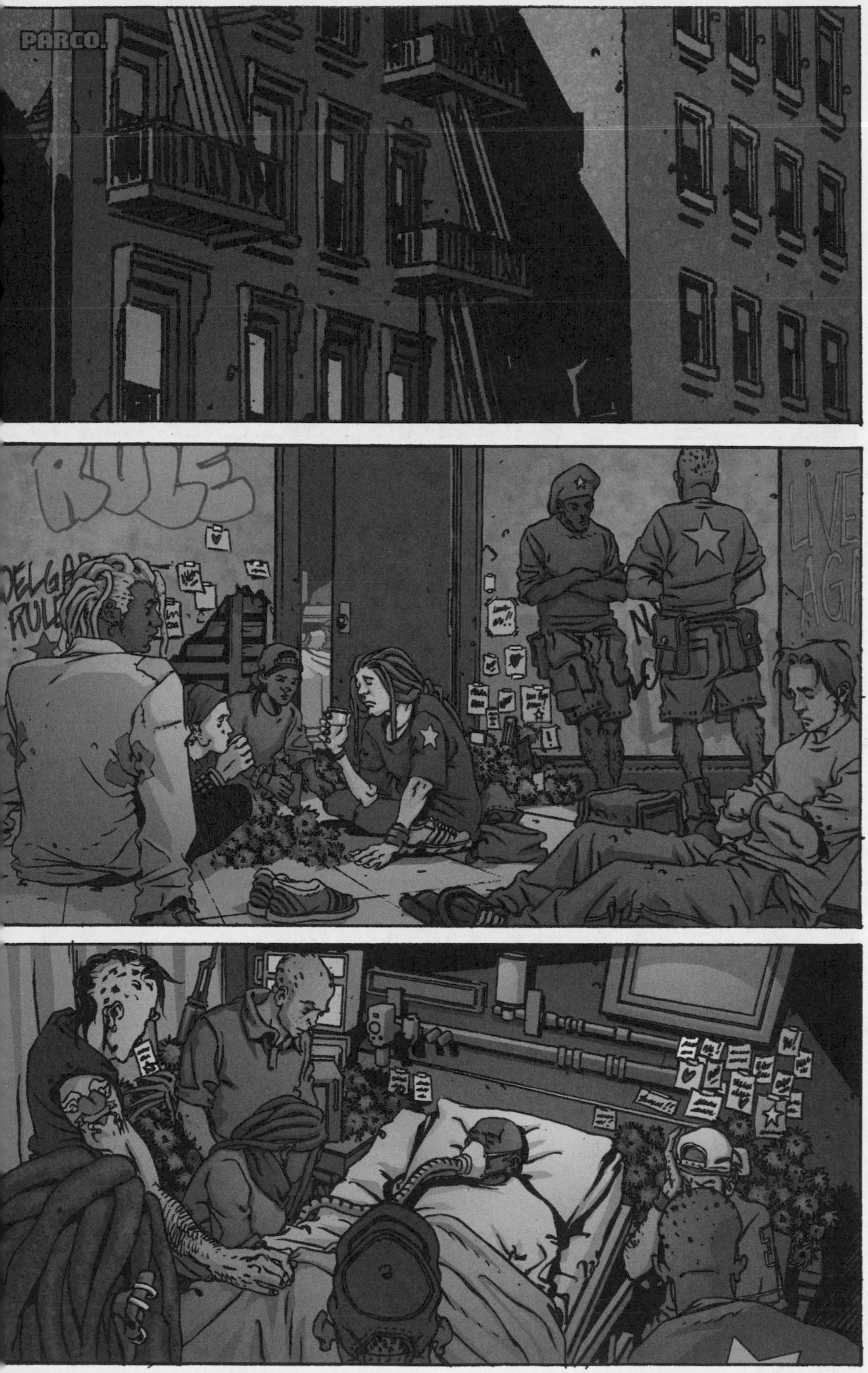
PARCO.

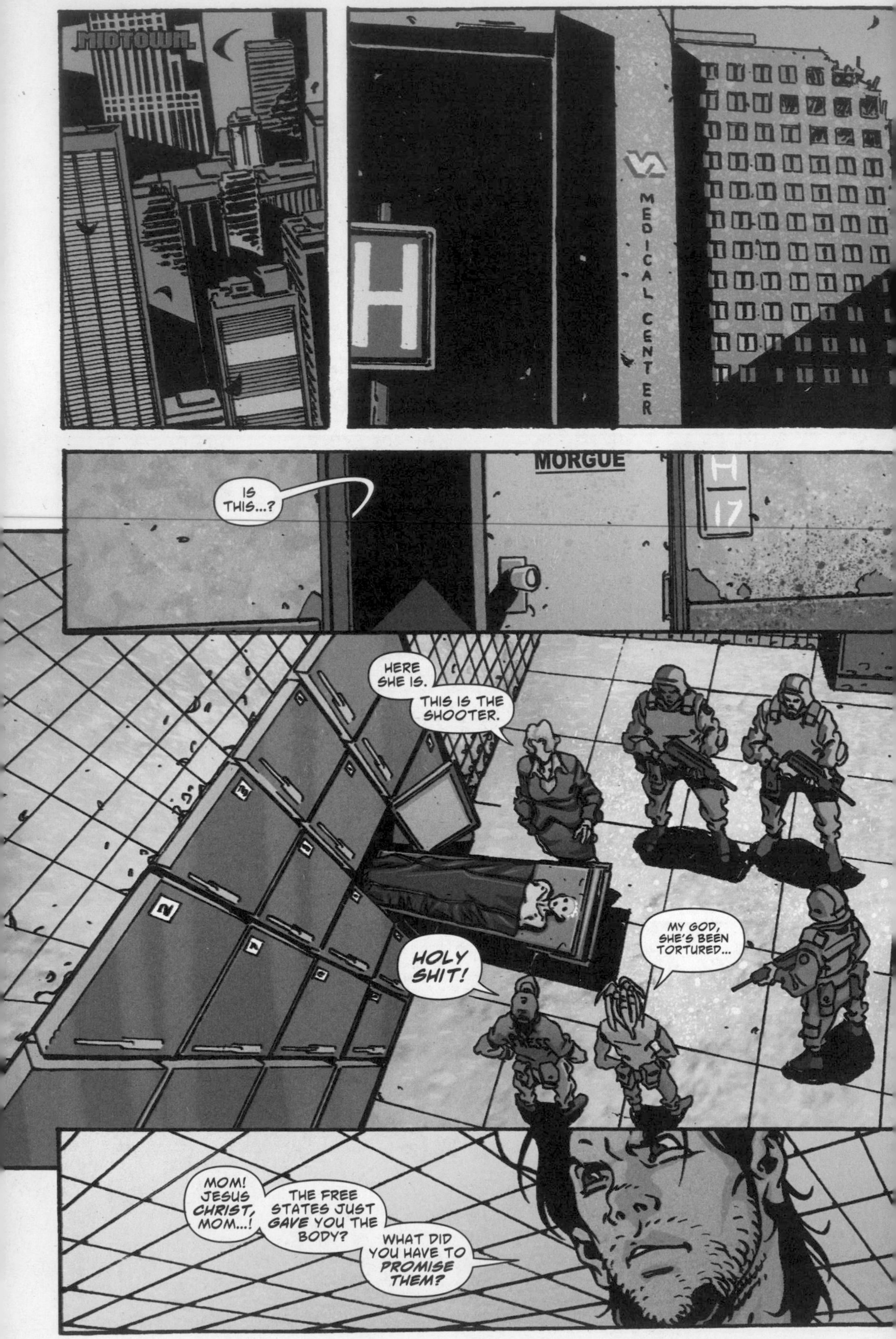
MIDTOWN
H
MEDICAL CENTER
MORGUE
H 17
IS THIS...?
HERE SHE IS.
THIS IS THE SHOOTER.
HOLY SHIT!
MY GOD, SHE'S BEEN TORTURED...
MOM! JESUS CHRIST, MOM...!
THE FREE STATES JUST GAVE YOU THE BODY?
WHAT DID YOU HAVE TO PROMISE THEM?

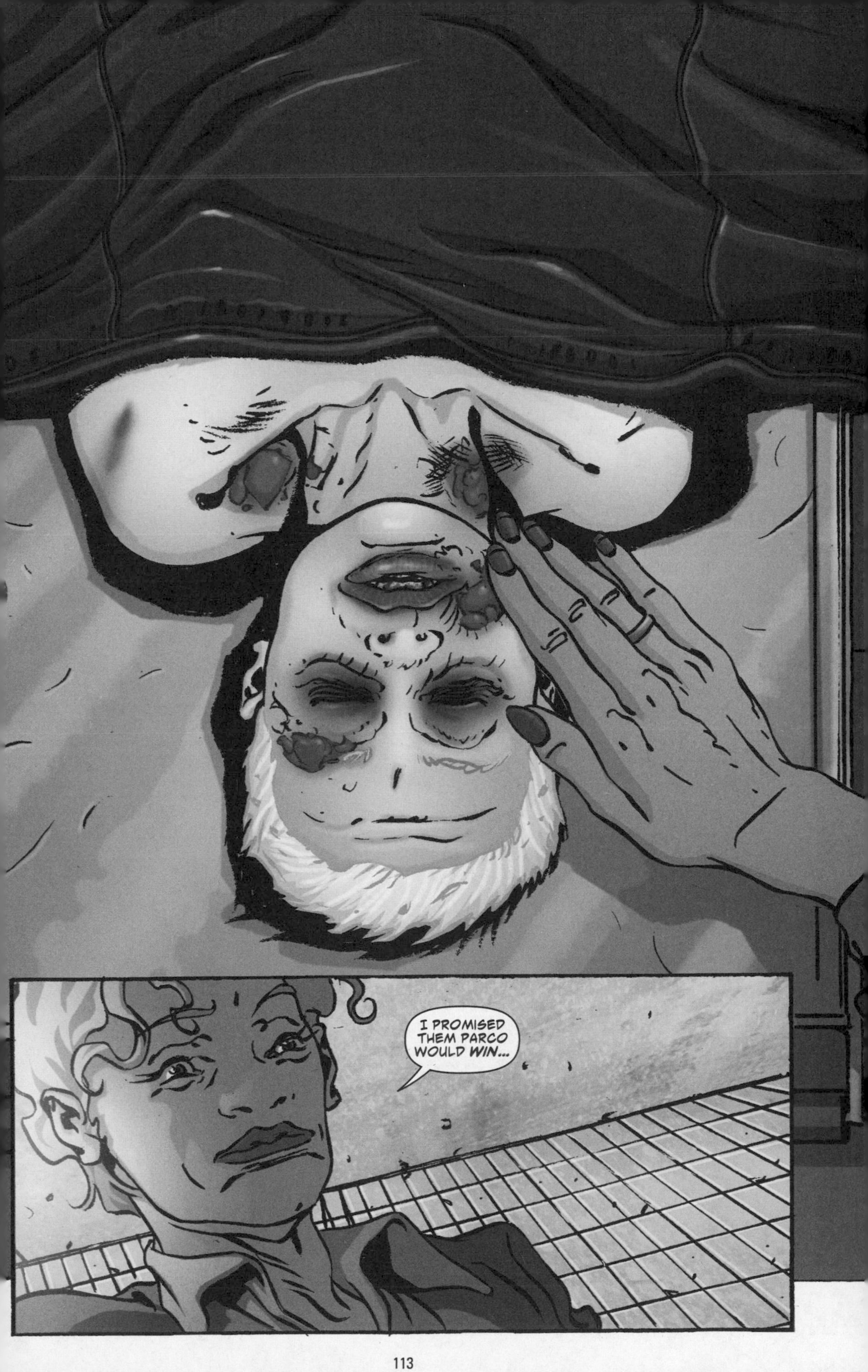
I PROMISED THEM PARCO WOULD WIN...

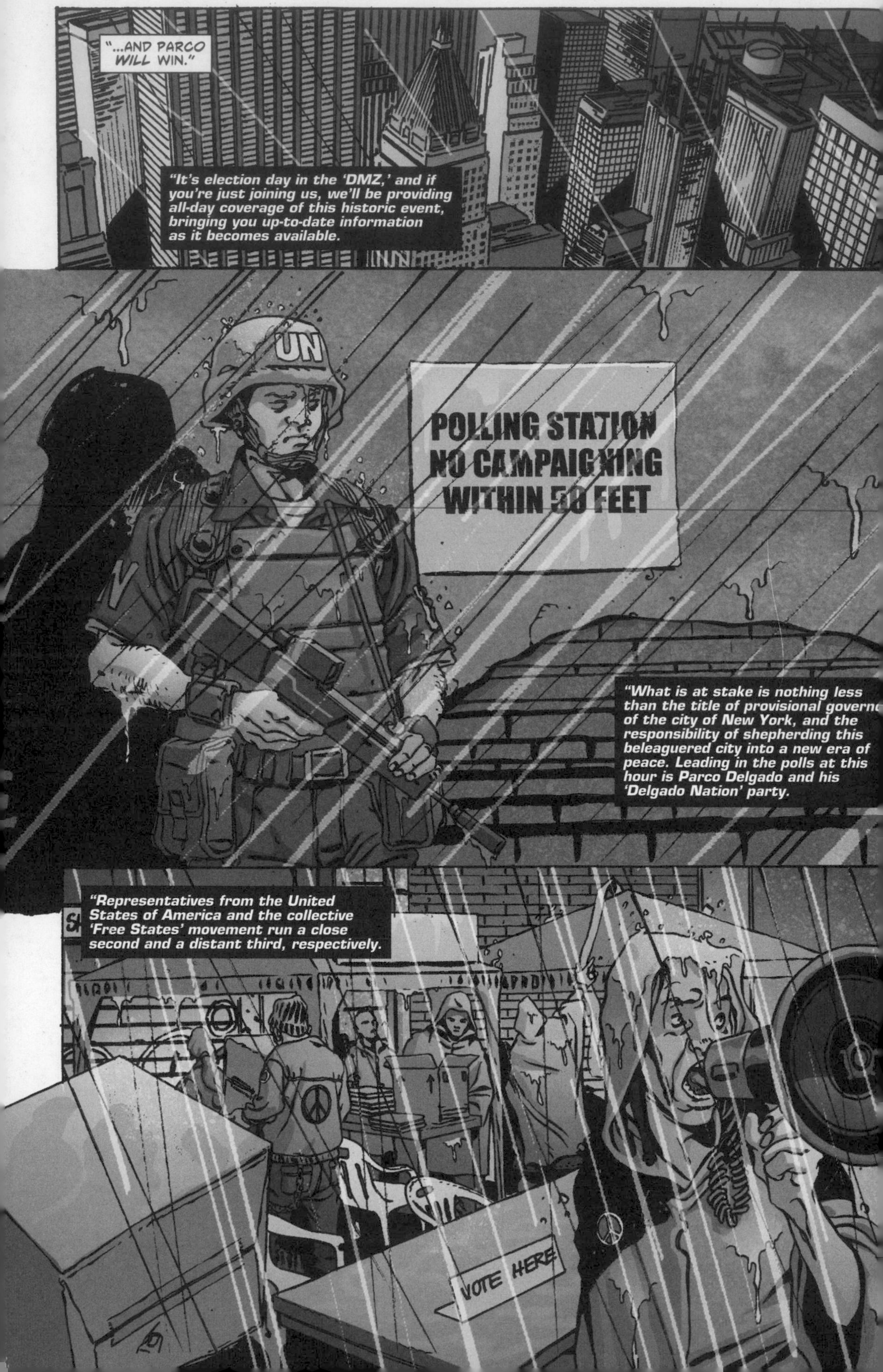
"...AND PARCO WILL WIN."
"It's election day in the 'DMZ,' and if you're just joining us, we'll be providing all-day coverage of this historic event, bringing you up-to-date information as it becomes available.
UN
POLLING STATION NO CAMPAIGNING WITHIN 50 FEET
"What is at stake is nothing less than the title of provisional governe of the city of New York, and the responsibility of shepherding this beleaguered city into a new era of peace. Leading in the polls at this hour is Parco Delgado and his 'Delgado Nation' party.
"Representatives from the United States of America and the collective 'Free States' movement run a close second and a distant third, respectively.
VOTE HERE

"After many weeks of hard campaigning, Mr. Delgado has proven to be a difficult opponent, and after the attempt on his life his popularity has only risen."

"But the question on everyone's lips is 'Where is Parco?' Will the candidate finally make a public appearance, especially on his own election day?"

"Liberty's own Matty Roth has been working close to the Delgado campaign and is reporting for us from the DMZ proper...do we have Matty on the line?"

"NO COMMENT."

OR "I QUIT." SURE, THAT WORKS TOO.

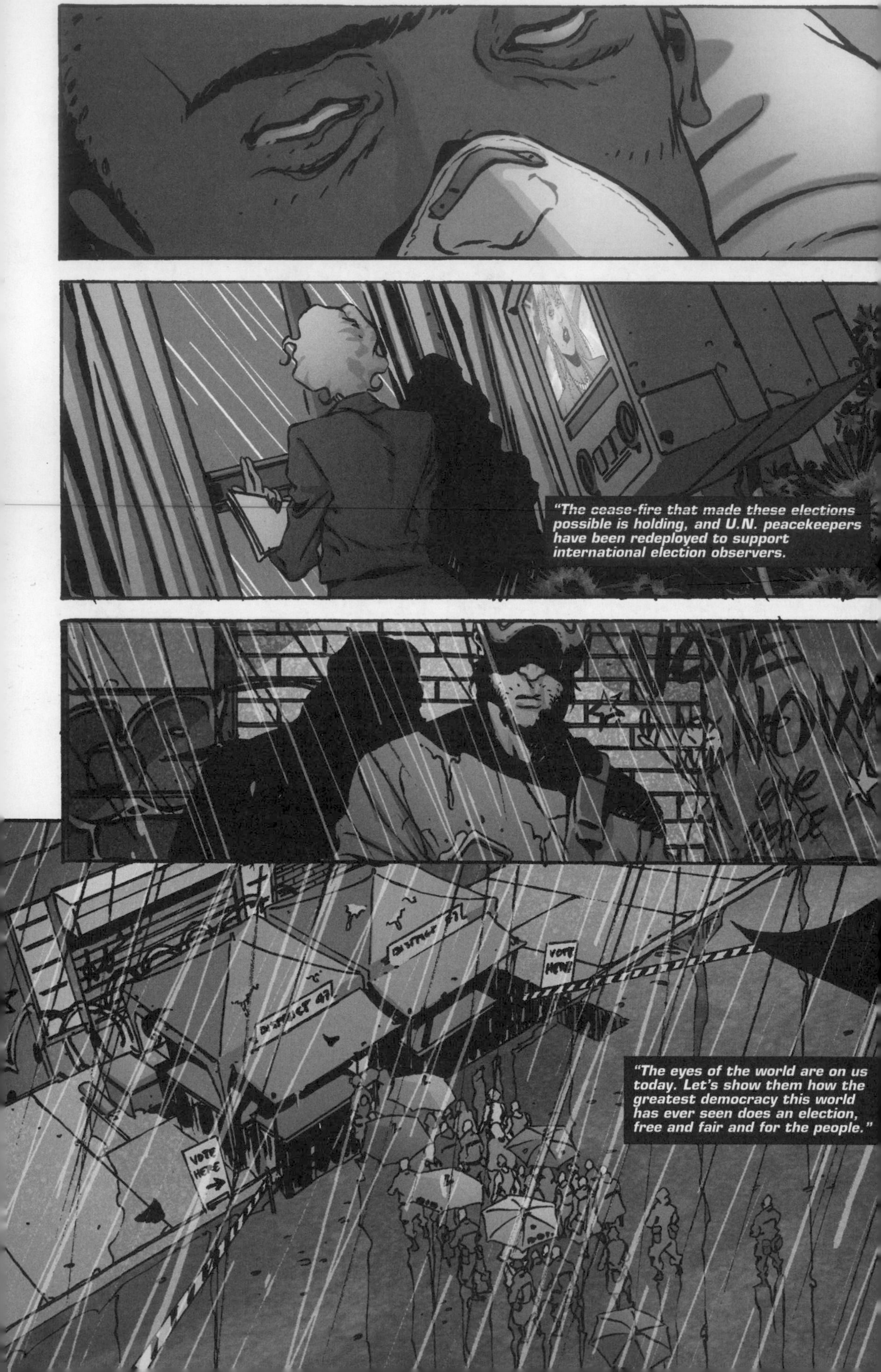
"The cease-fire that made these elections possible is holding, and U.N. peacekeepers have been redeployed to support international election observers.
DISTRICT 47
VOTE HERE
"The eyes of the world are on us today. Let's show them how the greatest democracy this world has ever seen does an election, free and fair and for the people."

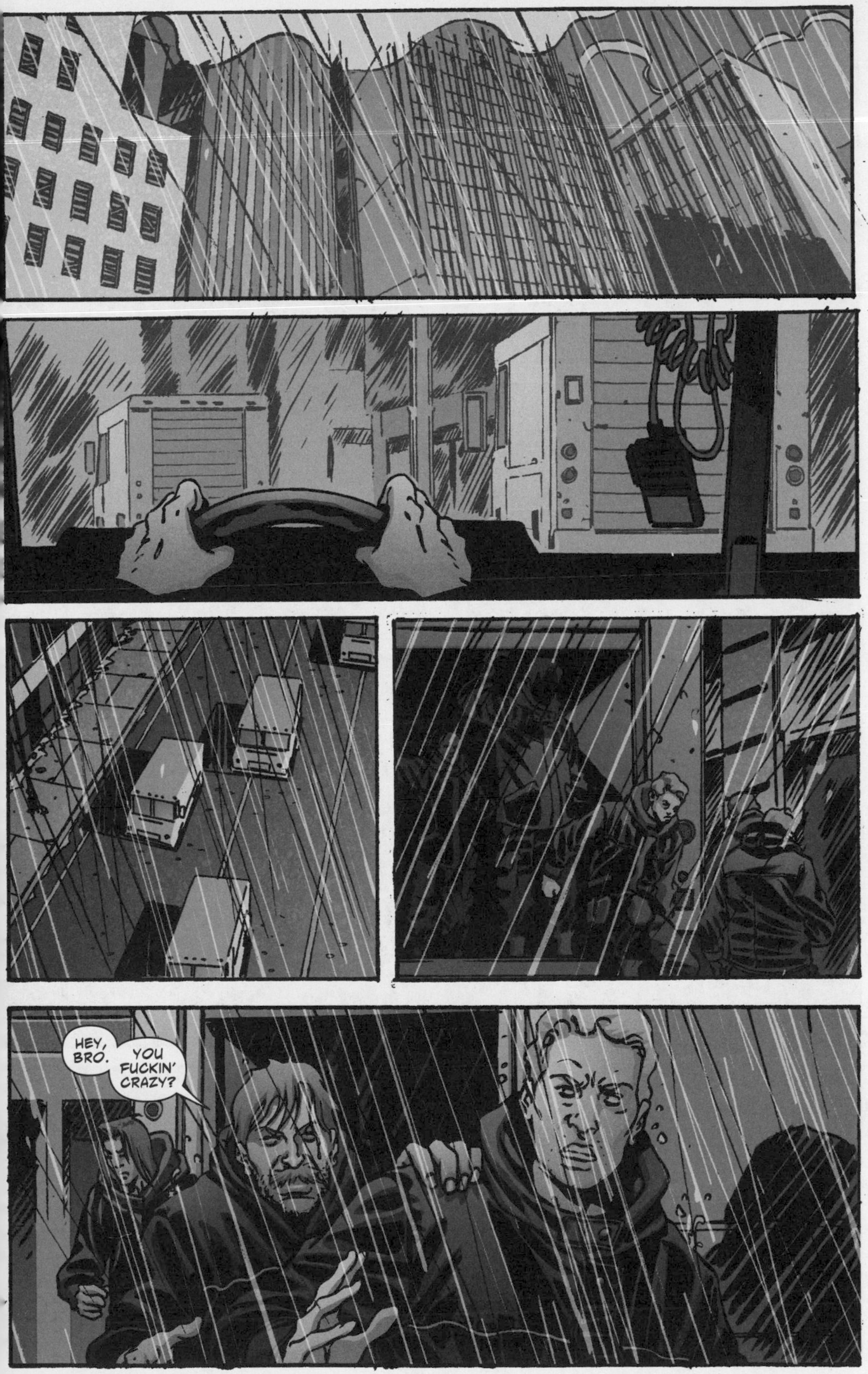
HEY, BRO.
YOU FUCKIN' CRAZY?

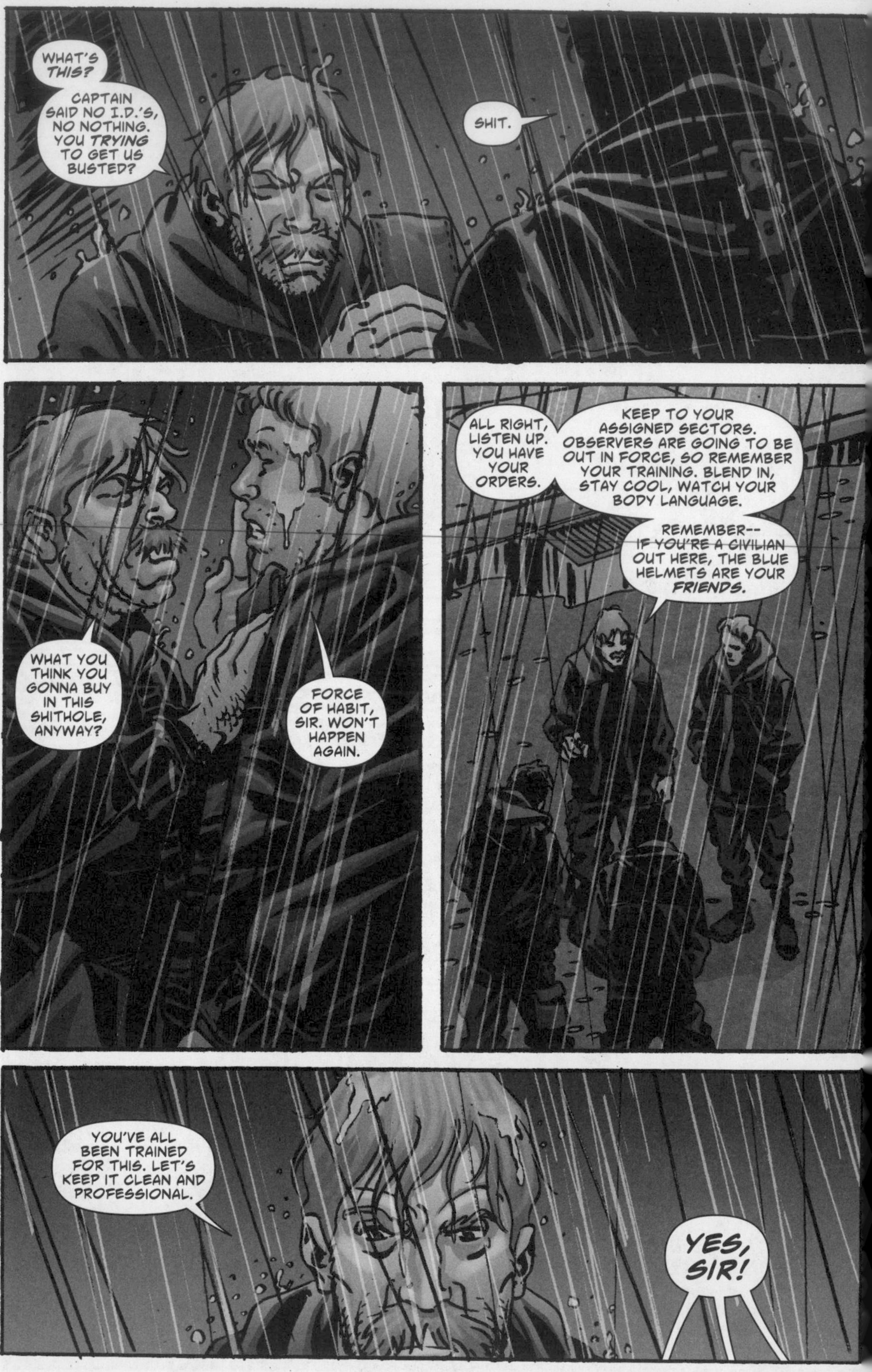
WHAT'S *THIS?*
CAPTAIN SAID NO I.D.'S, NO NOTHING. YOU *TRYING* TO GET US BUSTED?
SHIT.
WHAT YOU THINK YOU GONNA BUY IN THIS SHITHOLE, ANYWAY?
FORCE OF HABIT, SIR. WON'T HAPPEN AGAIN.
ALL RIGHT, LISTEN UP. YOU HAVE YOUR ORDERS.
KEEP TO YOUR ASSIGNED SECTORS. OBSERVERS ARE GOING TO BE OUT IN FORCE, SO REMEMBER YOUR TRAINING. BLEND IN, STAY COOL, WATCH YOUR BODY LANGUAGE.
REMEMBER-- IF YOU'RE A CIVILIAN OUT HERE, THE BLUE HELMETS ARE YOUR *FRIENDS.*
YOU'VE ALL BEEN TRAINED FOR THIS. LET'S KEEP IT CLEAN AND PROFESSIONAL.
YES, SIR!

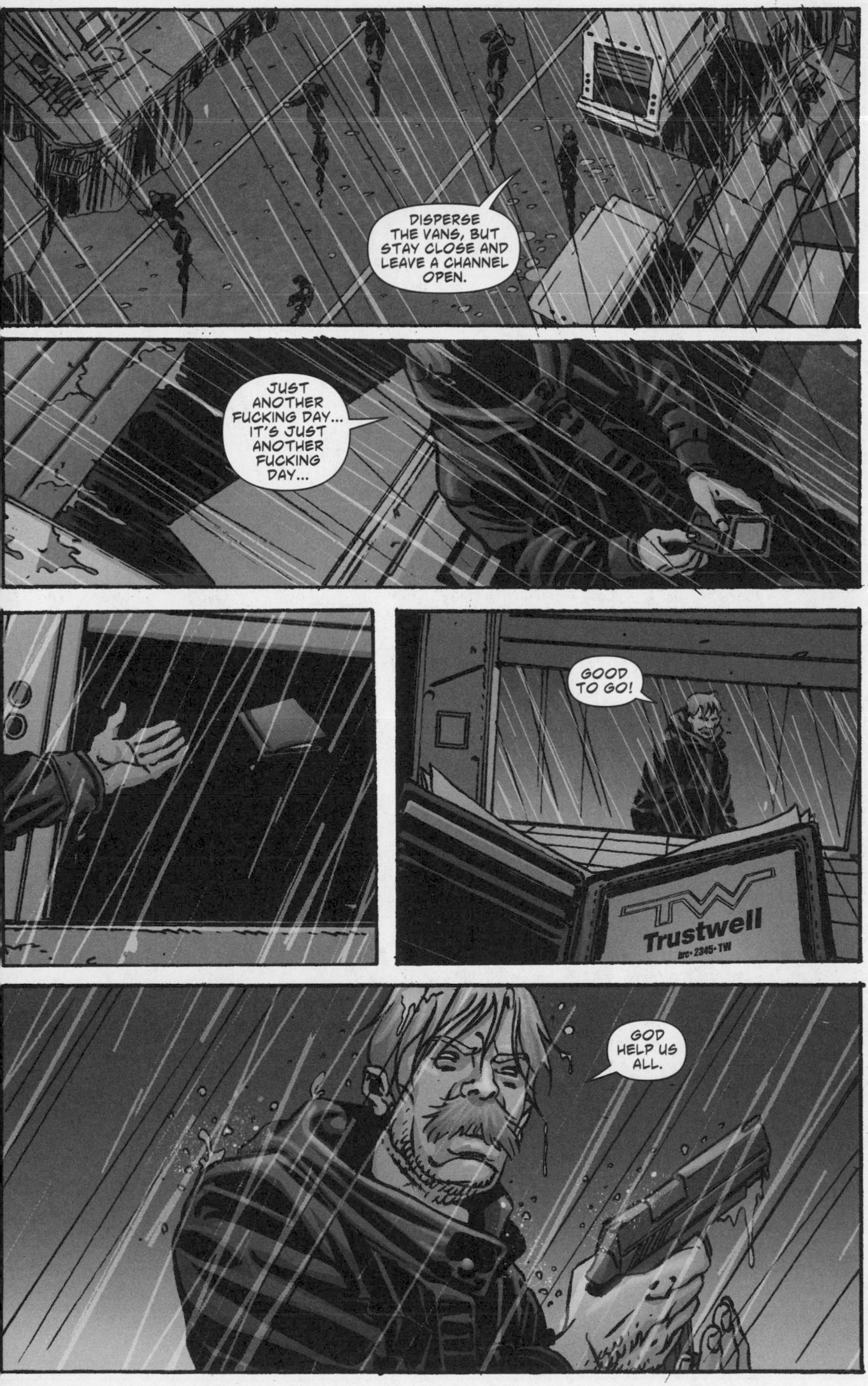
DISPERSE THE VANS, BUT STAY CLOSE AND LEAVE A CHANNEL OPEN.
JUST ANOTHER FUCKING DAY... IT'S JUST ANOTHER FUCKING DAY...
GOOD TO GO!
Trustwell
GOD HELP US ALL.

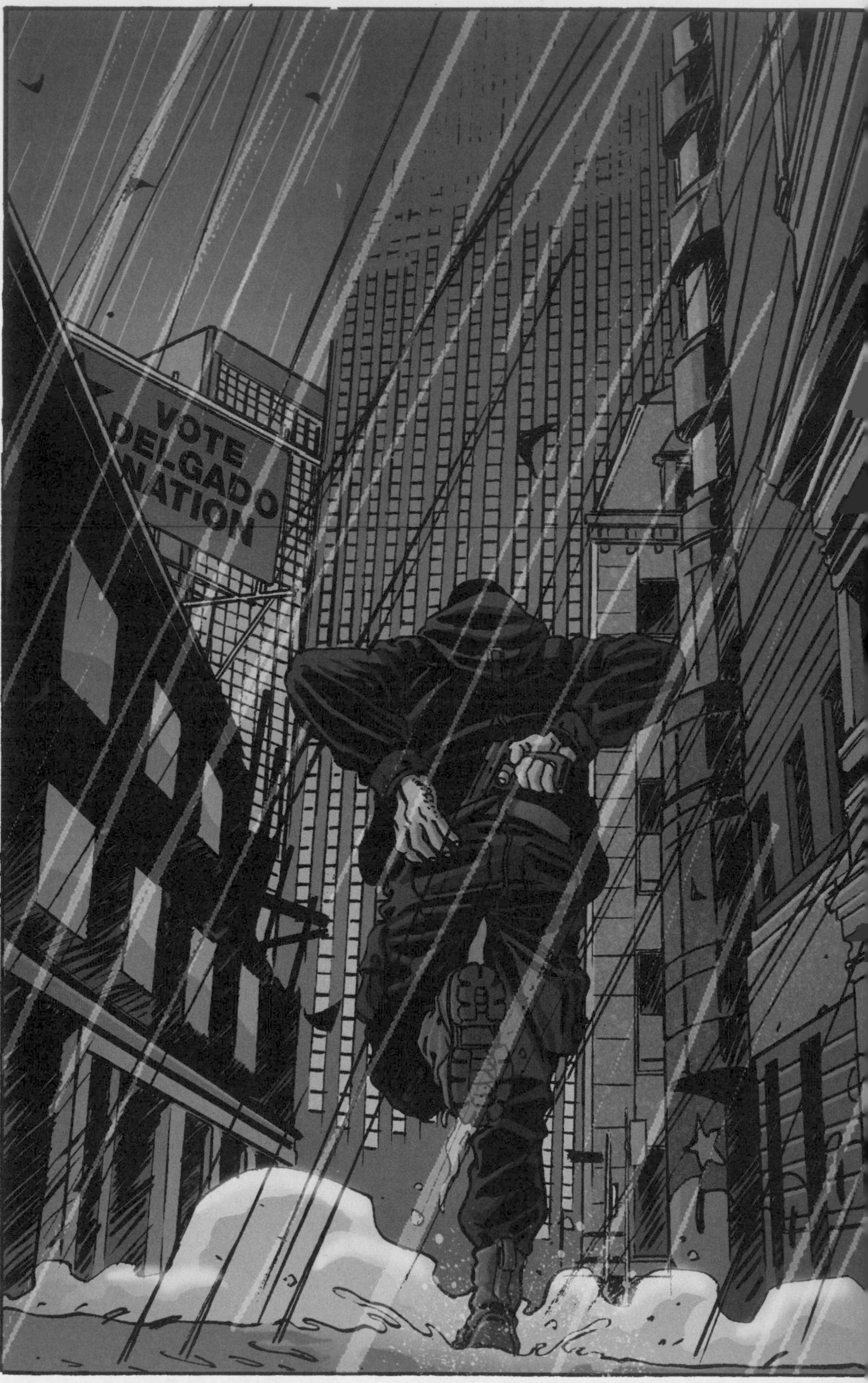
VOTE
DELGADO
NATION

DMZ VOTO

CHAPTER SIX

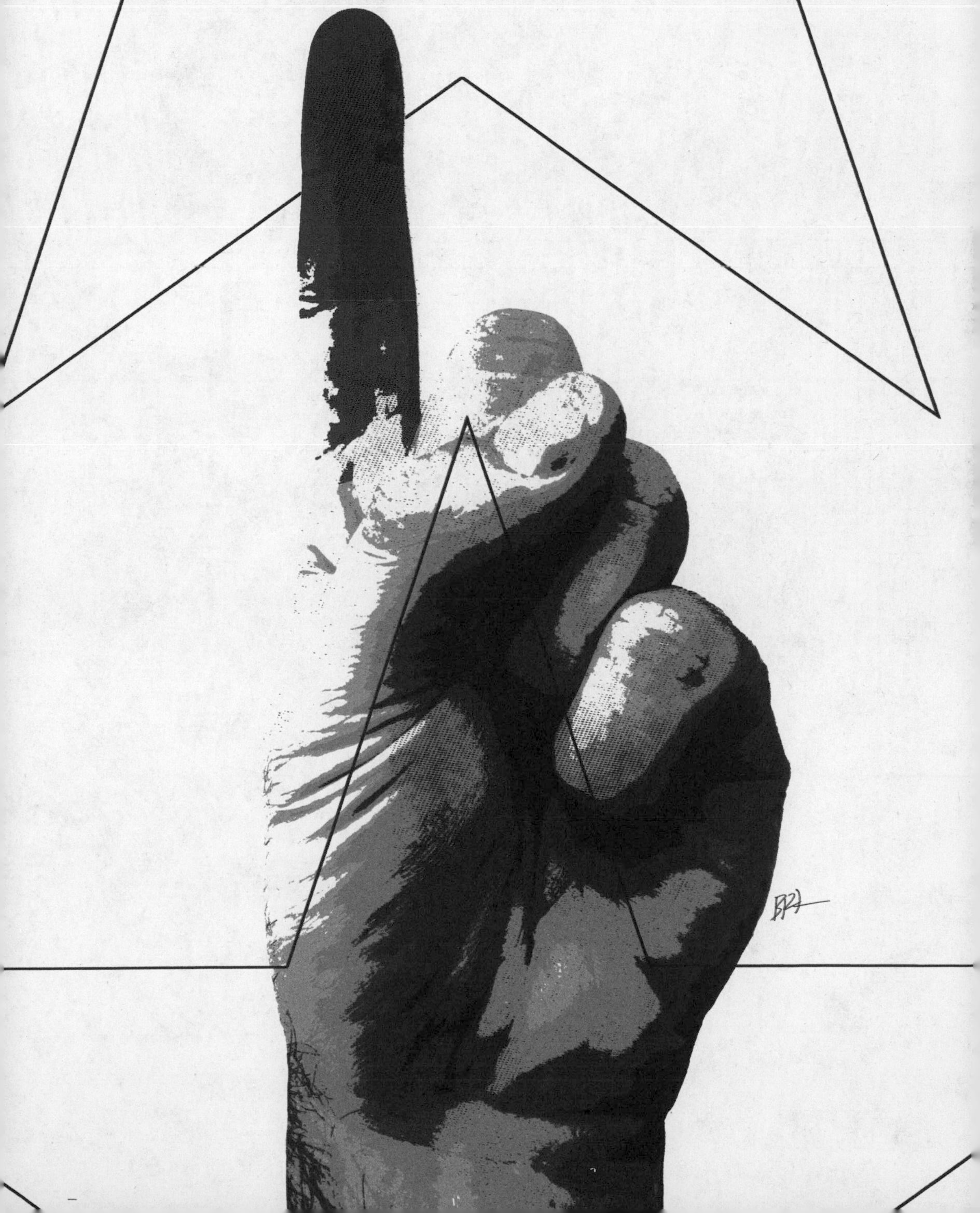

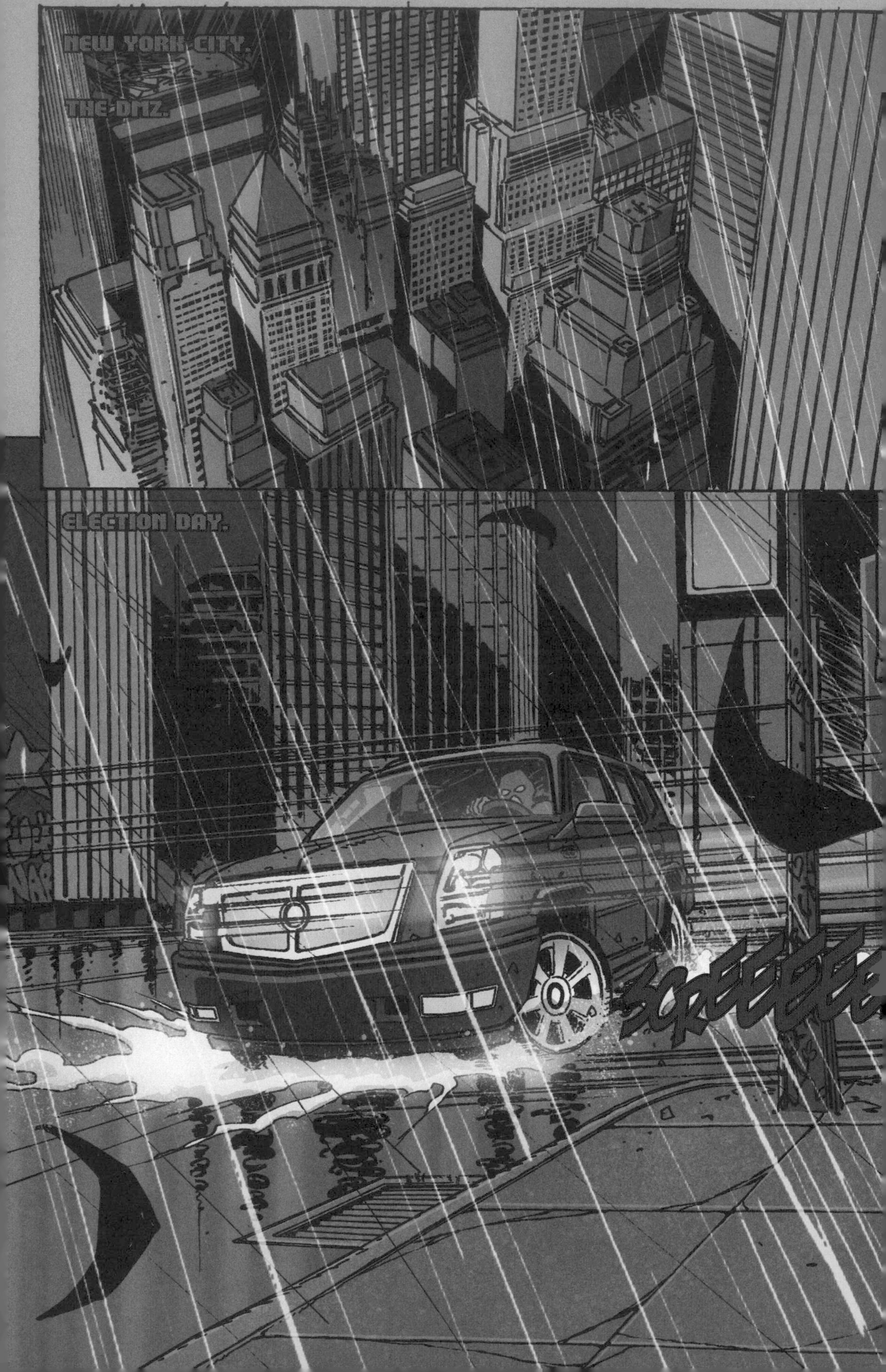
NEW YORK CITY.
THE DMZ.
ELECTION DAY.
SCREEEEE

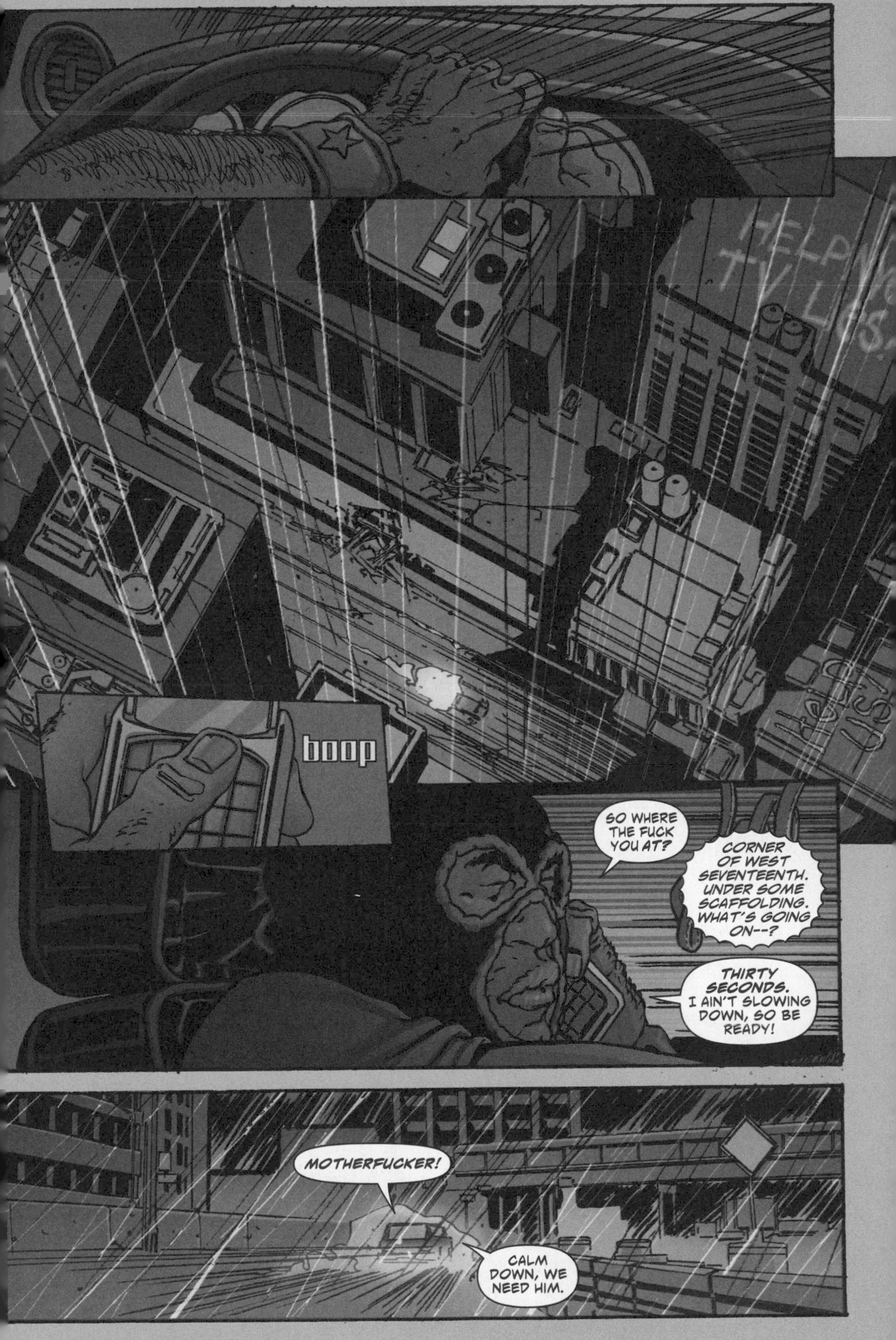
boop
SO WHERE THE FUCK YOU AT?
CORNER OF WEST SEVENTEENTH. UNDER SOME SCAFFOLDING. WHAT'S GOING ON--?
THIRTY SECONDS. I AIN'T SLOWING DOWN, SO BE READY!
MOTHERFUCKER!
CALM DOWN, WE NEED HIM.

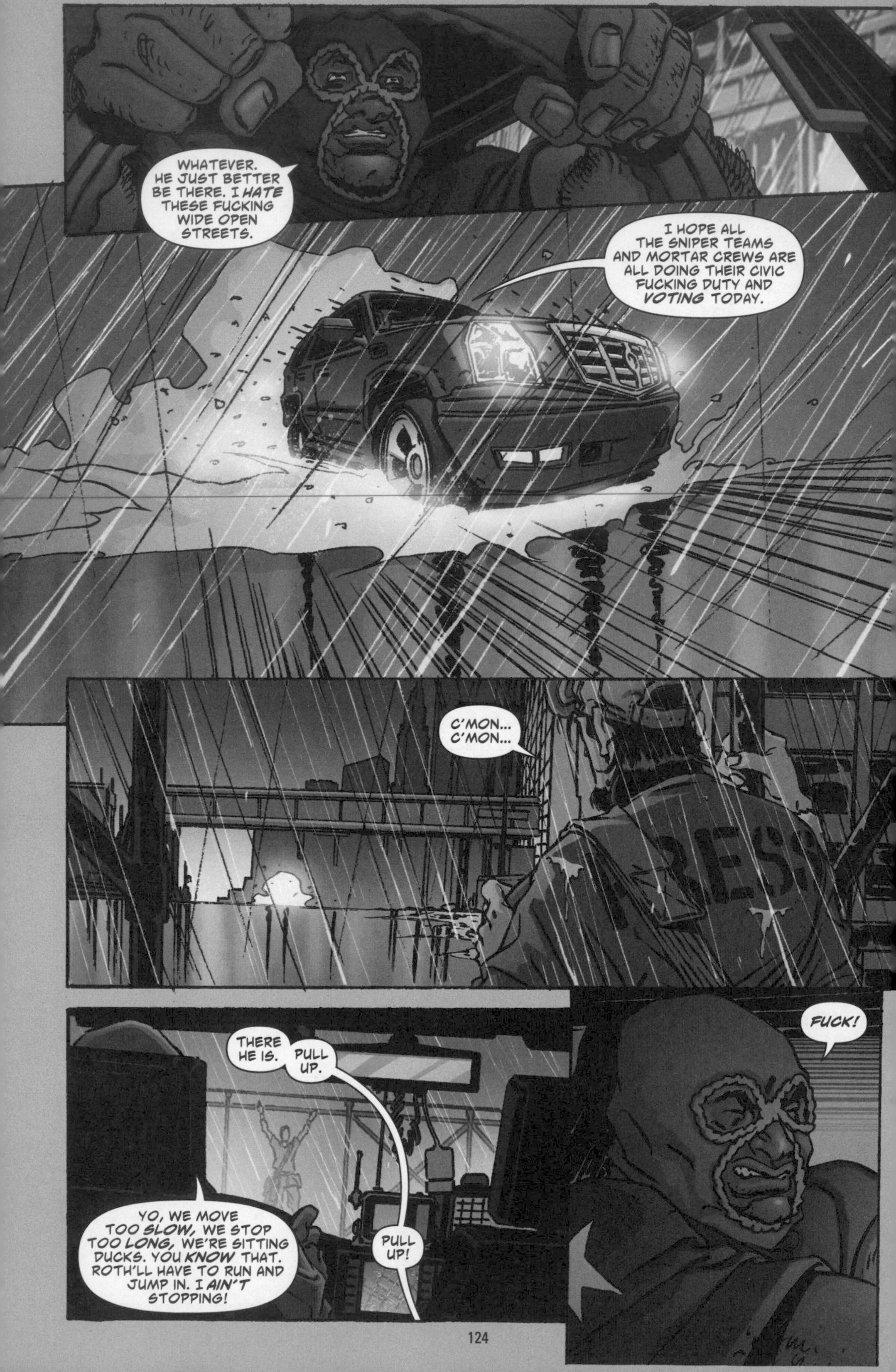
WHATEVER. HE JUST BETTER BE THERE. I HATE THESE FUCKING WIDE OPEN STREETS.
I HOPE ALL THE SNIPER TEAMS AND MORTAR CREWS ARE ALL DOING THEIR CIVIC FUCKING DUTY AND VOTING TODAY.
C'MON... C'MON...
THERE HE IS.
PULL UP.
YO, WE MOVE TOO SLOW, WE STOP TOO LONG, WE'RE SITTING DUCKS. YOU KNOW THAT. ROTH'LL HAVE TO RUN AND JUMP IN. I AIN'T STOPPING!
PULL UP!
FUCK!

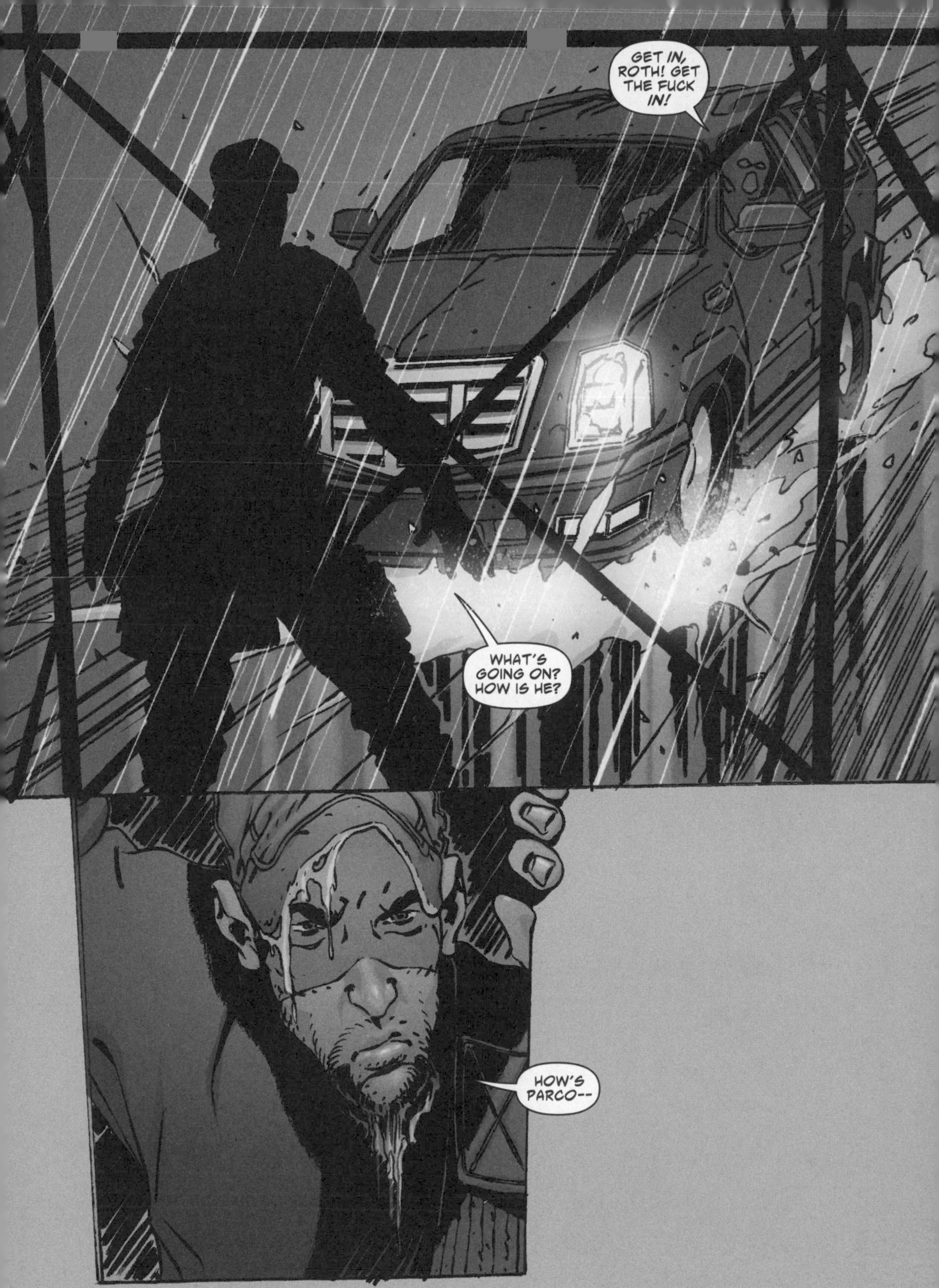
GET IN, ROTH! GET THE FUCK IN!
WHAT'S GOING ON? HOW IS HE?
HOW'S PARCO--

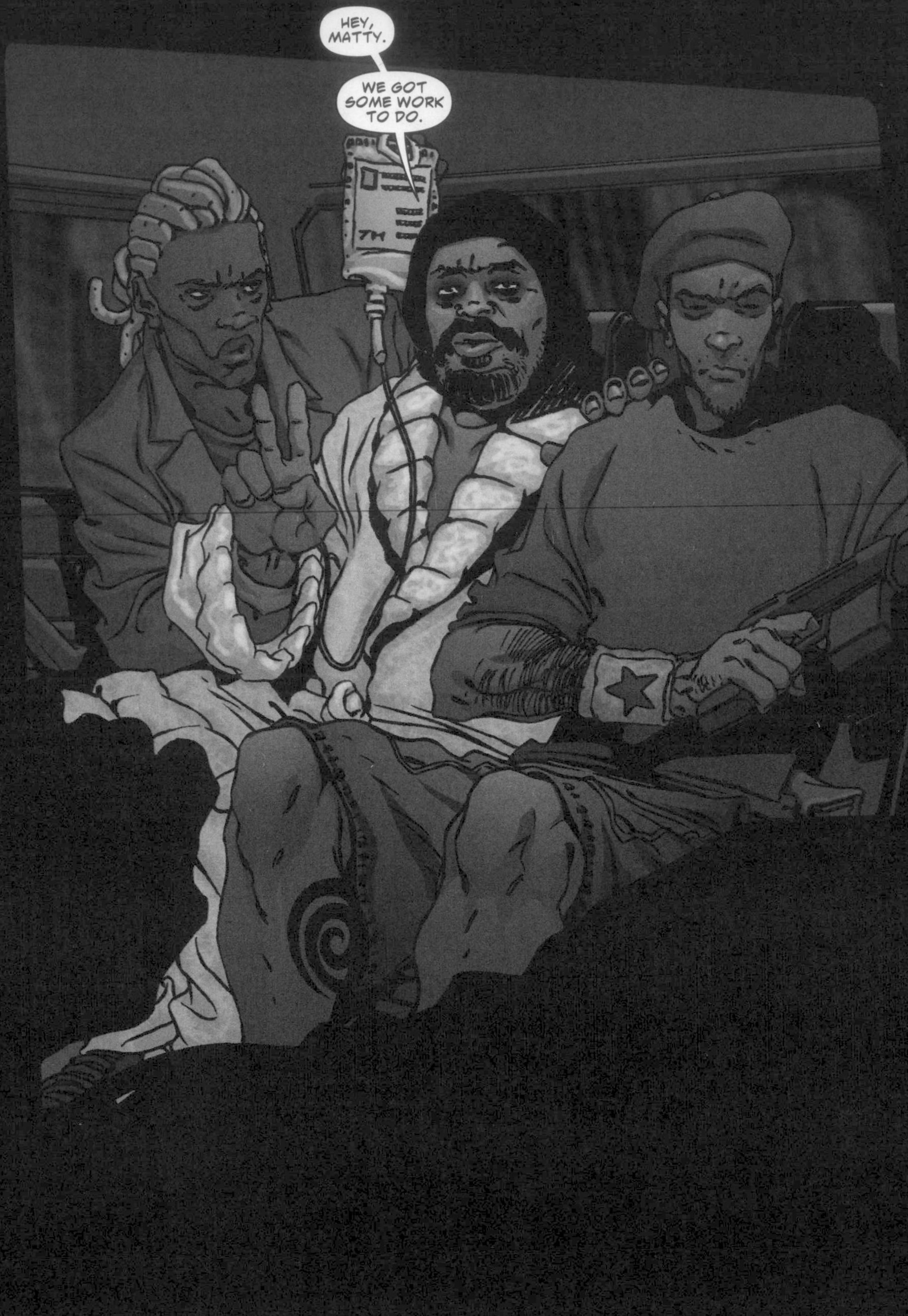
HEY, MATTY.
WE GOT SOME WORK TO DO.

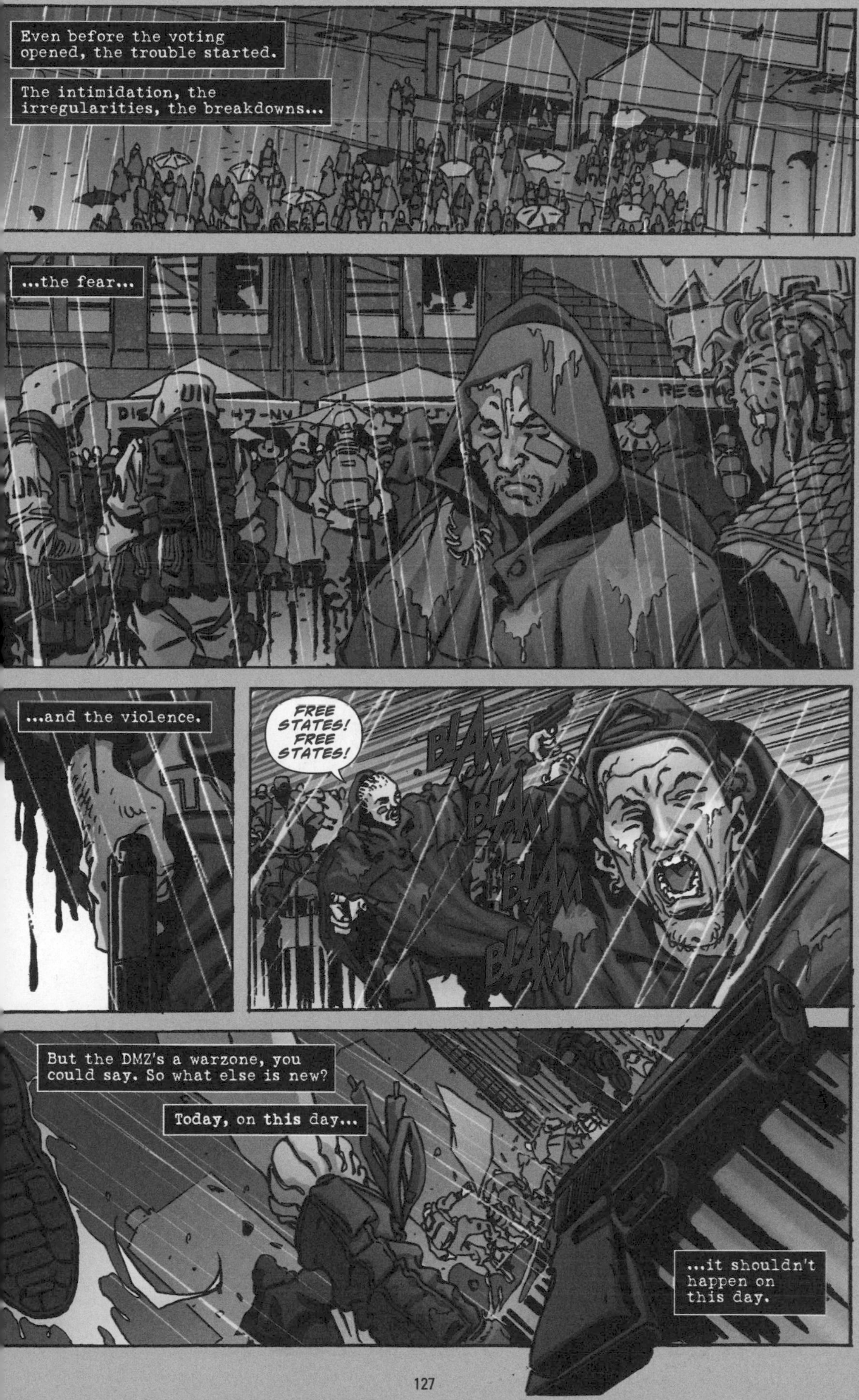
Even before the voting opened, the trouble started.
The intimidation, the irregularities, the breakdowns...
...the fear...
...and the violence.
FREE STATES! FREE STATES!
BLAM
BLAM
BLAM
BLAM
But the DMZ's a warzone, you could say. So what else is new?
Today, on this day...
...it shouldn't happen on this day.

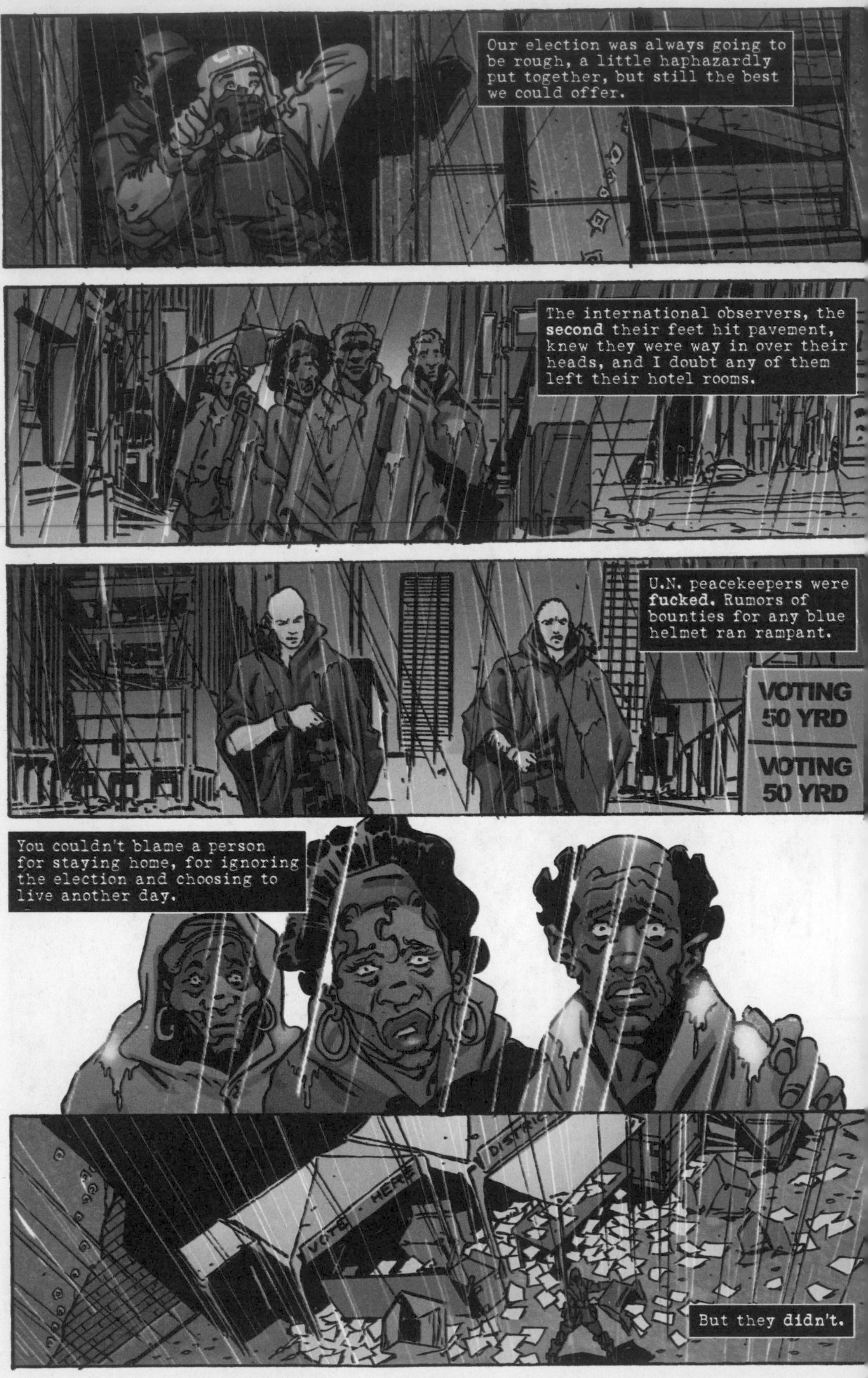

Our election was always going to be rough, a little haphazardly put together, but still the best we could offer.
The international observers, the **second** their feet hit pavement, knew they were way in over their heads, and I doubt any of them left their hotel rooms.
U.N. peacekeepers were **fucked.** Rumors of bounties for any blue helmet ran rampant.
VOTING 50 YRD
VOTING 50 YRD
You couldn't blame a person for staying home, for ignoring the election and choosing to live another day.
VOTE HERE
DISTRIC
But they **didn't.**

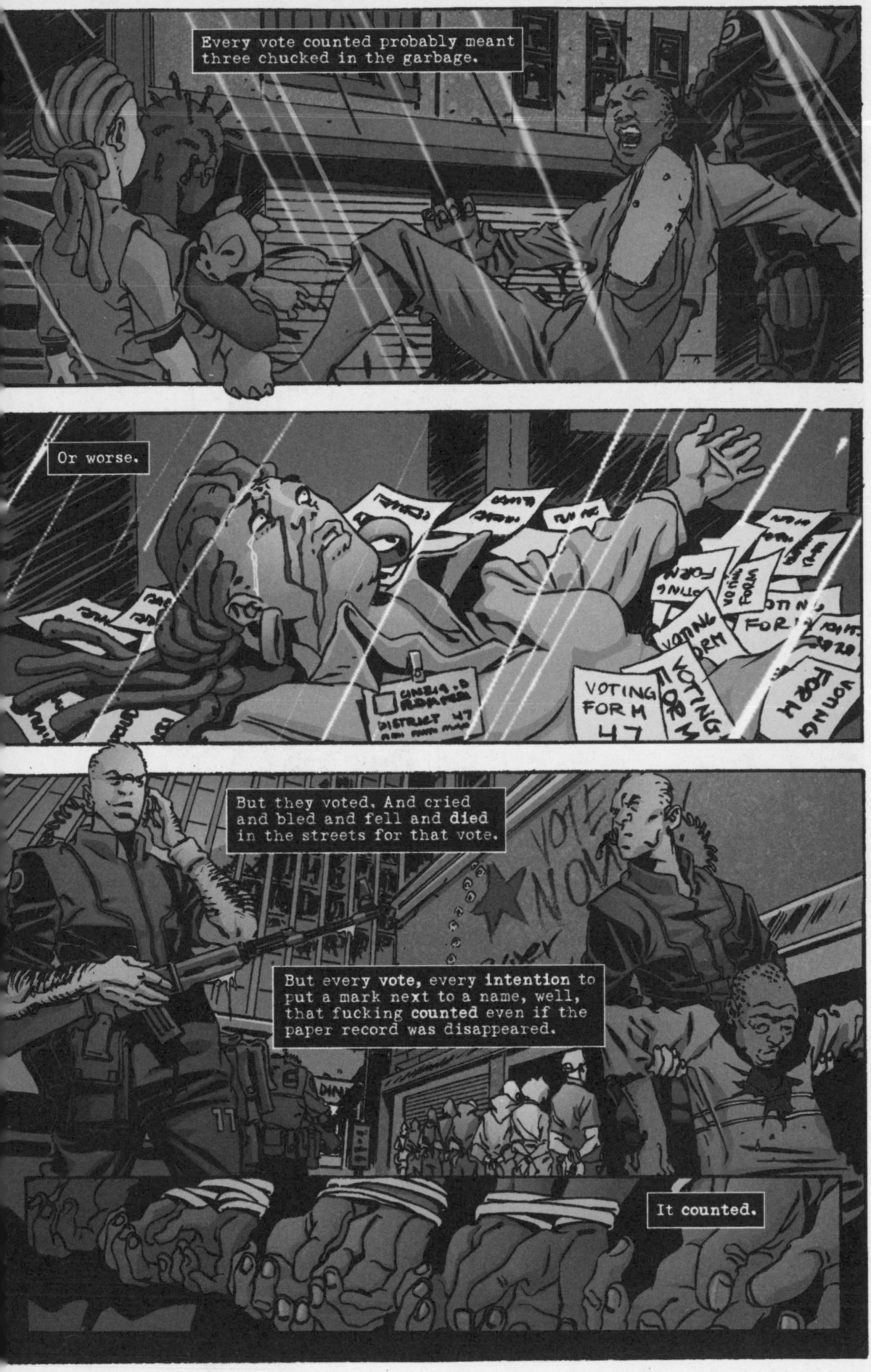
Every vote counted probably meant three chucked in the garbage.
Or worse.
VOTING FORM 47
DISTRICT 47
But they voted. And cried and bled and fell and died in the streets for that vote.
VOTE NOW
But every vote, every intention to put a mark next to a name, well, that fucking counted even if the paper record was disappeared.
It counted.

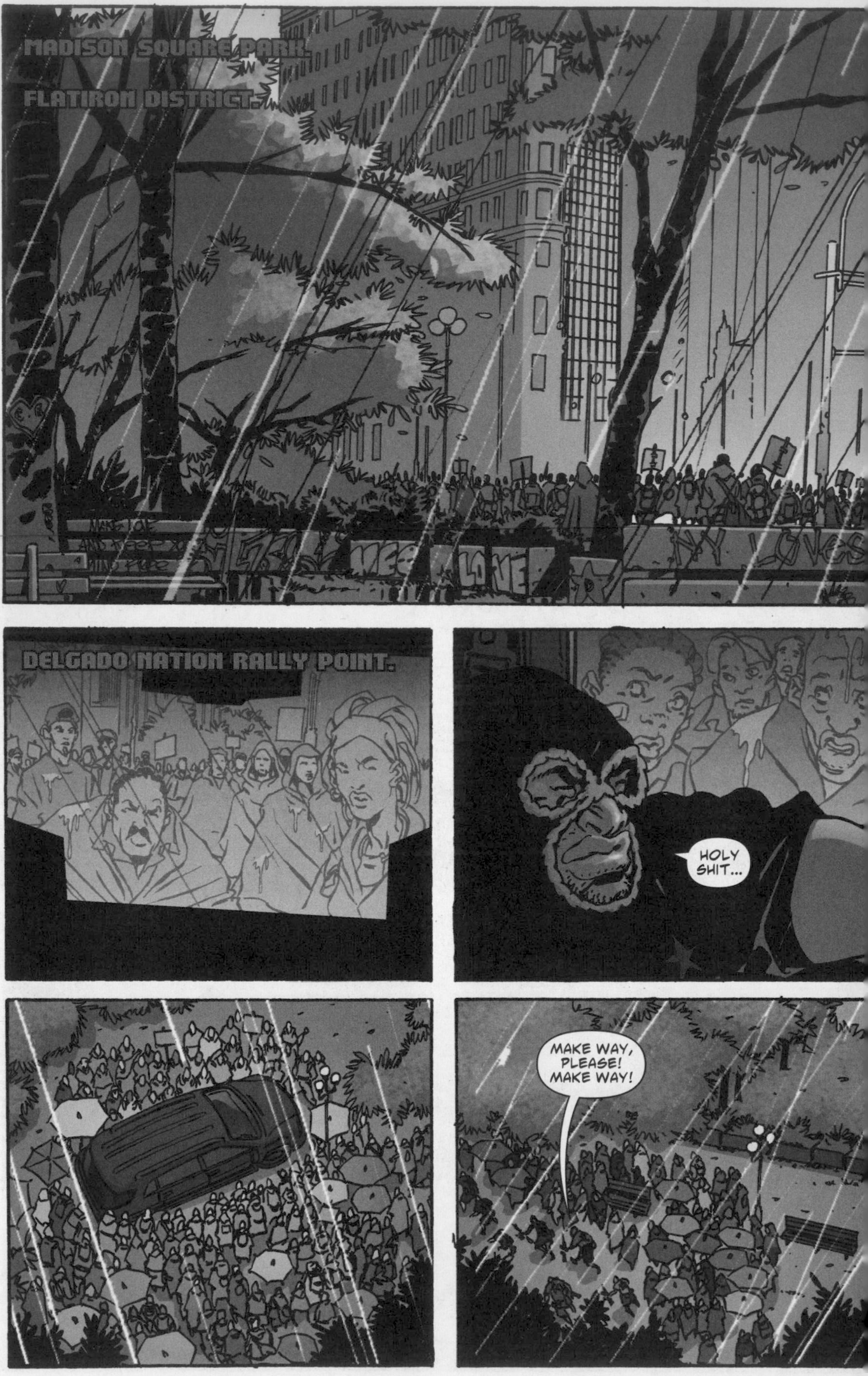
MADISON SQUARE PARK.
FLATIRON DISTRICT.
NY LOVES
DELGADO NATION RALLY POINT.
HOLY SHIT...
MAKE WAY, PLEASE! MAKE WAY!

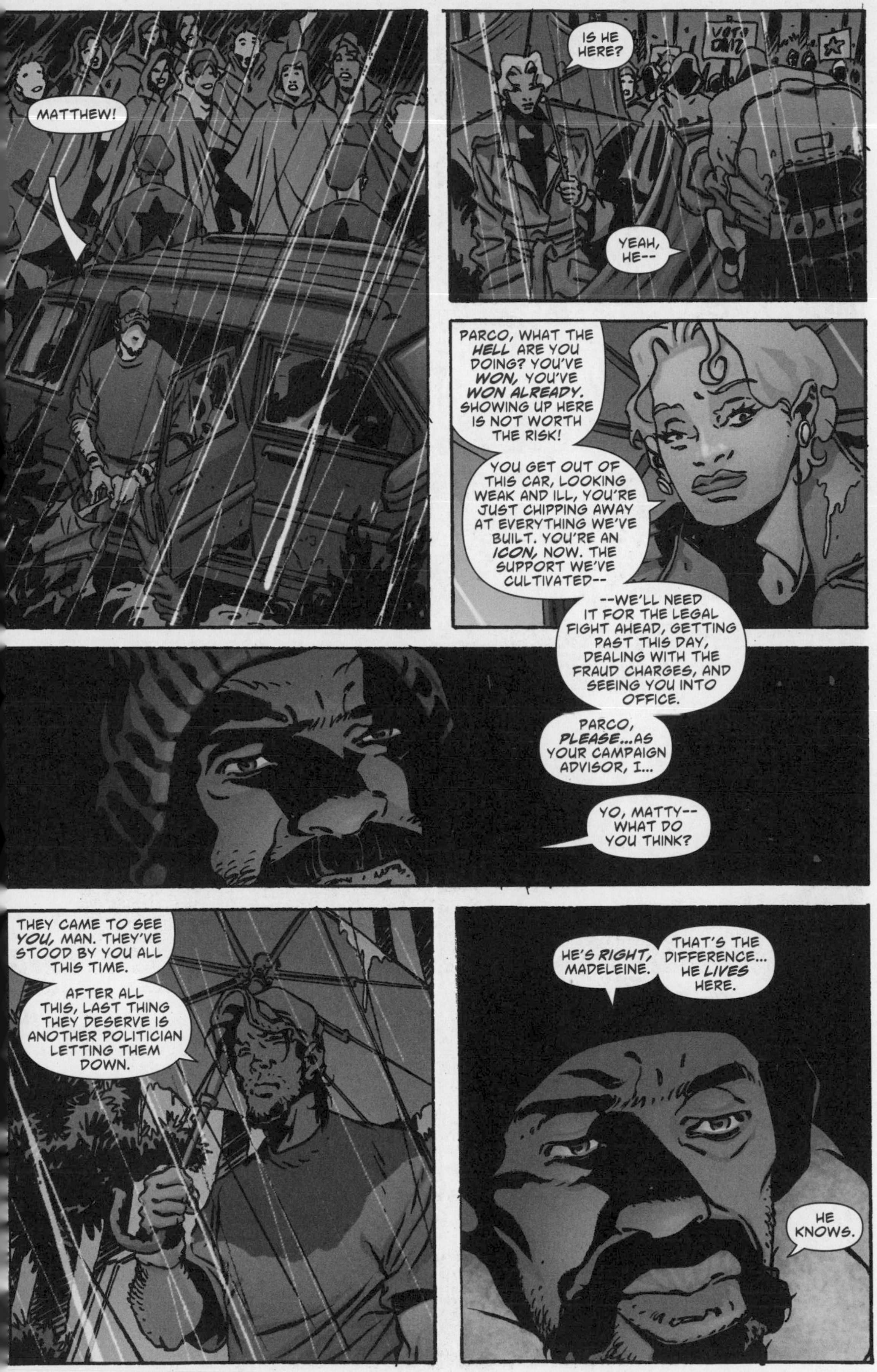
MATTHEW!
IS HE HERE?
YEAH, HE--
PARCO, WHAT THE HELL ARE YOU DOING? YOU'VE WON, YOU'VE WON ALREADY. SHOWING UP HERE IS NOT WORTH THE RISK!
YOU GET OUT OF THIS CAR, LOOKING WEAK AND ILL, YOU'RE JUST CHIPPING AWAY AT EVERYTHING WE'VE BUILT. YOU'RE AN ICON, NOW. THE SUPPORT WE'VE CULTIVATED--
--WE'LL NEED IT FOR THE LEGAL FIGHT AHEAD, GETTING PAST THIS DAY, DEALING WITH THE FRAUD CHARGES, AND SEEING YOU INTO OFFICE.
PARCO, PLEASE...AS YOUR CAMPAIGN ADVISOR, I...
YO, MATTY--WHAT DO YOU THINK?
THEY CAME TO SEE YOU, MAN. THEY'VE STOOD BY YOU ALL THIS TIME.
AFTER ALL THIS, LAST THING THEY DESERVE IS ANOTHER POLITICIAN LETTING THEM DOWN.
HE'S RIGHT, MADELEINE.
THAT'S THE DIFFERENCE... HE LIVES HERE.
HE KNOWS.

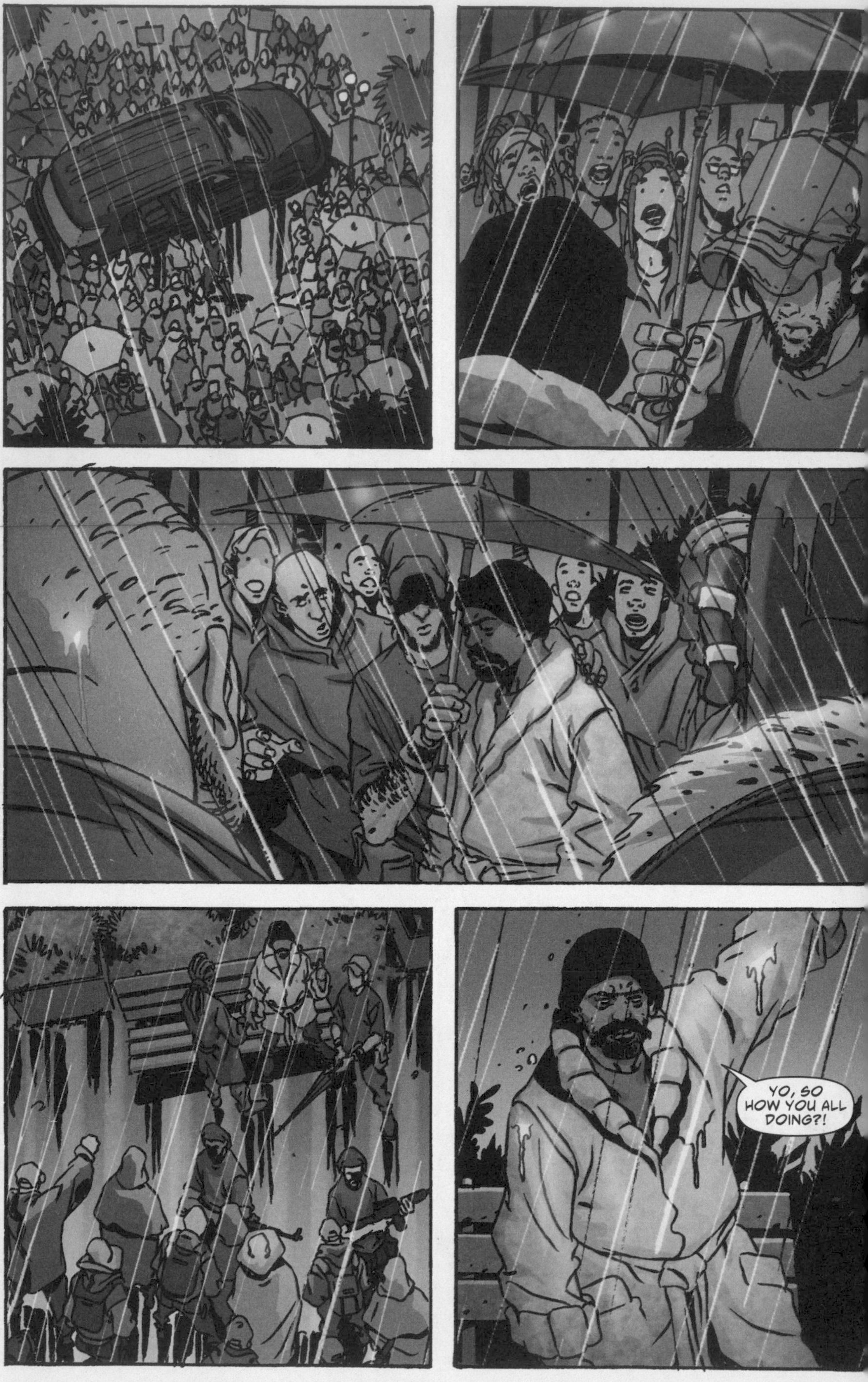
YO, SO
HOW YOU ALL
DOING?!

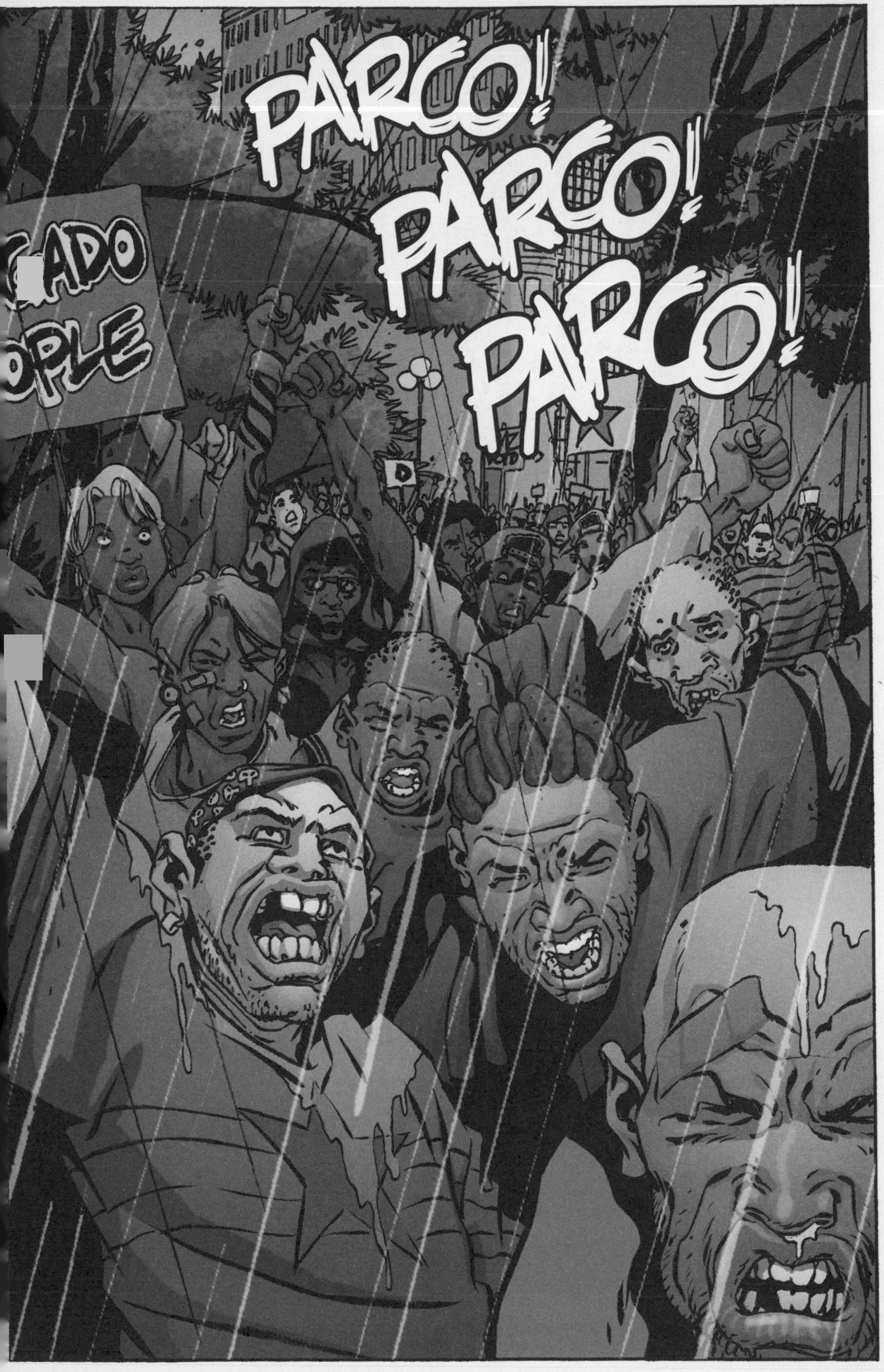
PARCO!
PARCO!
PARCO!

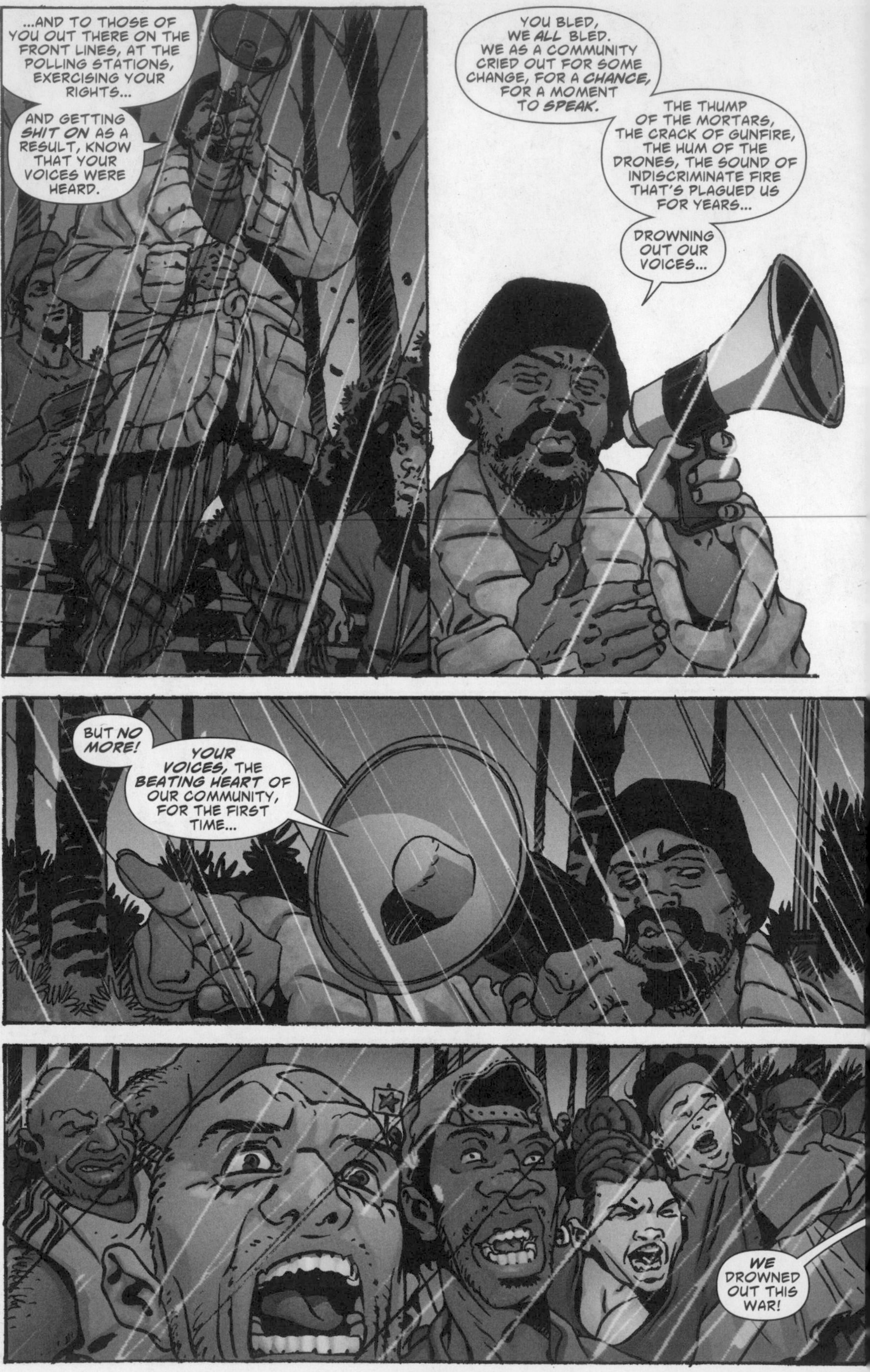
...AND TO THOSE OF YOU OUT THERE ON THE FRONT LINES, AT THE POLLING STATIONS, EXERCISING YOUR RIGHTS...
AND GETTING SHIT ON AS A RESULT, KNOW THAT YOUR VOICES WERE HEARD.
YOU BLED, WE ALL BLED. WE AS A COMMUNITY CRIED OUT FOR SOME CHANGE, FOR A CHANCE, FOR A MOMENT TO SPEAK.
THE THUMP OF THE MORTARS, THE CRACK OF GUNFIRE, THE HUM OF THE DRONES, THE SOUND OF INDISCRIMINATE FIRE THAT'S PLAGUED US FOR YEARS...
DROWNING OUT OUR VOICES...
BUT NO MORE!
YOUR VOICES, THE BEATING HEART OF OUR COMMUNITY, FOR THE FIRST TIME...
WE DROWNED OUT THIS WAR!

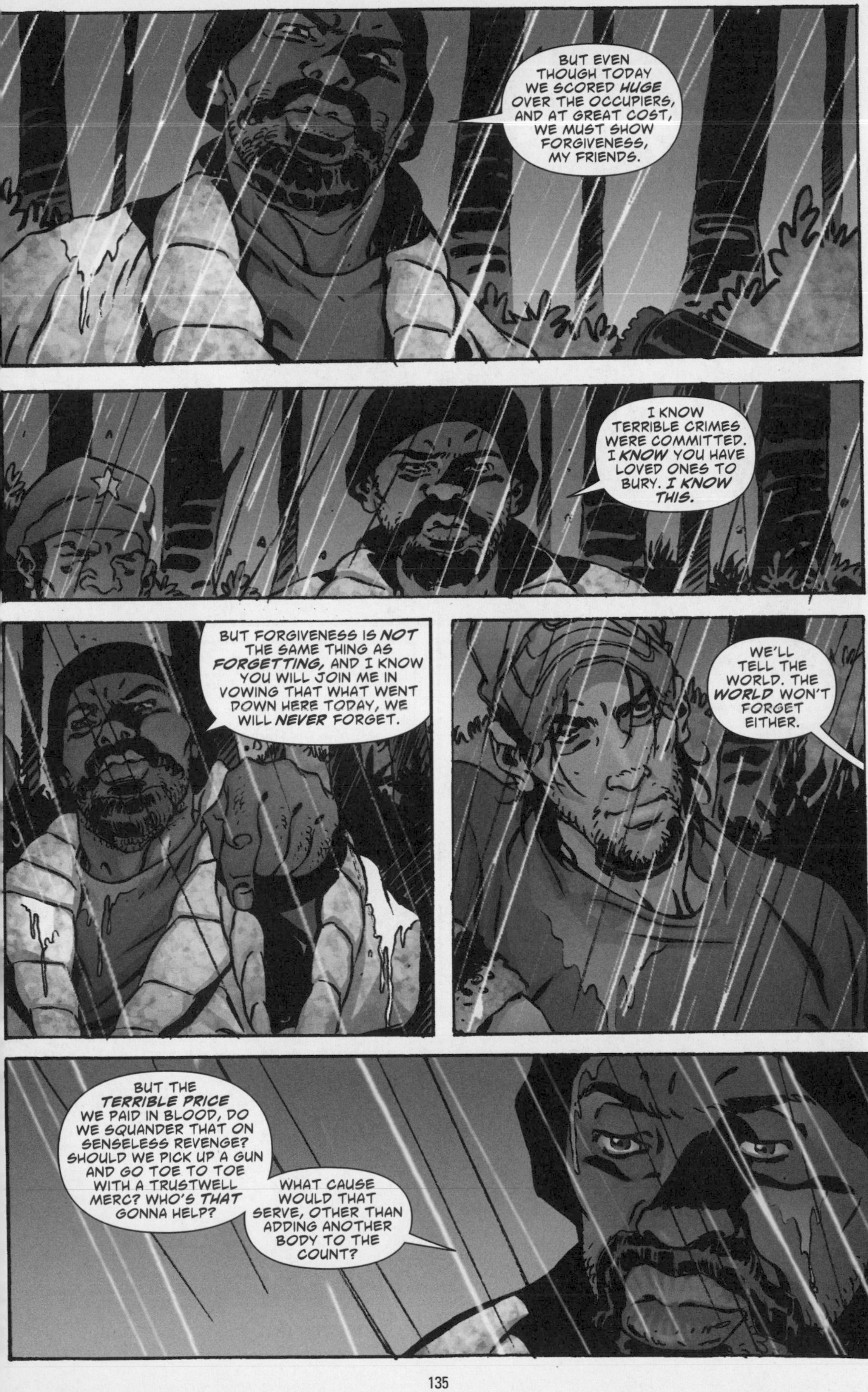
BUT EVEN THOUGH TODAY WE SCORED HUGE OVER THE OCCUPIERS, AND AT GREAT COST, WE MUST SHOW FORGIVENESS, MY FRIENDS.
I KNOW TERRIBLE CRIMES WERE COMMITTED. I KNOW YOU HAVE LOVED ONES TO BURY. I KNOW THIS.
BUT FORGIVENESS IS NOT THE SAME THING AS FORGETTING, AND I KNOW YOU WILL JOIN ME IN VOWING THAT WHAT WENT DOWN HERE TODAY, WE WILL NEVER FORGET.
WE'LL TELL THE WORLD. THE WORLD WON'T FORGET EITHER.
BUT THE TERRIBLE PRICE WE PAID IN BLOOD, DO WE SQUANDER THAT ON SENSELESS REVENGE? SHOULD WE PICK UP A GUN AND GO TOE TO TOE WITH A TRUSTWELL MERC? WHO'S THAT GONNA HELP?
WHAT CAUSE WOULD THAT SERVE, OTHER THAN ADDING ANOTHER BODY TO THE COUNT?

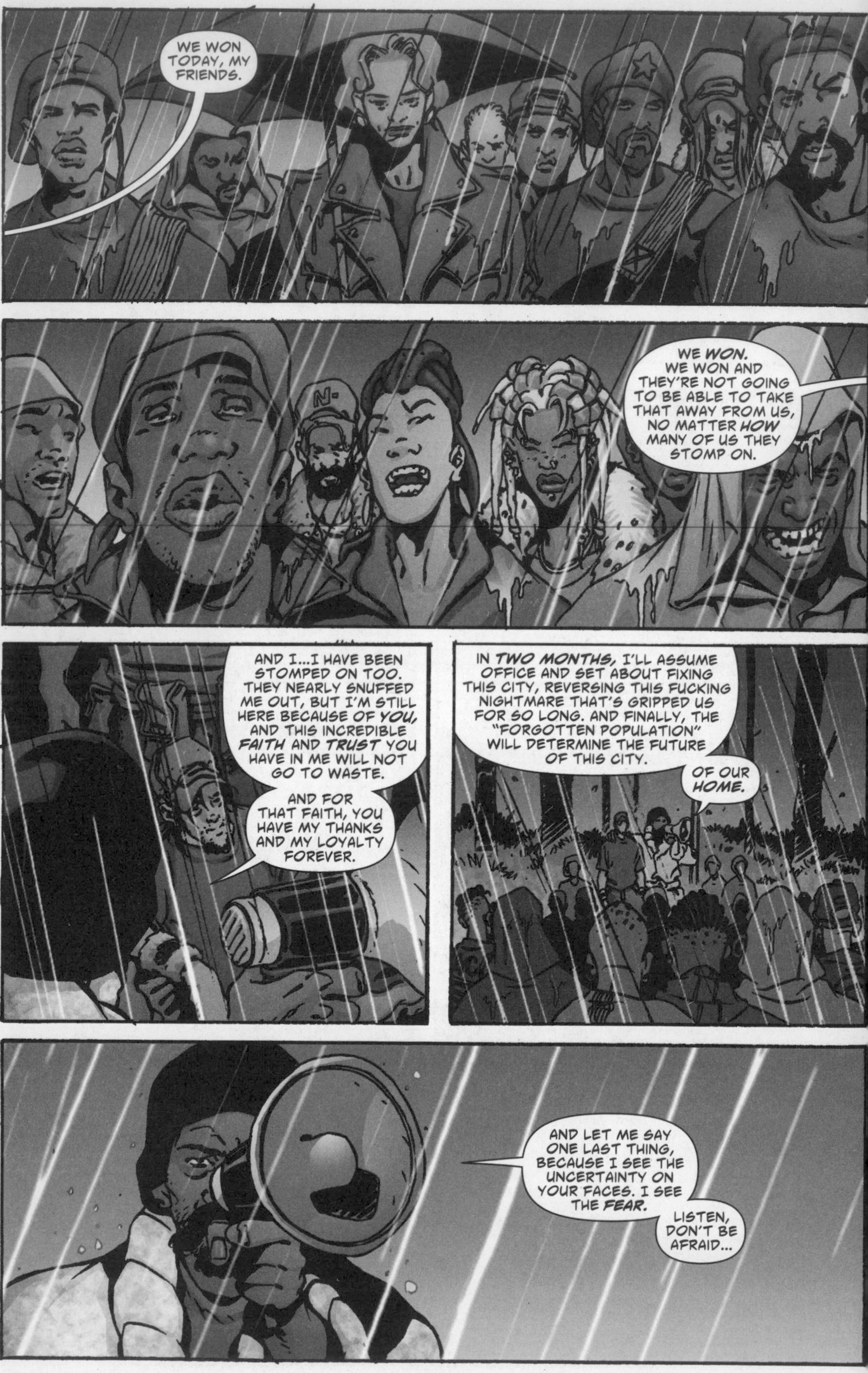
WE WON TODAY, MY FRIENDS.
WE *WON.* WE WON AND THEY'RE NOT GOING TO BE ABLE TO TAKE THAT AWAY FROM US, NO MATTER *HOW* MANY OF US THEY STOMP ON.
AND I...I HAVE BEEN STOMPED ON TOO. THEY NEARLY SNUFFED ME OUT, BUT I'M STILL HERE BECAUSE OF *YOU,* AND THIS INCREDIBLE *FAITH* AND *TRUST* YOU HAVE IN ME WILL NOT GO TO WASTE.
AND FOR THAT FAITH, YOU HAVE MY THANKS AND MY LOYALTY FOREVER.
IN *TWO MONTHS,* I'LL ASSUME OFFICE AND SET ABOUT FIXING THIS CITY, REVERSING THIS FUCKING NIGHTMARE THAT'S GRIPPED US FOR SO LONG. AND FINALLY, THE "FORGOTTEN POPULATION" WILL DETERMINE THE FUTURE OF THIS CITY.
OF OUR *HOME.*
AND LET ME SAY ONE LAST THING, BECAUSE I SEE THE UNCERTAINTY ON YOUR FACES. I SEE THE *FEAR.*
LISTEN, DON'T BE AFRAID...

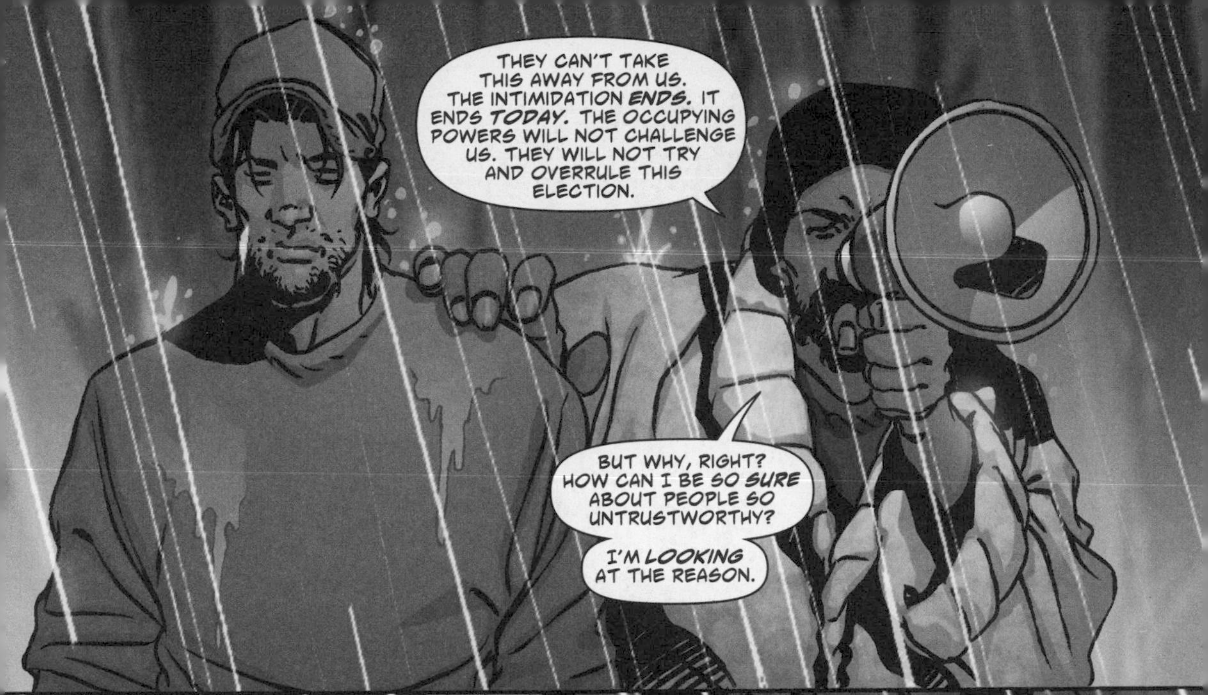
THEY CAN'T TAKE THIS AWAY FROM US. THE INTIMIDATION ENDS. IT ENDS TODAY. THE OCCUPYING POWERS WILL NOT CHALLENGE US. THEY WILL NOT TRY AND OVERRULE THIS ELECTION.
BUT WHY, RIGHT? HOW CAN I BE SO SURE ABOUT PEOPLE SO UNTRUSTWORTHY?
I'M LOOKING AT THE REASON.

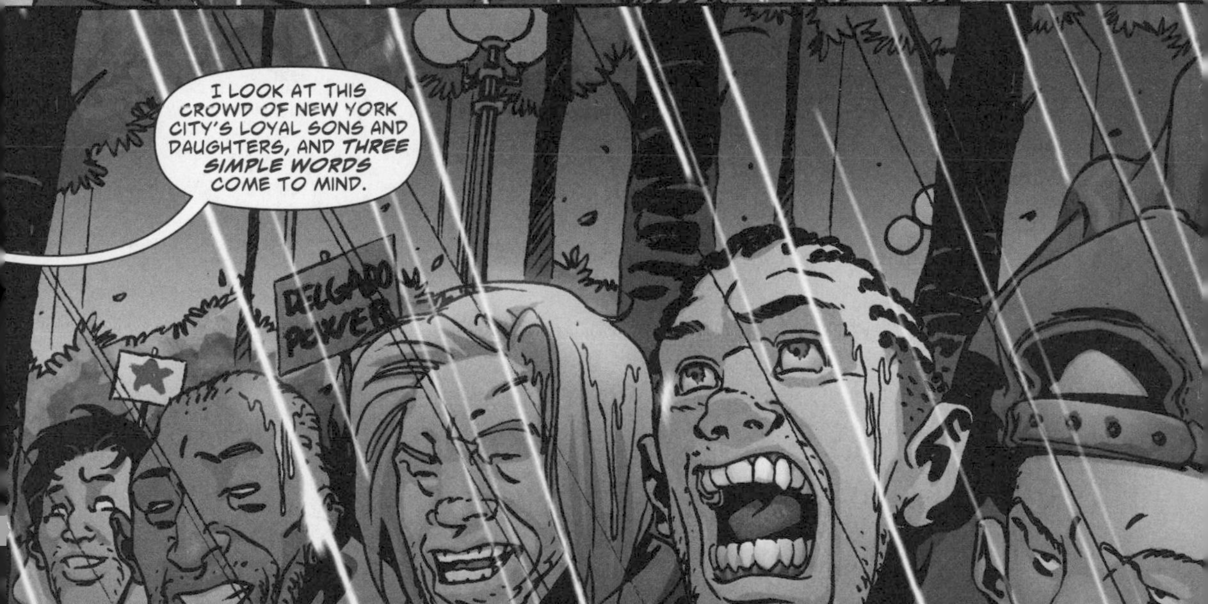
I LOOK AT THIS CROWD OF NEW YORK CITY'S LOYAL SONS AND DAUGHTERS, AND THREE SIMPLE WORDS COME TO MIND.
DELGADO POWER

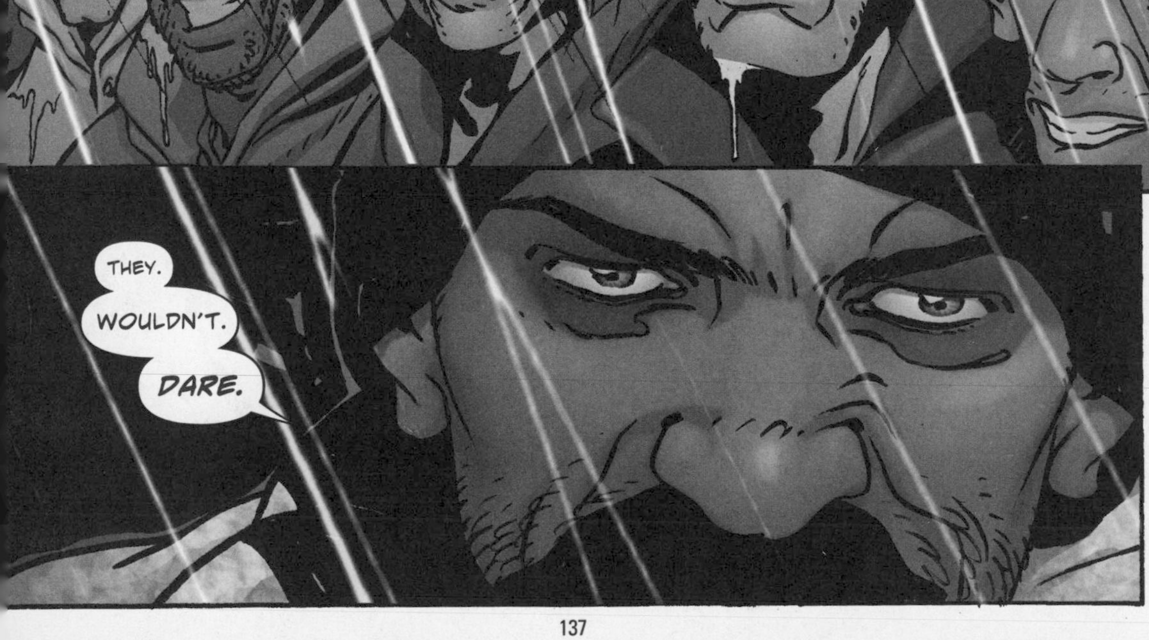
THEY.
WOULDN'T.
DARE.

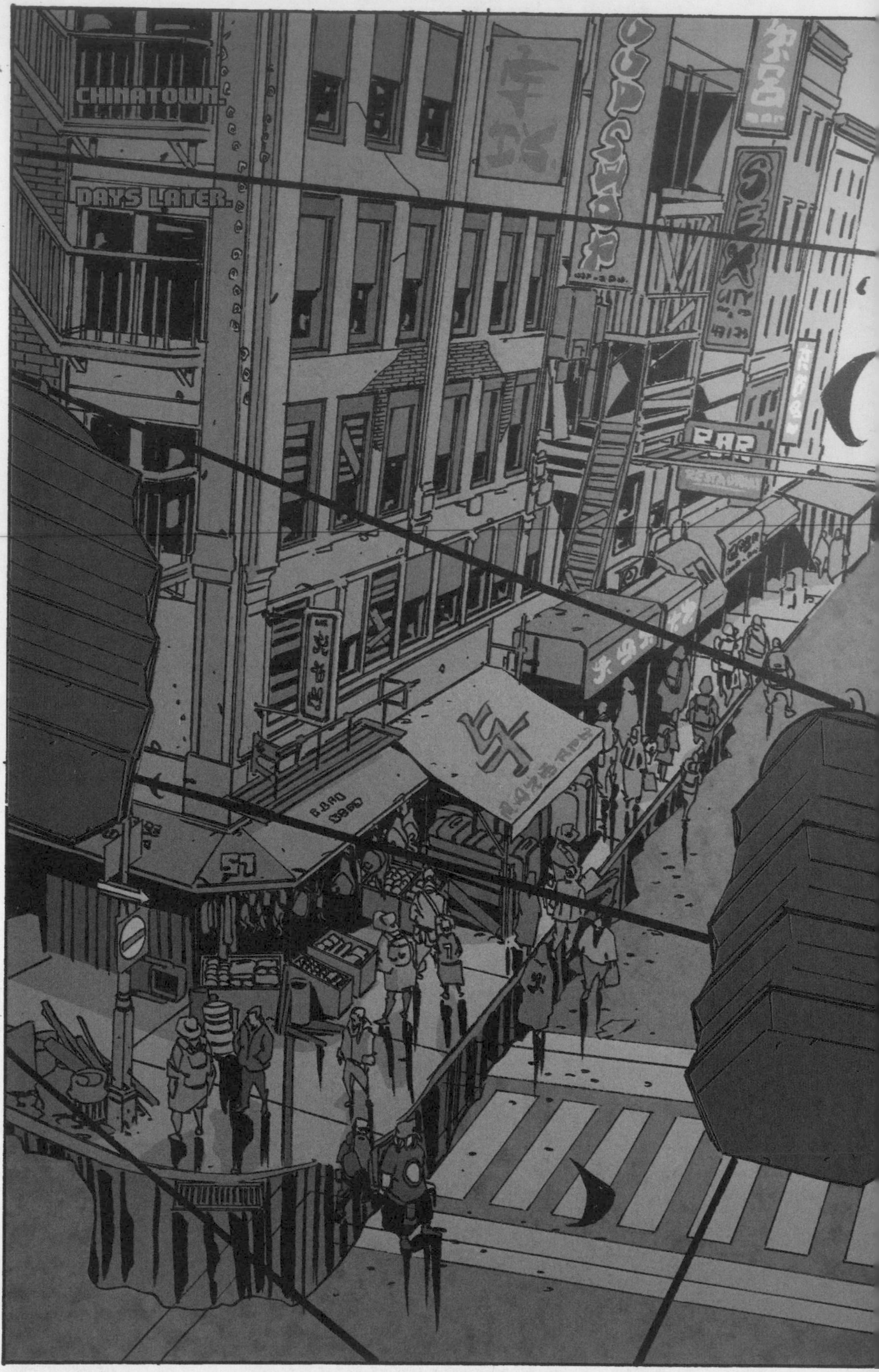
CHINATOWN.
DAYS LATER.
BAR

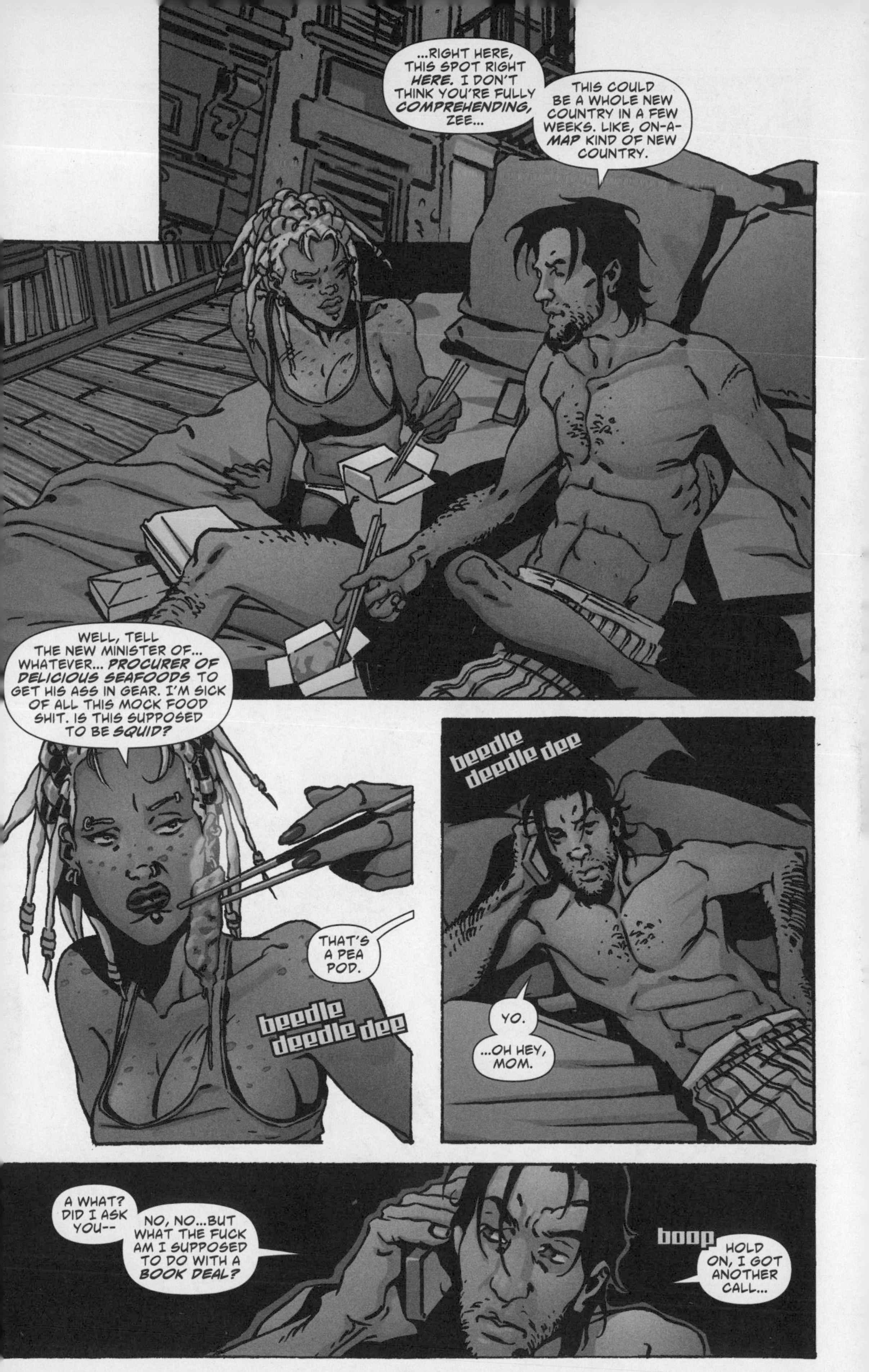
...RIGHT HERE, THIS SPOT RIGHT HERE. I DON'T THINK YOU'RE FULLY COMPREHENDING, ZEE...
THIS COULD BE A WHOLE NEW COUNTRY IN A FEW WEEKS. LIKE, ON-A-MAP KIND OF NEW COUNTRY.
WELL, TELL THE NEW MINISTER OF... WHATEVER... PROCURER OF DELICIOUS SEAFOODS TO GET HIS ASS IN GEAR. I'M SICK OF ALL THIS MOCK FOOD SHIT. IS THIS SUPPOSED TO BE SQUID?
THAT'S A PEA POD.
beedle deedle dee
beedle deedle dee
YO.
...OH HEY, MOM.
A WHAT? DID I ASK YOU--
NO, NO...BUT WHAT THE FUCK AM I SUPPOSED TO DO WITH A BOOK DEAL?
boop
HOLD ON, I GOT ANOTHER CALL...

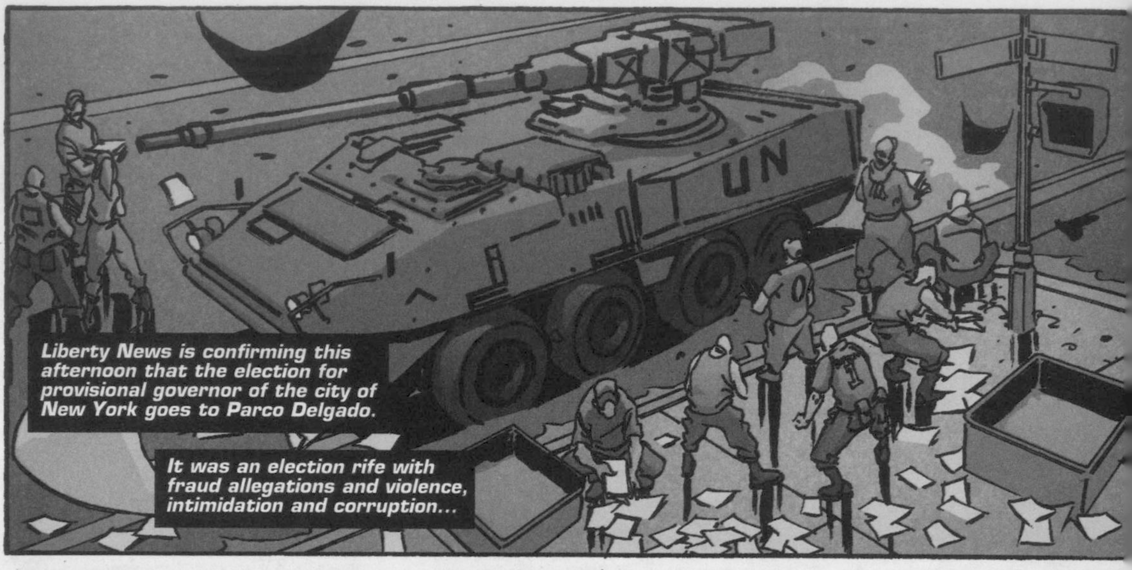
UN
Liberty News is confirming this afternoon that the election for provisional governor of the city of New York goes to Parco Delgado.
It was an election rife with fraud allegations and violence, intimidation and corruption...

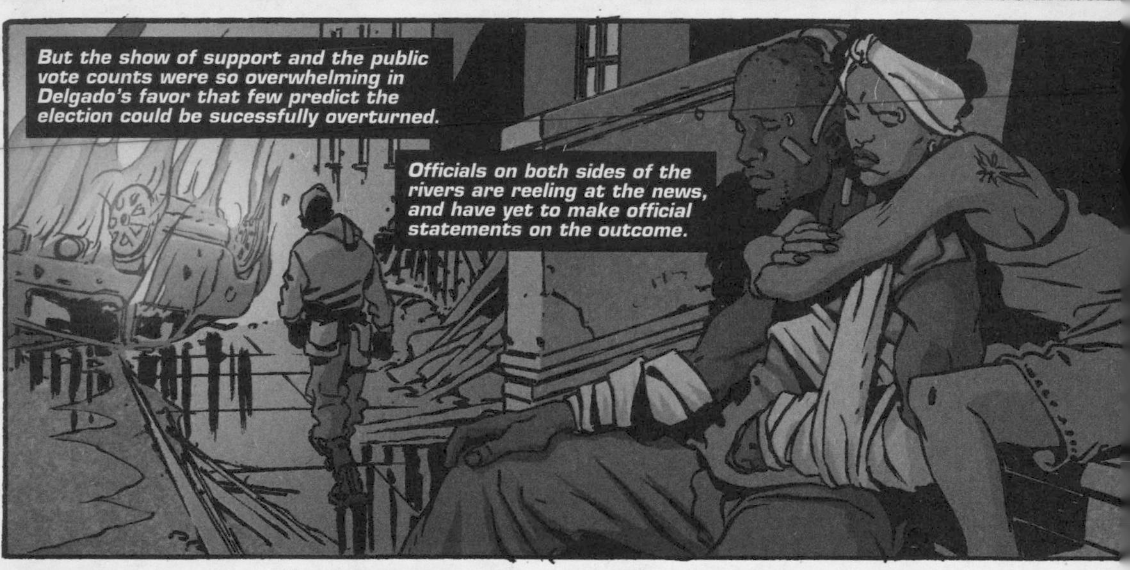
But the show of support and the public vote counts were so overwhelming in Delgado's favor that few predict the election could be sucessfully overturned.
Officials on both sides of the rivers are reeling at the news, and have yet to make official statements on the outcome.

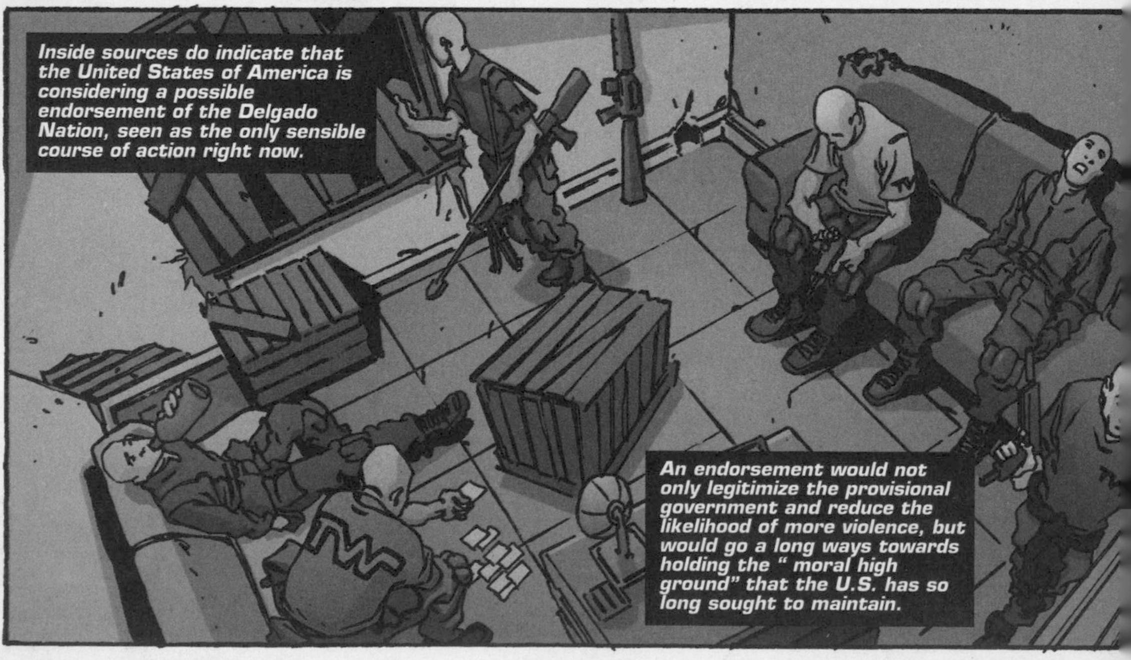
Inside sources do indicate that the United States of America is considering a possible endorsement of the Delgado Nation, seen as the only sensible course of action right now.
An endorsement would not only legitimize the provisional government and reduce the likelihood of more violence, but would go a long ways towards holding the " moral high ground" that the U.S. has so long sought to maintain.

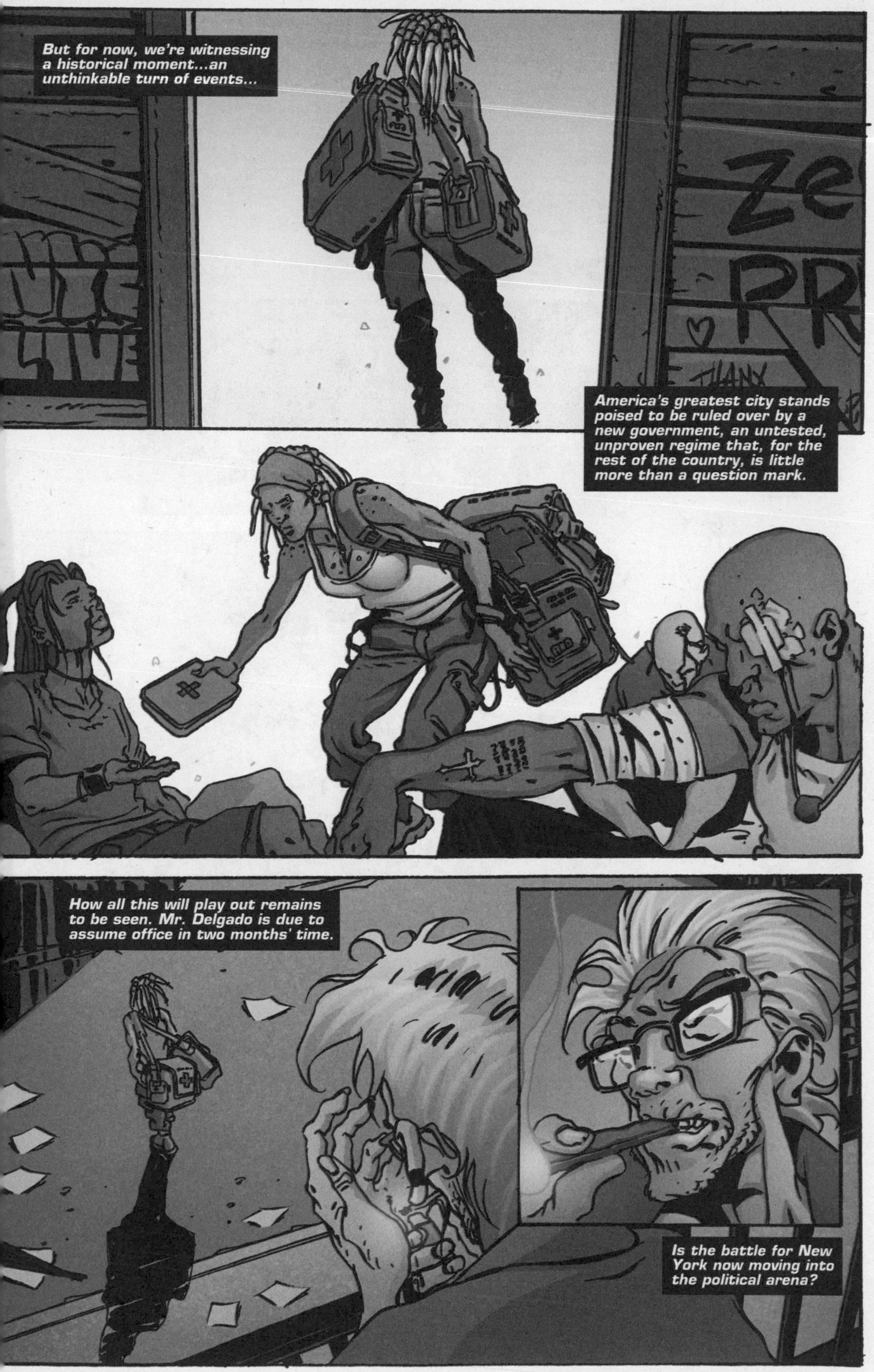

But for now, we're witnessing a historical moment...an unthinkable turn of events...
America's greatest city stands poised to be ruled over by a new government, an untested, unproven regime that, for the rest of the country, is little more than a question mark.
How all this will play out remains to be seen. Mr. Delgado is due to assume office in two months' time.
Is the battle for New York now moving into the political arena?

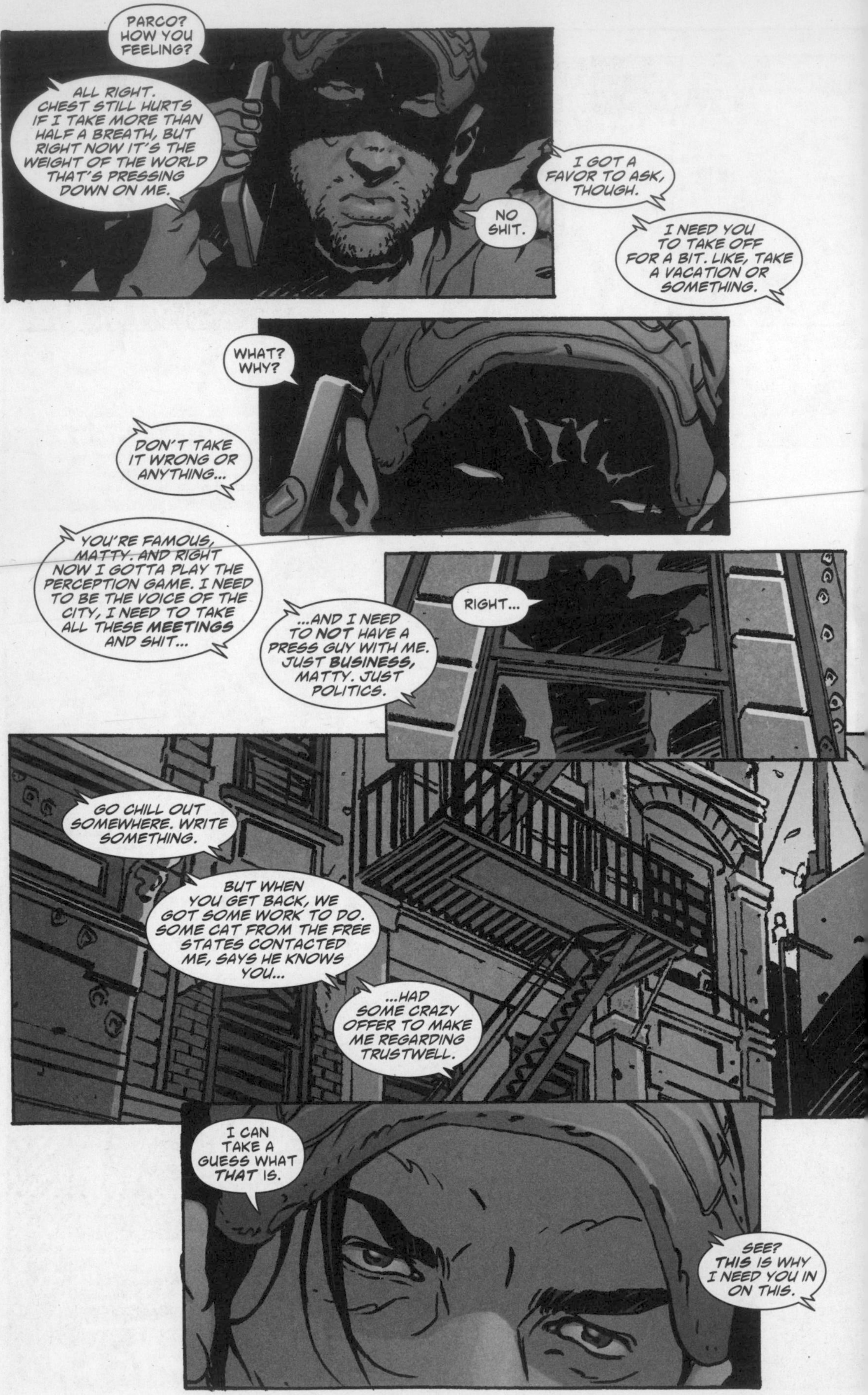
PARCO? HOW YOU FEELING?
ALL RIGHT. CHEST STILL HURTS IF I TAKE MORE THAN HALF A BREATH, BUT RIGHT NOW IT'S THE WEIGHT OF THE WORLD THAT'S PRESSING DOWN ON ME.
NO SHIT.
I GOT A FAVOR TO ASK, THOUGH.
I NEED YOU TO TAKE OFF FOR A BIT. LIKE, TAKE A VACATION OR SOMETHING.
WHAT? WHY?
DON'T TAKE IT WRONG OR ANYTHING...
YOU'RE FAMOUS, MATTY. AND RIGHT NOW I GOTTA PLAY THE PERCEPTION GAME. I NEED TO BE THE VOICE OF THE CITY, I NEED TO TAKE ALL THESE MEETINGS AND SHIT...
RIGHT...
...AND I NEED TO NOT HAVE A PRESS GUY WITH ME. JUST BUSINESS, MATTY. JUST POLITICS.
GO CHILL OUT SOMEWHERE. WRITE SOMETHING.
BUT WHEN YOU GET BACK, WE GOT SOME WORK TO DO. SOME CAT FROM THE FREE STATES CONTACTED ME, SAYS HE KNOWS YOU...
...HAD SOME CRAZY OFFER TO MAKE ME REGARDING TRUSTWELL.
I CAN TAKE A GUESS WHAT THAT IS.
SEE? THIS IS WHY I NEED YOU IN ON THIS.

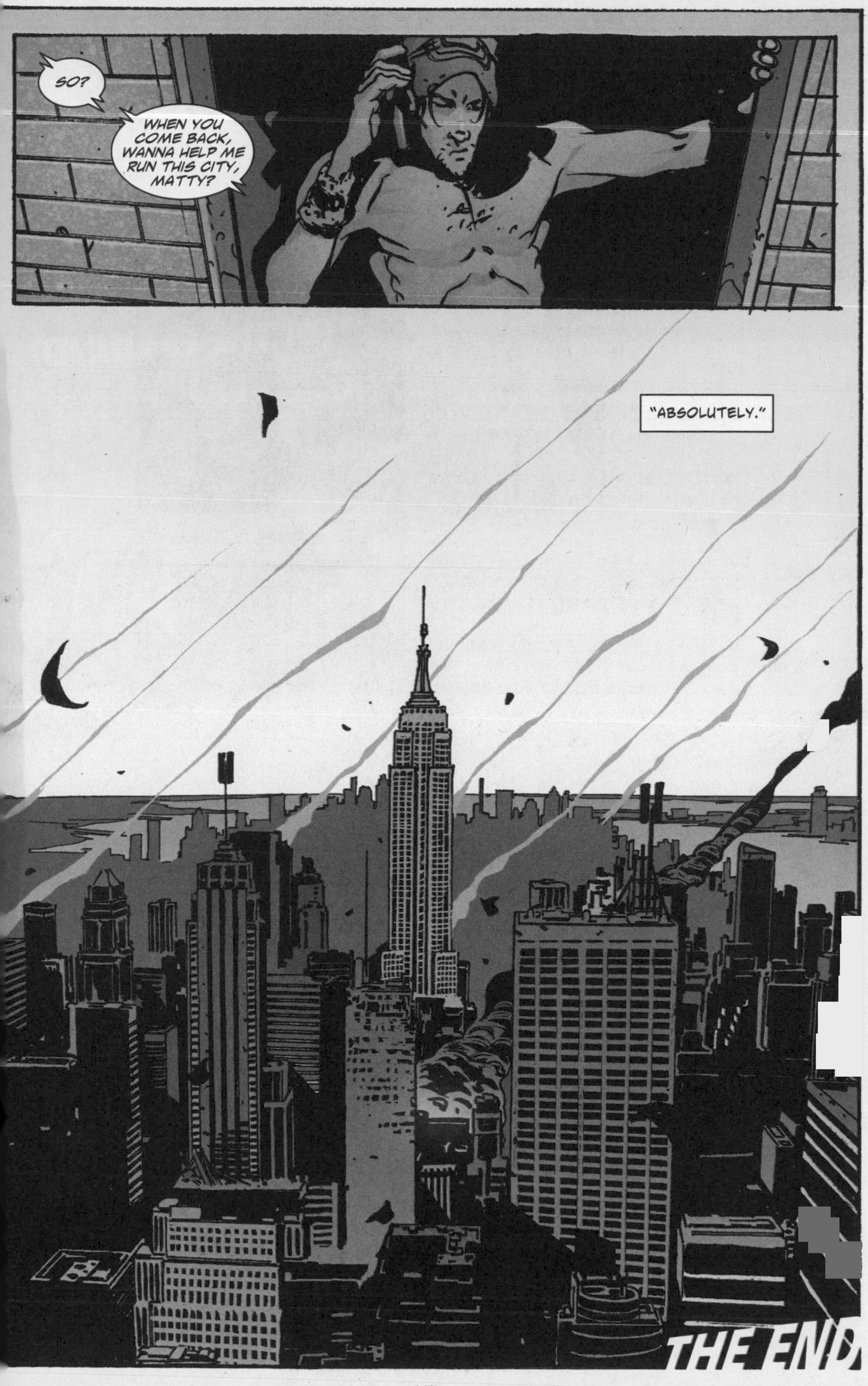
SO?
WHEN YOU COME BACK, WANNA HELP ME RUN THIS CITY, MATTY?
"ABSOLUTELY."
THE END

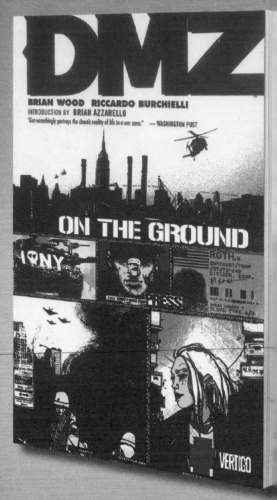
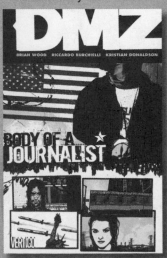

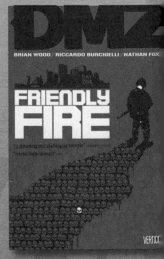